SUBURBAN

NATION

———

THE RISE OF SPRAWL

AND THE

DECLINE OF THE AMERICAN DREAM

North Point Press
A division of Farrar, Straus and Giroux
19 Union Square West, New York 10003

Copyright © 2000 by Andres Duany, Elizabeth Plater-Zyberk, and Jeff Speck
Distributed in Canada by Douglas & McIntyre Ltd.
Printed in the United States of America
Designed by Jonathan D. Lippincott
First edition, 2000

Library of Congress Cataloging-in-Publication Data
Duany, Andres.
    Suburban nation : the rise of sprawl and the decline of the American Dream / Andres
Duany, Elizabeth Plater-Zyberk, and Jeff Speck.—1st ed.
        p.   cm.
    Includes bibliographical references.
    ISBN 0-86547-557-1 (alk. paper)
    1. Urbanization—United States.   2. Suburbs—United States.   3. Community
development, Urban—United States.   4. Urban renewal—United States.   5. Urban
policy—United States.   I. Plater-Zyberk, Elizabeth.   II. Speck, Jeff.   III. Title.

HT384.U5 D83   2000
307.76'0973—dc21

                                                                                99-052186

To our parents

CONTENTS

INTRODUCTION

———

You're stuck in traffic again.

As you creep along a highway that was widened just three years ago, you pass that awful new billboard: COMING SOON: NEW HOMES! Already the bulldozers are plowing down pine trees, and a thin layer of mud is oozing onto the roadway. How could this be happening? Over the years, you've seen a lot of forest and farmland replaced by rooftops, but these one hundred acres had been left unscathed, at the whim of a wealthy owner. Now, it is said, the owner has passed on, the children have cashed out, and the property has fallen victim to the incessant pressures of growth.

These one hundred acres, where you hiked and sledded as a child, are now zoned for single-family housing. They have been bought and sold on that premise, and there is a strong demand for new houses. The developer is not about to go away. The anticipated buyers of these new homes, your future neighbors, are respectable professionals, families much like yours, people who could easily be your friends, relatives, or colleagues. These people are welcome to settle this land, to share your suburban dream—over your dead body.

Why, in this country in which growth is considered tantamount to well-being, in which economic health is measured in "housing starts," is the prospect of these particular houses starting near yours so threatening? What has happened to our manner of growth, such that the thought of new growth makes your stomach turn?

It is not just sentimental attachment to an old sledding hill that has you upset. It is the expectation, based upon decades of experience, that what will be built here you will detest. It will be sprawl: cookie-cutter houses, wide, treeless, sidewalk-free roadways, mindlessly curving cul-de-sacs, a streetscape of garage doors—a beige vinyl parody of *Leave It to Beaver*. Or, worse yet, a pretentious slew of McMansions, complete with the obligatory gatehouse. You will not be welcome there, not that you would ever have reason to visit its monotonous moonscape. Meanwhile, more cars will worsen your congested commute. The future residents will come in search of their American Dream, and in so doing will compromise yours.

You are against growth, because you believe that it will make your life worse. And you are correct in that belief, because, for the past fifty years, we Americans have been building a national landscape that is largely devoid of places worth caring about. Soulless subdivisions, residential "communities" utterly lacking in communal life; strip shopping centers, "big box" chain stores, and artificially festive malls set within barren seas of parking; antiseptic office parks, ghost towns after 6 p.m.; and mile upon mile of clogged collector roads, the only fabric tying our disassociated lives back together—this is growth, and you can find little reason to support it. In fact, so far as your hectic daily schedule allows, you fight it. Once a *citizen*, you have now become a *Nimby* (Not In My BackYard), or what professional planners dismissively term a *Banana* (Build Nothing Anywhere Near Anything). As such, you are hardly expected to be reasonable, or even polite. Still, it would be nice if there were a more constructive role to play—if only there were some third choice available other than *bad growth* and *no growth,* the former being difficult to stomach and the latter being difficult to sustain for more than a few years at a time.

Obviously, that third choice is *good growth,* but is there really such a thing? Do there exist man-made places that are as valuable as the nature they displaced? How about your hometown Main Street? Or Charleston? San Francisco? Few would dispute that man has proved himself capable of producing wonderful places, environments that people cherish no less than the untouched wilderness. They, too, are examples of growth, but they grew in a different way than the sprawl that threatens you now.

The problem is that one cannot easily build Charleston anymore, because it is against the law. Similarly, Boston's Beacon Hill, Nantucket, Santa Fe, Carmel—all of these well-known places, many of which have become tourist destinations, exist in direct violation of current zoning ordinances. Even the classic American main street, with its mixed-use buildings right up against the sidewalk, is now illegal in most municipalities. Somewhere along the way, through a series of small and well-intentioned steps, traditional towns became a crime in America. At the same time, one of the largest segments of our economy, the homebuilding industry, developed a comprehensive system of land development practices based upon sprawl, practices that have become so ingrained as to be second nature. It is these practices, and the laws that encourage them, which must be overcome if good growth is to become a viable alternative.

As daunting as such a task may seem, it is not impossible. Slowly but surely, often led by reformed Nimbys, cities and towns throughout North America are rewriting their zoning laws and demanding a higher standard of performance from their developers. Encouraged by the success of a few pioneering projects, homebuilders have begun to experiment with a form of development that grows its cities and towns in the traditional manner of the country's most successful older neighborhoods. The question is not whether or not such growth is possible but whether it will come in time to spare our countryside, small towns, and older cities from the march of suburbia.

Whether America grows into a placeless collection of subdivisions, strip centers, and office parks, or a real town with real neighborhoods, will depend on whether its citizens understand the difference between those two alternatives, and whether they can argue effectively for healthy growth. Toward that end, we offer this book. It is a summing up of our experiences, as designers and citizens, over the past two decades all across our land.

Since 1979, when we were first asked by Robert Davis to design Seaside, Florida, we have been intimately involved in the creation and revitalization of villages, towns, and cities from Cape Cod to Los Angeles. Everywhere we've visited, we have observed and studied urban and suburban life: walked the downtowns, cruised the suburbs, enjoyed meals in homes, given lectures in university theaters, corporate boardrooms, and high school cafeterias. Most of all, we have talked to the residents of these places, and we have listened intently. Almost without exception, the message we have heard, a message of deep concern, has been the same: the American Dream just doesn't seem to be coming true anymore. Life at the dawn of the millennium isn't what it should be. It seems that our economic and technological progress has not succeeded in bringing about the good society. A higher standard of living has somehow failed to result in a better quality of life.

And from mayors to average citizens, we have heard expressed a shared belief in a direct causal relationship between the character of the physical environment and the social health of families and the community at large. For all of the household conveniences, cars, and shopping malls, life seems less satisfying to most Americans, particularly in the ubiquitous middle-class suburbs, where a sprawling, repetitive, and forgettable landscape has replaced the original promise of suburban life with a hollow imitation. In an architectural version of *Invasion of the Body Snatchers,* our main streets and neighborhoods have been replaced by alien substitutes, similar but not the same. Life once spent enjoying the richness of community has increasingly become life spent alone behind the wheel. Lacking a physical framework conducive to public discourse, our family and communal institutions struggle to persist in our increasingly *sub*-urban surroundings. And, sadly, suburban growth seems to have also drained much of the vitality from our inner cities, where a carless underclass finds itself with diminishing access to jobs and services.

It doesn't have to be this way. After many successes, a number of failures, and, most important, prolonged collaboration with residents of every part of this country, we believe more strongly than ever in the power of good design to overcome the ills created by bad design, or, more accurately, by design's conspicuous absence.

We live today in cities and suburbs whose form and character we did not choose. They were imposed upon us, by federal policy, local zoning laws, and the demands of the automobile. If these influences are reversed—and they can be—an environment designed around the true needs of individuals, conducive to the formation of community and preservation of the landscape, becomes possible. Unsurprisingly, this environment would not look so different from our old American neighborhoods before they were ravaged by sprawl.

Historically, we have rebuilt our nation every fifty to sixty years, so it is not too late. The choice is ours: either a society of homogeneous pieces, isolated from one another in often fortified enclaves, or a society of diverse and memorable neighborhoods, organized into mutually supportive towns, cities, and regions. This book is a primer on how design can help us untangle the mess we have made and once again build and inhabit places worth caring about.

SUBURBAN NATION

1

WHAT IS SPRAWL, AND WHY?

TWO WAYS TO GROW; THE FIVE COMPONENTS OF SPRAWL; A BRIEF HISTORY OF SPRAWL; WHY VIRGINIA BEACH IS NOT ALEXANDRIA; NEIGHBORHOOD PLANS VERSUS SPRAWL PLANS

The cities will be part of the country; I shall live 30 miles from my office in one direction, under a pine tree; my secretary will live 30 miles away from it too, in the other direction, under another pine tree. We shall both have our own car.

We shall use up tires, wear out road surfaces and gears, consume oil and gasoline. All of which will necessitate a great deal of work . . . enough for all.

—LE CORBUSIER, *THE RADIANT CITY* (1967)

TWO WAYS TO GROW

This book is a study of two different models of urban growth: the traditional neighborhood and suburban sprawl. They are polar opposites in appearance, function, and character: they look different, they act differently, and they affect us in different ways.

The traditional neighborhood was the fundamental form of European settlement on this continent through the Second World War, from St. Augustine to Seattle. It continues to be the dominant

The traditional neighborhood: naturally occurring, pedestrian-friendly, and diverse. Daily needs are located within walking distance

Suburban sprawl: an invention, an abstract system of carefully separated pods of single use. Daily needs are located within driving distance

pattern of habitation outside the United States, as it has been throughout recorded history. The traditional neighborhood—represented by mixed-use, pedestrian-friendly communities of varied population, either standing free as villages or grouped into towns and cities—has proved to be a sustainable form of growth. It allowed us to settle the continent without bankrupting the country or destroying the countryside in the process.

Suburban sprawl, now the standard North American pattern of growth, ignores historical precedent and human experience. It is an invention, conceived by architects, engineers, and planners, and promoted by developers in the great *sweeping aside of the old* that occurred after the Second World War. Unlike the traditional neighborhood model, which evolved organically as a response to human needs, suburban sprawl is an idealized artificial system. It is not without a certain beauty: it is rational, consistent, and comprehensive. Its performance is largely predictable. It is an outgrowth of modern problem solving: a system for living. Unfortunately, this system is already showing itself to be unsustainable. Unlike the traditional neighborhood, sprawl is not healthy growth; it is essentially self-destructive. Even at relatively low population densities, sprawl tends not to pay for itself financially and consumes land at an alarming rate, while producing insurmountable traffic problems and exacerbating social inequity and isolation. These particular outcomes were not predicted. Neither was the toll that sprawl exacts from America's cities and towns, which continue to decant slowly into the countryside. As the ring of suburbia grows around most of our cities, so grows the void at the center. Even while the struggle to revitalize deteriorated downtown neighborhoods and business districts continues, the inner ring of suburbs is already at risk, losing residents and businesses to fresher locations on a new suburban edge.•

THE FIVE COMPONENTS OF SPRAWL

If sprawl truly is destructive, why is it allowed to continue? The beginning of an answer lies in sprawl's seductive simplicity, the fact that it consists of very few homogeneous components—five in all— which can be arranged in almost any way. It is appropriate to review these parts individually, since they always occur independently. While one component may be adjacent to another, the dominant characteristic of sprawl is that each component is strictly segregated from the others.

Housing subdivisions, also called *clusters* and *pods.* These places consist only of residences. They are sometimes called *villages, towns,* and *neighborhoods* by their developers, which is misleading, since those terms denote places which are not exclusively residential and which provide an experiential richness not available in a housing tract. Subdivisions can be identified as such by their contrived names, which tend toward the romantic—Pheasant Mill Crossing—and often pay tribute to the natural or historic resource they have displaced.■

A residential subdivision: houses and parking

• Bill Morrish and Catherine Brown have done much to document this new frontier of decline, the "inner ring," at the Design Center for American Urban Landscape at the University of Minnesota. Los Angeles journalist Mike Davis describes this evolving phenomenon in his book *City of Quartz: Excavating the Future in Los Angeles.*
■ Housing subdivisions are not the only components of sprawl with ridiculous names. Our favorite is a new section of Atlanta called Perimeter Center, a moniker that aptly sums up the confusion inherent in the suburban landscape.

A strip center: stores and parking

A corporate park: offices and parking

A public high school: classrooms and parking

Shopping centers, also called *strip centers, shopping malls,* and *big-box retail.* These are places exclusively for shopping. They come in every size, from the Quick Mart on the corner to the Mall of America, but they are all places to which one is unlikely to walk. The conventional shopping center can be easily distinguished from its traditional main-street counterpart by its lack of housing or offices, its single-story height, and its parking lot between the building and the roadway.

Office parks and business parks. These are places only for work. Derived from the modernist architectural vision of the building standing free in the park, the contemporary office park is usually made of boxes in parking lots. Still imagined as a pastoral workplace isolated in nature, it has kept its idealistic name and also its quality of isolation, but in practice it is more likely to be surrounded by highways than by countryside.

Civic institutions. The fourth component of suburbia is public buildings: the town halls, churches, schools, and other places where people gather for communication and culture. In traditional neighborhoods, these buildings often serve as neighborhood focal points, but in suburbia they take an altered form: large and infrequent, generally unadorned owing to limited funding, surrounded by parking, and located nowhere in particular. The school pictured here shows what a dramatic evolution this building type has undergone in the past thirty years. A comparison between the size of the parking lot and the size of the building is revealing: this is a school to which no child will ever walk. Because pedestrian access is usually nonexistent, and because the dispersion of surrounding homes often makes school buses impractical, schools in the new suburbs are designed based on the assumption of massive automotive transportation.

Roadways. The fifth component of sprawl consists of the miles of pavement that are necessary to connect the other four disassociated components. Since each piece of suburbia serves only one type of activity, and since daily life involves a wide variety of activities, the residents of suburbia spend an unprecedented amount of time and money moving from one place to the next. Since most of this motion takes place in singly occupied automobiles, even a sparsely populated area can generate the traffic of a much larger traditional town.

The traffic load caused by the many disassociated pieces of suburbia is most clearly visible from above. As seen in this image of Palm Beach County, Florida, the amount of pavement (public infrastructure) per building (private structure) is extremely high, especially when compared to the efficiency of a section of an older city like Washington, D.C. The same economic relationship is at work underground, where low-density land-use patterns require greater lengths of pipe and conduit to distribute municipal services. This high ratio of public to private expenditure helps explain why suburban municipalities are finding that new growth fails to pay for itself at acceptable levels of taxation.

The modern city (Palm Beach County, Florida): low density, high dependence on automotive infrastructure

The traditional city (Washington, D.C.): higher density, low dependence on automotive infrastructure

A BRIEF HISTORY OF SPRAWL

How did sprawl come about? Far from being an inevitable evolution or a historical accident, suburban sprawl is the direct result of a number of policies that conspired powerfully to encourage urban dispersal. The most significant of these were the Federal Housing Administration and Veterans Administration loan programs which, in the years following the Second World War, provided mortgages for over eleven million new homes. These mortgages, which typically cost less per month than paying rent, were directed at new single-family suburban construction.[*] Intentionally or not, the FHA and VA programs discouraged the renovation of existing housing stock, while turning their back on the construction of row houses, mixed-use buildings, and other urban housing types. Simultaneously, a 41,000-mile interstate highway program, coupled with federal and local subsidies for road improvement and the neglect of mass transit, helped make automotive commuting affordable and convenient for the average citizen.[■] Within the new economic framework, young families made the financially rational choice: Levittown. Housing gradually migrated from historic city neighborhoods to the periphery, landing increasingly farther away.

The shops stayed in the city, but only for a while. It did not take long for merchants to realize that their customers had relocated and

---

[*] Kenneth Jackson, *Crabgrass Frontier*, 205–8. "Quite simply, it often became cheaper to buy than to rent" (205). Interestingly, Jackson notes that "the primary purpose of the legislation . . . was the alleviation of unemployment, which stood at about a quarter of the total work force in 1934 and which was particularly high in the construction industry" (203).

[■] Ibid., 249. The Interstate Highway act of 1956 provided for 41,000 miles of roadway, 90 percent paid for by the federal government, at an initial cost of $26 billion (249–50). Jackson notes that, "according to Senator Gaylord Nelson of Wisconsin, 75 percent of government expenditures for transportation in the United States in the postwar generation went for highways as opposed to 1 percent for urban mass transit" (250). Still, "the government pays seven times as much to support the operation of the private car as to support public transportation" (Jane Holtz Kay, "Stuck in Gear," D1). The preference in Washington for roads over rails was due in no small part to influence peddling by the auto industry, as continues to be the case. With and without the government's blessing, the automakers have a history of mercenary acts, the most notorious of which was portrayed in the film *Who Framed Roger Rabbit?* In what Jim Kunstler describes as "a systematic campaign to put streetcar lines out of business all over America," a consortium of auto, tire, and oil companies purchased and tore up over one hundred streetcar systems nationwide, an act for which General Motors was ultimately convicted of criminal conspiracy and fined a grand total of $5,000 (James Howard Kunstler, *The Geography of Nowhere*, 91–92).

to follow them out. But unlike America's prewar suburbs, the new subdivisions were being financed by programs that addressed only homebuilding, and therefore neglected to set aside any sites for corner stores. As a result, shopping required not only its own distinct method of financing and development but also its own locations. Placed along the wide high-speed collector roads between housing clusters, the new shops responded to their environment by pulling back from the street and constructing large freestanding signage. In this way the now ubiquitous strip shopping center was born.

For a time, most jobs stayed downtown. Workers traveled from the suburbs into the center, and the downtown business districts remained viable. But, as with the shops, this situation could not last; by the 1970s, many corporations were moving their offices closer to the workforce—or, more accurately, closer to the CEO's house, as ingeniously diagrammed by William Whyte.[*] The CEO's desire for a shorter commute, coupled with suburbia's lower tax burden, led to the development of the business park, completing the migration of each of life's components into the suburbs. As commuting patterns became predominantly suburb to suburb, many center cities became expendable.

While government programs for housing and highway promoted sprawl, the planning profession, worshipping at the altar of zoning, worked to make it the law. Why the country's planners were so

---

[*] William Whyte, *City: Rediscovering the Center*, 288. Whyte noted: "Of thirty-eight companies that moved out of New York City to better quality-of-life needs of their employees, thirty-one moved to the Greenwich-Stamford area. . . . Average distance from the CEO's home: eight miles." Whyte also documented how, over the next eleven years, those thirty-eight companies that moved experienced less than half the stock appreciation of thirty-six randomly chosen comparable companies that chose to remain in the city (294–95).

uniformly convinced of the efficacy of zoning—the segregation of the different aspects of daily life—is a story that dates back to the previous century and the first victory of the planning profession. At that time, Europe's industrialized cities were shrouded in the smoke of Blake's "dark, satanic mills." City planners wisely advocated the separation of such factories from residential areas, with dramatic results. Cities such as London, Paris, and Barcelona, which in the mid-nineteenth century had been virtually unfit for human habitation, were transformed within decades into national treasures. Life expectancies rose significantly, and the planners, fairly enough, were hailed as heroes.

The successes of turn-of-the-century planning, represented in America by the City Beautiful movement, became the foundation of a new profession, and ever since, planners have repeatedly attempted to relive that moment of glory by separating everything from everything else. This segregation, once applied only to incompatible uses, is now applied to every use. A typical contemporary zoning code has several dozen land-use designations; not only is housing separated from industry but low-density housing is separated from medium-density housing, which is separated from high-density housing. Medical offices are separated from general offices, which are in turn separated from restaurants and shopping. [•]

As a result, the new American city has been likened to an unmade omelet: eggs, cheese, vegetables, a pinch of salt, but each

---

[•] The strict separation of housing types actually hints at a more insidious cause of sprawl, economic discrimination, or sometimes simple racism. In the words of F. J. Popper: "The basic purpose of zoning was to keep Them where They belonged—Out. If They had already gotten in, then its purpose was to confine Them to limited areas. The exact identity of Them varied a bit around the country. Blacks, Latinos and poor people qualified. Catholics, Jews and Orientals were targets in many places" (Peter Hall, *Cities*

consumed in turn, raw. Perhaps the greatest irony is that even industry need not be isolated anymore. Many modern production facilities are perfectly safe neighbors, thanks to evolved manufacturing processes and improved pollution control. A comprehensive mix of diverse land uses is once again as reasonable as it was in the preindustrial age.

The planners' enthusiasm for single-use zoning and the government's commitment to homebuilding and highway construction were supported by another, more subtle ethos: the widespread application of management lessons learned overseas during the Second World War. In this part of the story, members of the professional class—called the Whiz Kids in John Byrne's book of that name—returned from the war with a whole new approach to accomplishing large-scale tasks, centered on the twin acts of classifying and counting. Because these techniques had been so successful in building munitions and allocating troops, they were applied across the board to industry, to education, to governance, to wherever the Whiz Kids found themselves. In the case of cities, they took a complex human tradition of settlement, said "Out with the old," and replaced it with a rational model that could be easily understood through systems analysis and flow charts. Town planning, until 1930 considered a humanistic discipline based upon history, aesthetics, and culture, became a technical profession based upon numbers. As a result, the American city was reduced into the simplistic categories and quantities of sprawl.

---

of Tomorrow, 60). It has been well documented by Robert Fishman and others how racism was a large factor in the disappearance of the middle class from the center city ("white flight"), and how zoning law clearly manifests the desire to keep away what one has left behind.

Because these tenets still hold sway, sprawl continues largely unchecked. At the current rate, California alone grows by a Pasadena every year and a Massachusetts every decade.[•] Each year, we construct the equivalent of many cities, but the pieces don't add up to anything memorable or of lasting value. The result doesn't look like a place, it doesn't act like a place, and, perhaps most significant, it doesn't feel like a place. Rather, it feels like what it is: an uncoordinated agglomeration of standardized single-use zones with little pedestrian life and even less civic identification, connected only by an overtaxed network of roadways. Perhaps the most regrettable fact of all is that exactly the same ingredients—the houses, shops, offices, civic buildings, and roads—could instead have been assembled as new neighborhoods and cities. Countless residents of unincorporated counties could instead be citizens of real towns, enjoying the quality of life and civic involvement that such places provide.

WHY VIRGINIA BEACH IS NOT ALEXANDRIA

Because sprawl is so unsatisfying, it remains tempting to think of it as an accident. For those who wish to take refuge in that thought, the caption under this photograph may come as a surprise: "Becoming a Showcase: Virginia Beach Boulevard–Phase I celebrated its

Becoming a Showcase: Virginia Beach Boulevard-Phase I celebrated its completion in December. This project involved the removal of

A modern town center: the apotheosis of suburban zoning laws

[•] Data given by Nelson Rising at the second Congress for the New Urbanism, Los Angeles, May 21, 1994. From 1970 to 1990, Los Angeles grew 45 percent in population and 300 percent in size (Christopher Leinberger, Robert Charles Lesser & Co. original research). According to the *Population Environment Balance* newsletter, we pave an area equal to the size of the state of Delaware every year. All told, seven thousand acres of forests, farms, and countryside are lost to sprawl each day, totaling well over 50,000 square miles since 1970 (Will Rogers, *The Trust for Public Land* membership letter, 1–2).

completion . . ." This "city center" is regarded with pride, for it is the successful attainment of a specific vision: eleven lanes of traffic and plenty of parking.

What is pictured here is the direct outcome of regulations governing modern engineering and development practice. Every detail of this environment comes straight from technical manuals. After reading them one might easily conclude that they are organized, written, and enforced in the name of a single objective: making cars happy. Indeed, at Virginia Beach they should be happy: no more than eight cars ever stack at the light, and the huge corner radius of the intersection means that turning requires minimal use of the brake. The parking lots are typically half-empty, since they have been sized for the Saturday before Christmas. Such excess is inevitable; anyone who has shopped in suburbia knows that the inability to find a parking space makes the entire proposition unworkable. As a result, the typical suburban building code has ten or twenty pages of rules on the design of parking lots alone, with different requirements for each land use. For retail locations, the square footage of parking often exceeds the square footage of leasable space.

Perhaps surprisingly, the creation of this environment is also guided by rules pertaining to aesthetics. These mostly came about during the sixties, when Lady Bird Johnson's beautification campaign and the nascent environmental movement opened the door for tree and sign ordinances. Notice the trees preserved in the parking lot, and the absence of large signs. These regulations result in suburban settlements that are neat, clean, and often more appealing than their deteriorating counterparts in the older city. In truth, a lot of sprawl—primarily affluent areas—could be considered beautiful.

This raises a fundamental point: the problem with suburbia is not that it is ugly. The problem with suburbia is that, in spite of all its regulatory controls, it is not functional: it simply does not efficiently serve society or preserve the environment.

A clue to this dysfunction can be found in the same photograph: the thin ribbon of concrete between roadway and parking lot. It is a safe bet that, in the years since that sidewalk was built, it has never been used by anyone except indigents and those experiencing serious car trouble. We have witnessed this phenomenon ourselves. Walking alongside a street near Orlando's Disney World, we were intercepted by a minivan—"Are you all right?"—and whisked aboard. It was a security vehicle, the roving patrol for stray pedestrians.

The virgin sidewalk—the physical embodiment of sprawl's guilty conscience—reveals the true failure of suburbia, a landscape in which automobile use is a prerequisite to social viability. For those who cannot drive, cannot afford a car, or simply wish to spend less time behind the wheel, Virginia Beach Boulevard will never be a satisfactory place to live.• But even those who love driving must acknowledge that there is an inherent inequity in sprawl, an environment of outsize physical dimensions determined by automotive motion. Public funds build and support sprawl's far-flung infrastructure. Pavement, pipes, patrols, ambulances, and the other costs of unhealthy growth are paid for by taxing drivers and non-drivers

---

• There is no arguing that the automobile is a wonderful instrument of freedom for those who are able to drive one. Indeed, it is hard to beat the sheer physical enjoyment of moving quickly through space in command of 200 horsepower and two tons of steel. As of this writing, the three authors have yet to give up their cars. This does not blind them, however, to the fact that what was once our servant has become our master, and that an instrument of freedom is a very different thing from an instrument of survival. The problem with cars is not the cars themselves but that they have produced an environment of dependence.

alike, whether they are the inhabitants of sprawl or the citizens of more efficient environments, such as our core cities and older neighborhoods.•

Not far from Virginia Beach is Alexandria, a fine example of the traditional neighborhood pattern. It is an old place, laid out by, among others, a seventeen-year-old George Washington. It was built following six fundamental rules that distinguish it from sprawl:

Alexandria, Virginia: efficient, beloved, and illegal

1. The center. Each neighborhood has a clear center, focused on the common activities of commerce, culture, and governance. This is downtown Alexandria, understood by residents and tourists alike as a unique place to visit to engage in civilized activity.

2. The five-minute walk. A local resident is rarely more than a five-minute walk from the ordinary needs of daily life: living, working, and shopping. In the downtown, these three activities may be found in the same building. By living so close to all that they need, Alexandria's residents can drive much less, if they have to drive at all.

3. The street network. Because the street pattern takes the form of a continuous web—in this case, a grid—numerous paths connect one location to another. Blocks are relatively small, rarely exceeding a quarter mile in perimeter. In contrast to suburbia, where walking routes are scarce and traffic is concentrated on a small number of highways, the traditional network provides the pedestrian and the driver with a choice. This condition is not only more interesting but more useful. A person who lives in Alexandria is able to adjust her path minutely to and from work on a daily basis, to drop off a child

---

• The cost of suburban growth is financed through federal, state, and local taxes, which are levied on all citizens irrespective of their location. Even at the local level, city and county taxes often relocate resources within a jurisdiction from its older center to its newer edge. It has been demonstrated time and time again that most new suburban growth is heavily subsidized by older sections of the city, often unwittingly.

at daycare, pick up the dry cleaning, or visit a coffeehouse. If she chooses to drive, she can constantly alter her route—at every intersection if necessary—to avoid heavy traffic.

4. Narrow, versatile streets. Because there are so many streets to accommodate the traffic, each street can be small. Of all the streets pictured here, only one is more than two lanes wide. This slows down the traffic, as does the parallel parking along the curb, resulting in a street that is pleasant and safe to walk along. This pedestrian-friendly environment is enhanced by wide sidewalks, shade trees, and buildings close to the street. Traditional streets, like all organic systems, are extremely complex, in contrast to the artificial simplicity of sprawl. On Alexandria's streets, cars drive and park while people walk, enter buildings, meet, converse under trees, and even dine at sidewalk cafés. In Virginia Beach, only one thing happens on the street: cars moving. There is no parallel parking, no pedestrians, and certainly no trees. Like many state departments of transportation, Virginia's discourages its state roads from being lined with trees, which are considered dangerous. In fact, they are not called trees at all but FHOs: Fixed and Hazardous Objects.*

5. Mixed Use. In contrast to sprawl's single-use zoning, almost all of downtown Alexandria's blocks are of mixed use, as are many of the buildings. Despite this complexity, it is not a design free-for-all. All of the above characteristics are the intended consequence of a town plan with carefully prescribed details. There is an essential discipline regarding two factors: the size of the building and its relationship to the street. Large buildings sit in the company of other

---

* Virginia Department of Transportation Regulations, 8/95 edition, table A-3-1. The manual adds that "every effort should be made to remove the tree rather than shield it with a guardrail."

large buildings, small buildings sit alongside other small buildings, and so on. This organization is a form of zoning, but buildings are arranged by their physical type more often than by their use. When buildings of different size do adjoin, they still collaborate to define the space of the street, usually by pulling right up against the sidewalk. Parking lots, if any, are hidden at the back. In those rare cases where a building sits back from the sidewalk, it does so in order to create a public plaza or garden, not a parking lot.

6. *Special sites for special buildings.* Finally, traditional neighborhoods devote unique sites to civic buildings, those structures that represent the collective identity and aspirations of the community. Alexandria's City Hall sits back from the street on a plaza, the site of a thriving farmers' market on Sundays. Even within a fairly uniform grid, schools, places of worship, and other civic buildings are located in positions that contribute to their prominence. In this way, the city achieves a physical structure that both manifests and supports its social structure.

All the above rules work together to make Alexandria a delight, the kind of place that people visit just to be there. While some of the design principles applied there were simply common sense, many others were spelled out in the early settlers' building codes, which dictated such items as building setbacks and gable orientation.[•]

[•] One of the things that make Alexandria special was the rule that only public buildings were allowed to face the gable end of a roof toward the street. All private buildings were required to face the eaves to the front, creating a calm and steady background for the more important civic buildings. The codes for Williamsburg, Virginia, were equally stringent, specifying the location of civic buildings and mandating setbacks and fences for much of the private property (Witold Rybczynski, *City Life*, 71).

These rules are still available to us today, and provide a fully valid framework for the design and redesign of our communities. Unfortunately, in most jurisdictions around the country, all the old rules are precluded by the new rules dictating sprawl.

NEIGHBORHOOD PLANS VERSUS SPRAWL PLANS

The zoning plan of Coral Gables: a fine grain of mixed land uses and densities within an interconnected street network

A modern zoning plan: a strict separation of land uses, a few big roads, and little else

Since places are built from plans, it is important to understand what distinguishes plans for neighborhoods from plans for sprawl. On the left is the plan of Coral Gables, one of the large successful new towns of the early twentieth century. Coral Gables was designed when the American town planning movement was at its apogee, in the 1920s. The great planners of this era determined the form of their new cities by studying the best traditional towns and adjusting their organizational principles only as necessary to accommodate the automobile. A modern city, Coral Gables is zoned by use, but the zoning is as tightly grained as an Oriental rug. Different uses, represented by different shades, are often located directly adjacent to one another. Mansions sit just down the street from apartment houses, which are around the corner from shops and office buildings. It takes a sharp pencil to draw plans this intricate.

Below, in fat marker pen, is a land-use plan—more accurately referred to as a bubble diagram—typical of those being produced for greenfield sites across the country. All the municipal government cares to know—and all the developer is held to—is that growth will take the form of single-use pods along a collector road. Is it any wonder that the result is sprawl? This plan guarantees it, since a mix of uses is not allowed in any one zone.

This sort of plan manifests the public sector's abrogation of responsibility for community-making to the private sector. Many would argue that its only purpose is to give the developer the utmost flexibility to build whatever physical environment he wants, at the public's expense. It is an irony of modern zoning that this plan is, in effect, much more restrictive than Coral Gables'. While it is dangerously imprecise about urban form, it is utterly inflexible about land use. A developer who owns a twenty-acre pod of sprawl can provide only one thing. If there is no demand for that one thing, he is out of business.

The bubble diagram is not the only restriction that the developer has to deal with. It is supplemented by a pile of planning codes many inches thick. As exposed in Philip Howard's *The Death of Common Sense,* these lengthy codes can be burdensome to the point of farce. But the problem with the current development codes is not just their size; they also seem to have a negative effect on the quality of the built environment. Their size and their result are symptoms of the same problem: they are hollow at their core. They do not emanate from any physical vision. They have no images, no diagrams, no recommended models, only numbers and words. Their authors, it seems, have no clear picture of what they want their communities to be. They are not imagining a place that they admire, or buildings that they hope to emulate. Rather, all they seem to imagine is what they *don't* want: no mixed uses, no slow-moving cars, no parking shortages, no overcrowding. Such prohibitions do not a city make.

In the end, perhaps this is the most charitable way to consider sprawl. It wasn't an accident, but neither was it based on a specific vision of its physical form or of the life that form would generate. As such, it remains an innocent error, but nonetheless an error that should not continue to be promoted. There is currently more sprawl covering American soil than was ever intended by its inventors. While there are some people who truly enjoy living in this environment, there are many others who would prefer to walk to school, bicycle to work, or simply spend less time in the car. It is for these people, who have access to ever fewer places that can accommodate their choice, that an alternative must be provided. And the only proven alternative to sprawl is the traditional neighborhood.

2

THE DEVIL IS IN THE DETAILS

WHY TRAFFIC IS CONGESTED; WHEN NEARBY IS STILL FAR AWAY;

THE CONVENIENCE STORE VERSUS THE CORNER STORE;

THE SHOPPING CENTER AND THE OFFICE PARK VERSUS MAIN

STREET; USELESS AND USEFUL OPEN SPACE; WHY CURVING ROADS

AND CUL-DE-SACS DO NOT MAKE MEMORABLE PLACES

———

People say they do not want to live near where they work, but that they would like to work near where they live.

—ZEV COHEN, LECTURE (1995)

———

Let us take a closer look at sprawl to see how it compares to the traditional neighborhood at the level of the pavement. In doing so, it will be difficult not to conclude that many of the vexations of life in the new suburbs are the outcome of their physical design. This chapter and the next will inspect the components of sprawl, comparing them to the traditional elements that they replaced.

The first complaint one always hears about suburbia is the traffic congestion. More than any other factor, the perception of excessive traffic is what causes citizens to take up arms against growth in suburban communities. This perception is generally justified: in most American cities, the worst traffic is to be found not downtown but in the surrounding suburbs, where an "edge city" chokes highways that were originally built for lighter loads. In newer cities such as Phoenix and Atlanta, where there is not much of a downtown to speak of, traffic congestion is consistently cited as the single most frustrating aspect of daily life.

Why have suburban areas, with their height limits and low density of population, proved to be such a traffic nightmare? The first reason, and the obvious one, is that everyone is forced to drive. In modern suburbia, where pedestrians, bicycles, and public transportation are rarely an option, the average household currently generates thirteen car trips per day. Even if each trip is fairly short—and few are—that's a lot of time spent on the road, contributing to congestion, especially when compared to life in traditional neighborhoods. Traffic engineer Rick Chellman, in his landmark study of Portsmouth, New Hampshire, applied standard suburban trip-generation rates to that town's historic core, and found that they predicted twice as much traffic as actually existed there. Owing to its pedestrian-friendly plan—and in spite of its pedestrian-unfriendly weather—Portsmouth generates half the automobile trips of a modern-day suburb.[*]

---

[*] Rick Chellman, *Portsmouth Traffic/Trip Generation Study,* overview. Actually, half the trips here means less than half the traffic, as urban trips are generally considerably shorter than suburban trips. Interestingly, during the morning and evening rush hours, the number of trips was 60 to 70 percent lower than predicted.

But even if the suburbs were to generate no more trips than the city, they would still suffer from traffic to a much greater extent because of the way they are organized. The diagram shown here illustrates how a suburban road system, what engineers call a *sparse hierarchy,* differs from a traditional street network. The components of the suburban model are easy to spot in the top half of the diagram: the shopping mall in its sea of parking, the fast-food joints, the apartment complex, the looping cul-de-sacs of the housing subdivision.• Buffered from the others, each of these components has its own individual connection to a larger external road called the *collector.* Every single trip from one component to another, no matter how short, must enter the collector. Thus, the traffic of an entire community may rely on a single road, which, as a result, is generally congested during much of the day. If there is a major accident on the collector, the entire system is rendered useless until it is cleared.

A typical neighborhood is shown in the bottom half of the diagram. It accommodates all the same components as the suburban model, but they are organized as a web, a densely interconnected system that reduces demand on the collector road. Unlike suburbia, the neighborhood presents the opportunity to walk or bicycle. But even if few do so, its gridded network is superior at handling

Sprawl (above) versus the traditional neighborhood (below): in contrast to the traditional network of many walkable streets, the sprawl model not only eliminates pedestrian connections but focuses all traffic onto a single road

---

The suburban model presents us with a whole series of vicious circles. Traffic congestion results in the construction of additional roadways, which encourage people to drive more, generating more traffic. Engineering standards that respond to automobile dependence create environments in which walking is even less viable. Parking lots built to contain all the cars necessitated by an automotive environment cause buildings to be located increasingly farther apart, again making walking less likely. In every case, techniques developed in response to suburban land-use patterns end up perpetuating those very patterns.

• These single-use suburban pods are the real-estate equivalent of what biologists call a *monoculture,* characterized by its genetic poverty (Jonathan Rose, "Violence, Materialism, and Ritual," 144). Environments this simple and homogeneous are not considered fertile ground for continued evolution.

automobile traffic, providing multiple routes between destinations.[*] Because the entire system is available for local travel, trips are dispersed, and traffic on most streets remains light. If there is an accident, drivers simply choose an alternate path. The efficiency of the traditional grid explains why Charleston, South Carolina, at 2,500 acres, handles an annual tourist load of 5.5 million people with little congestion, while Hilton Head Island, ten times larger, experiences severe backups at 1.5 million visitors. Hilton Head, for years the suburban planners' exemplar, focuses all its traffic on a single collector road.

The suburban model does offer one advantage over the neighborhood model: it is much easier to analyze statistically. Because every single trip follows a predetermined path, traffic can be measured and predicted accurately. When the same measurement techniques are applied to an open network, the statistical chart goes flat; prediction becomes impossible and, indeed, unnecessary. But the suburban model still holds sway, and traffic engineers enjoy a position of unprecedented influence, often determining single-handedly what gets built and what doesn't. That traffic can occupy such a dominant position in the public discourse is indication enough that planning needs to be rethought from top to bottom.

WHEN NEARBY IS STILL FAR AWAY

Another paradox of suburban planning is the distinction that it creates between adjacency and accessibility. While many of the desti-

---

[*] Interestingly, the suburban system, with its overly wide streets, requires no less pavement than the traditional network; often, it requires more. But it typically seems the opposite, since most roads are dead ends serving no connective function.

nations of daily life are often next to each other, only rarely are they easy to reach directly.

For example, even though the houses pictured here are adjacent to the shopping center, in experience they are considerably more distant. Local ordinances have forced the developers to build a wall between the two properties, discouraging even the most intrepid citizen from walking to the store. The resident of a house just fifty yards away must still get into the car, drive half a mile to exit the subdivision, drive another half mile on the collector road back to the shopping center, and then walk from car to store. What could have been a pleasant two-minute walk down a residential street becomes instead an expedition requiring the use of gasoline, roadway capacity, and space for parking.

Adjacency versus accessibility: thanks to the code requirements for walls, ditches, and other buffers, even nearby shopping is not reachable on foot

Supporters of this separatist single-use zoning argue that people do not want to live near shopping. This is only partially true. Some don't, and some do. But suburbia does not provide that choice, because even adjacent uses are contrived to be distant. The planning model that does provide citizens with a choice can be seen in the New England town pictured here. One can live above the store, next to the store, five minutes from the store, or nowhere near the store, and it is easy to imagine the different age groups and personalities that would prefer each alternative. In this way and others, the traditional neighborhood provides for an array of lifestyles. In suburbia, there is only one available lifestyle: to own a car and to need it for everything.

The traditional town: its organization allows citizens to choose how close they wish to live to shopping and other mixed uses

THE CONVENIENCE STORE
VERSUS THE CORNER STORE

The suburban debasement of the corner store: plastic signs and parking lots

The 7-Eleven as designed by Norman Rockwell: a retail building that is compatible with its residential neighbors

The suburbanites' aversion to living close to shopping is strong. For a number of years, Miami–Dade County, Florida, has permitted developers to place up to five acres of shopping in their otherwise exclusively residential subdivisions, but that option has never been exercised. County planners point to this as evidence of the undesirability of retail. Actually, this tendency arises not out of an aversion to retail per se but from a loathing of the form that retail takes in suburbia: the drive-in Quick Mart. Many planners can tell horror stories about attempting to place a store in an existing residential development, only to have the terrified neighbors threaten civil action. While these designers may be proposing a traditional corner store, what the neighbors are picturing instead is a Quick Mart: an aluminum and glass flat-topped building bathed in fluorescent light, surrounded by asphalt, and topped by a glowing plastic sign. It's not that these people don't need convenient access to orange juice and cat food like everyone else; they just know that the presence of a Quick Mart nearby will make their environment uglier and their property values lower.

But what if the Quick Mart were really to take the form of a traditional corner store? Judging by popular reaction to the two models, one might never suspect that they both sell the same things. They are both small places to pick up small amounts of convenience goods. Yet one is a welcome neighbor, a social center, and a contributor to property values, while the other is considered a blight. The critical difference between the two is the volume of the building and its relationship to the street, two factors that can be combined under the heading of *building typology*. The building type of this corner store is essentially the same as the town houses next to it: two stories high, three windows wide, built of brick, and situated directly against the sidewalk, which its entrance faces. One could imagine it may even have been a town house once, so well does it blend in among its neighbors.

In contrast, the Quick Mart—one story tall and facing a parking lot[*]—has little in common with its residential neighbors and is therefore unwelcome. Compatibility has less to do with use than with building type. When typology is compatible, a variety of activities can coexist side by side.

THE SHOPPING CENTER VERSUS MAIN STREET

Big-box suburban retail presents the same problems writ large. Many people, when they come across a scene like the one pictured at the top of the next page, assume that the developer has somehow gotten away with something. Sadly, this shopping center and others like it are examples of the developers following the rules, building such retail the only way it is allowed. Almost every aspect of what is

---

[*] The presence of the parking lot in front of the building, in addition to damaging the pedestrian quality of the street, gives the signal that the store is oriented less toward its local neighbors than toward strangers driving by. This impression is further fueled by the likelihood that the store is owned by a national chain—an absentee landlord—with no local ties. While one would hope that the national chains might eventually replace their anti-neighborhood building types with more compatible designs, an even happier solution would involve the replacement of the chain stores by local businesses. In most places, however, it is naïve to hope for such an outcome. Given the realities of modern business—people's apparent preference for chain stores—it is far more productive to promote good design to the national retailers than to try to put them out of business.

Suburban retail, by the book: what developers build if they follow the rules

Mizner Park in Boca Raton, Florida: the shopping mall rearranged as Main Street, with offices and apartments above

pictured here has been taken straight out of the code books: the size of the sign, the number of spaces in the parking lot, the placement of the lighting fixtures, the thickness of the asphalt, even the precise hue of the yellow stripes between the parking spaces. A considerable amount of time, energy, and care goes into creating an environment that most find unpleasant and tawdry.

Mizner Park in Boca Raton, Florida, represents a different way to organize a large-scale retail center. This new main street far outperforms the suburban competition; it has even become a tourist destination. Mizner Park offers a superior physical environment that attracts people whether or not they need to shop. Its desirability stems from the carefully shaped public space it provides, as well as its traditional mix of uses: shops downstairs, offices and apartments above. Parking is neatly tucked away in garages to the rear. When well designed and well managed, this sort of mixed-use main-street retail is more profitable to own than the strip center or the shopping mall.•

Another success story is Mashpee Commons, in Massachusetts. It may be hard to believe, but the lively downtown pictured below was once the defunct strip center shown above it. This retrofit demonstrates not only the superiority of main street over the strip but also the ease with which some parts of suburbia can be reclaimed.

Its allure has not escaped the attention of the leading retailers. National merchants such as The Gap and Banana Republic, once focused exclusively on malls, have reoriented themselves toward

---

• "Well designed" means characterized by a harmonious architecture and streetscape. "Well managed" means clean and safe, with a truly useful mix of stores. In any case, it must be acknowledged that highway-oriented commercial properties will always constitute some small part of the American landscape. A traditional town center is capable of incorporating one or two big-box retailers, but aggregations of auto dealers, homebuilding suppliers, and discount warehouses will probably always seek locations on the outskirts of town, as is appropriate. What is odd about the present situation is that, with few exceptions, all scales of retail are currently relegated to highway locations.

traditional main streets. And some of the country's largest real estate developers, such as Federal Realty, are now routinely investing in downtowns such as Bethesda's and Santa Barbara's in order to develop main-street shopping districts. While the days of the shopping mall are not over, main streets are experiencing a resurgence.[•] When they are smart enough to appropriate management experience from the malls, traditionally designed downtowns can be quite competitive as retail locations.

Mashpee Commons, before: the strip center, unloved and short-lived

THE OFFICE PARK VERSUS MAIN STREET

Today, Mizner Park represents the latest in urban design innovation. Seventy-five years ago, these techniques were nothing more than common sense. The close proximity of living, working, and shopping was the most economic and convenient way to build. An exemplary version of this previous generation of mixed-use downtowns is Palmer Square in Princeton, New Jersey. This apparently historic collection of colonial buildings was actually constructed in the thirties as a real estate venture by a single developer.[■] Like Mizner Park, it derives its popularity in part from its lively combination of shops, offices, apartments, and even a substantial hotel.

Palmer Square is an unusually satisfying place because it contains, in close proximity, all the destinations of daily life. The

Mashpee Commons, after: reclaimed by the forces of urbanity

[•] An extreme example would be in Winter Park, Florida, where an aging suburban-era mall was "killed" by a resurgence in the city's downtown shops. Credit for many main-street revivals is due to the National Trust for Historic Preservation's Main Street Program, which provides funding and advice to communities across the country.
[■] The fact that most visitors mistake this ensemble for something much older, and enjoy it for that reason, throws into question the current professional distaste for historical replication. Even architects and preservationists have been fooled.

Palmer Square, Princeton: shops and restaurants below offices and apartments

The standard suburban office park: offices and parking, but nothing to do at lunchtime

workplace is an especially vital component here because it contributes to the viability of the shops by providing a daytime customer base for cafés, restaurants, and convenience shopping. It also offers employees the option of living in the same neighborhood where they work, a benefit that is not lost on New Jersey's weary commuters.

Offices above shops constitute one of the traditional urban workplace building types. In suburbia, the workplace is typically located in the office park. The accompanying illustration of a proposed office park, not so far from most workers' reality, stands in startling contrast to Palmer Square. This artist's rendering was presumably commissioned in order to make the project as attractive as possible. Unfortunately, the image is immediately suspect, for the artist has included something that is only a theoretical possibility: a pedestrian, flanked on one side by a vast parking lot and on the other by a barreling semi. Can one imagine that this person would actually choose to be there?

Pedestrian activity in such an environment is a fantasy. It feels unsafe, because there is no layer of parked cars or landscape to protect the pedestrian, physically and psychologically, from the onrush of traffic. Also, it is an incredibly boring place to walk, as the only distraction is provided by the grilles of the cars in the parking lot. Most important, it is a good bet that the pedestrian is not within easy walking distance of any destination worth walking to.

Whether or not one accepts the presence of a pedestrian in this scene, it is worth considering the quality of life of a typical employee in this office park. She can get to work only by car. Her valuable lunch hour provides precisely two choices: she can either eat in the company cafeteria or do what most people do: spend twenty-five minutes out of sixty fighting traffic in order to rush through a meal at a chain restaurant. In Palmer Square, workers are able to walk out onto the street and choose from a dozen local restaurants and cafés, enjoy a proper meal, and then use the extra time to run errands or just sit in the sun on the square. It may not be crepes on the Rive Gauche, but the Palmer Square experience makes the office-park lunch hour seem bleak indeed.

USELESS AND USEFUL OPEN SPACE

What do the suburbs offer that might compensate for what appears to be a compromised quality of life? Many people would say that the suburb's main advantage over the city is its generous provision of open space. Identified as a way to ensure a healthy environment, open space is mandated in copious quantities by suburban codes, and there is a long history behind this requirement. Nineteenth-century city planning wisely promoted landscape as a solution to a widespread urban health crisis. By the mid-twentieth century, this approach had generated an image of the ideal city as fully integrated with the natural environment, made up of vast conservation areas, continuous waterways, agricultural greenbelts, recreational trails, frequent parks, and yards surrounding every building. But, like many modern planning ideals, this one, too, has come to life in a dramatically compromised form. In today's conventional suburbs, man's relationship to nature is represented by engineered drainage pits surrounded by chain-link fences, exaggerated building setbacks at road frontages, useless buffers of green between compatible land uses, and a tree requirement for parking lots.

Suburban open space: residual and unused

The degeneration of the suburban landscape can be blamed on the fact that the current requirements for public open space, although derived from a rich and varied tradition of qualitative prescriptions, have been reduced to a set of regulations that are primarily statistical. These requirements say little about the configuration and quality of open space;* usually, the main specification is a percentage of the site area. Because there is no stipulation about its design, developers often distribute this required acreage along the houses' backyards, in order to provide residents with a longer view. The resulting swath of green is rarely used, precisely because it feels like a backyard; to occupy it violates the privacy of the houses.

The assumption that the residue left over after the roads and buildings are laid out can be satisfactory open space neglects the fact that people use open space in specific ways. Preserves, greenways, parks, plazas, squares, and promenades represent a regional to local hierarchy of open-space types that serve a variety of uses: nature conservation and continuity, active recreation, playgrounds for the youngest, strolling ground for the oldest, and so on. It is only by providing this full range of specific open spaces that planning authorities can ensure citizens the quality of life that their codes were originally intended to provide.

To truly improve quality of life, the planning codes must define open space with the same degree of precision and concern that they now apply to the design of parking lots. As an example, let us

---

*An exception to this rule is the municipal park for active recreation, typically the only type of park that suburban municipalities provide. Like the new schools already described, these sports fields are often designed for ease of maintenance rather than for accessibility. As a result, they tend to be consolidated into excessively large parcels well beyond pedestrian range.

consider the square, as pictured here. What makes a square? It is the size of a small city block. It is surrounded by public streets lined by buildings with entries and windows, for maximum activity and visual supervision. It has trees at its edge to define the space and to provide shade on hot days, and it is sunny and open at its center for cooler days. It has paved areas for strolling and grassy areas for sports. If any of these elements were missing, then this open space could not be called a square.

Traditional open space: carefully derived from proven models

Equally precise standards could be established for the full range of traditional open spaces so notably absent in conventional suburbia. Rules regarding the design of these social places should be administered by the same authority that now controls the design of parking lots, and with equal vigor. Only specific standards will produce the specific places that support specific activities. Without them, the term *open space* will only describe the dribble of green that is left over after the developer has finished laying out the houses.

WHY CURVING ROADS AND CUL-DE-SACS DO NOT MAKE MEMORABLE PLACES

Another detail of sprawl that merits reconsideration is its predisposition toward exclusively curvilinear streets. How did curves come to be considered the hallmark of good street design, when most of the world's great places have streets that are primarily straight? The conventional belief that straight streets are rigid and boring holds little water when one considers Savannah, San Francisco, and any number of other places.

The origin of the curved street can be found in those pathways across the landscape that respond to steep topography by following the undulating patterns of the land. Similarly, cul-de-sacs, those lollipop-shaped dead-end roads found throughout suburbia, derive from terrain in which steep and frequent valleys do not allow streets to connect across them. Historically, both techniques were used only where required by topography, as they limit connectivity and make smaller lots awkward to build on. Placing excessive curves and cul-de-sacs on flat land makes about as much sense as driving off-road vehicles around the city. Yet the curve and cul-de-sac subdivision is as common on flat land as it is on hills, one of the great clichés of our time.

Indeed, it is difficult to recall a residential area less than fifty years old that has straight streets, which is one reason suburban subdivisions all seem the same. But there is a more serious problem: unrelenting curves create an environment that is utterly disorienting. It is no wonder that so many people associate visiting suburbia with getting lost. Experience would suggest that the real purpose of the ubiquitous suburban gatehouse is not to keep out burglars but to give directions. Even Rand McNally appears overwhelmed by the onslaught of sprawling curlicues; its maps, normally direct and confident, often seem to devolve into hopeless chicken scratch at the suburban fringes.*

SITE DATA

	Acres	Units
Single Family #1	215.2 AC	300 Lots
Single Family #2	382.3 AC	493 Lots
Single Family #3	38.4 AC	44 Lots
Single Family #4	149.4 AC	249 Lots
Fayette County	9.2 AC	13 Lots

Chicken scratch: the typically disorienting suburban street pattern that winds back on itself

---

* It bears mentioning that this disorientation is by no means unintentional. Designers of the first curvilinear subdivisions, before the days of gated communities, promoted confusingly curvy streets as a means to discourage unwelcome cruising by strangers. Similarly, cul-de-sacs first became popular as a means to eliminate cut-through traffic from residential neighborhoods, and there are still instances where they may be appropriate to establish territoriality in high-crime areas. But none of this explains why the curve and the cul-de-sac have become so ubiquitous.

That said, curved streets can serve a valuable aesthetic purpose: they provide a constantly changing view as one moves through space, rather than the boring and endless vista that can result from a long straight road. This problem, usually the outcome of a gridiron street pattern, is easily avoided by modifying the grid so that continuous streets are slightly bent while maintaining their general cardinal directions. Curves, per se, are not the problem; the problem is driving along on a street that heads north and finding oneself heading east, then south, then west.

In fact, the use of a controlled curve to terminate a vista is a sophisticated design technique, and should not be avoided. It dependably provides the sense of intimacy that generates feelings of identity, belonging, and ownership. But there are other ways to terminate a vista, such as the careful placement of a public building, a hallmark of traditional town planning. The scene pictured here, St. Philip's Episcopal Church in Charleston, did not happen by accident. As already mentioned, the builders of historic towns customarily reserved their most noble sites for civic buildings. The top of a hill, the end of a street, the side of a plaza—these would be set aside for the church, the town hall, the library, and other public structures worthy of honor.

A terminated vista: traditional street networks provide orientation through the celebration of significant buildings

In suburbia, there are no honorable sites for honorable institutions. Civic buildings are sited like any other land use: behind a parking lot off the collector road. Compare that location with the placement of St. Philip's, which terminates vistas in two directions. This is a view that gives a unique identity to its neighborhood and its city, a view that tourism officials put on posters to inspire people to spend their vacations in Charleston. Unfortunately, this sort of siting is now typically impossible, thanks to the traffic engineers who

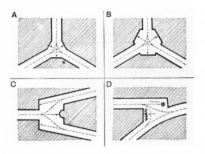

Currently illegal: traditional intersections designed to create memorable places

The safety of perceived danger: older, difficult intersections are actually safer than their carefully engineered counterparts because they cause drivers to slow down

maintain that if you place a building at the termination of a vista, someone will surely run into it. Never mind that no one has driven into St. Philip's in a hundred years.

The honorable placement of civic buildings benefits from the use of traditional intersections designed for just that purpose. A catalogue of these intersections was published in 1909 by the town planner Raymond Unwin. *Town Planning in Practice* is still the best planning manual available. It provides page after page of intersection geometries that designers still study with admiration. Making use of them, however, is another matter altogether, as the local official, planning for the "drunk driver at midnight," rejects them on sight. Even in old towns that are full of them, these intersections are typically illegal. Meanwhile, those that do still exist are usually safer statistically than the latest Department of Transportation model, precisely because they don't feel safe at high speeds. The geometries tell drivers that extra care is required, and drivers respond by slowing down.

An extreme example of the safe "unsafe" intersection is Confusion Corner in Stuart, Florida, where seven streets and an at-grade railroad track all meet at odd angles. The state D.O.T. was prepared to spend hundreds of thousands of dollars to reconfigure the entire area because their manuals suggested that it must be dangerous. Local citizens, however, defended their notorious intersection, the community's prime postcard-worthy location. Despite the intersection's reputation, studies revealed that it was among the region's safest major intersections, with only one accident in its multidecade history. The deadliest local intersections were all the standard D.O.T. models.

Those readers who are skeptical that unusual intersections are actually safer will be surprised to learn that traffic accidents in Sweden dropped by 17 percent when the country switched from driving on the left side of the street to the right. As motorists slowly became accustomed to the new rule, accidents returned to their earlier rate.[•]

The practice of using roadway geometry to improve safety has come to be known as *traffic calming,* which is developing into a fairly elaborate discipline with many tools at its disposal. Speed bumps, rumble strips, hammerheads, flare-outs, doglegs, and other combinations of geometry, landscape, and street furniture can be effective in lowering drivers' speed on local streets. Following successes in Europe, American communities have begun to install these devices, with good results. While this development is encouraging, it is important to note that traffic calming is often necessary only because streets have been built the wrong way to begin with, unnecessarily wide and with too much distance between intersections. Rather than continuing to build local roads like highways and subsequently hobbling them with speed bumps, municipalities could instead control their traffic by once again allowing narrow roads and artful intersections. This would be an important first step toward creating public spaces worthy of habitation.

[•] Malcolm Gladwell, "Blowup," 36. In another study, taxi operators in Munich, Germany, were given anti-lock brakes and secretly observed over a three-year period. Initially safer drivers, they were found to drive more and more recklessly until they regained their prior accident rate. This type of phenomenon has been termed *risk homeostasis.* People naturally adjust their behavior to the level of risk that they are comfortable with.

Narrow streets and difficult intersections are useful in communicating to drivers that they do not, in fact, own the road. Under ideal circumstances, drivers passing through a well-designed residential neighborhood are made to feel that they are *borrowing* the street space from the people who live there.

3

THE HOUSE THAT SPRAWL BUILT

THE ODDITY OF AMERICAN HOUSING; PRIVATE REALM VERSUS
PUBLIC REALM; THE SEGREGATION OF SOCIETY BY INCOME; TWO
ILLEGAL TYPES OF AFFORDABLE HOUSING; TWO FORGOTTEN RULES
OF AFFORDABLE HOUSING; THE MIDDLE-CLASS HOUSING CRISIS

———

Does anyone suppose that, in real life, answers to any of the great
questions that worry us today are going to come out of homogeneous
settlements?

—JANE JACOBS, *THE DEATH AND LIFE
OF GREAT AMERICAN CITIES* (1961)

———

THE ODDITY OF AMERICAN HOUSING

Sprawl is made up mostly of housing. Its ubiquity alone makes it an
important subject to study, but there are other reasons to consider
the way America provides housing. While the current suburban
model may seem natural enough to most Americans, it appears
quite odd when viewed in a global context. There is not another
nation on earth that houses its citizens as we do, and few could
afford to. Nevertheless, the proliferation of large-lot single-family
housing has begun around the world, despite our awareness of its
negative social and environmental consequences. The fact that

other nations, enamored of American culture and commercial methods, are beginning to emulate these practices should not validate them for us. Indeed, the frightening prospect of worldwide suburbia makes it all the more essential that we examine the ways that contemporary American housing deviates from its global and historical counterparts. It will become clear that there are powerful implications to the unprecedented way that we choose to locate and design our homes.

Today's suburban reality finds its origins in the pastoral dream of the autonomous homestead in the countryside. Articulated throughout U.S. history, from Jefferson through Limbaugh, this vision has been equated with a democratic economy, in which homeownership equals participation. However, this equation seems to have its limits, as only a small number of people can achieve that dream without compromising it for all involved. As the middle class rushes to build its countryside cottages at the same time on the same land, the resulting environment is inevitably unsatisfying, its objective self-contradictory: isolation en masse.

The diminishing returns of successive flights toward bucolic serenity have been well documented. Inner-ring suburbs, the previous generation's great escape, have begun to decay as newer subdivisions are built at the suburban fringe. These subdivisions will in turn lose their populations to new housing yet farther out. Meanwhile, as existing infrastructure becomes underused, new infrastructure is built at great expense, and traffic worsens daily. The central, yet unstated, assumptions of this centrifugal system of growth are the abandonment of existing neighborhoods and the mandatory purchase of one car per adult.

PRIVATE REALM VERSUS PUBLIC REALM

In the sparse universe of sprawl, the elementary particle is the single-family house. The current model is the fast-food version of the American dream—some call it the McMansion. Its roots can be traced back to the manse on the agricultural estate, or the cabin in the woods. Unlike its predecessors, however, the McMansion is located in the center of a small plot of land, surrounded at close quarters by more of the same. The aesthetic deficiencies of this form of housing are so obvious that a number of well-known architects have made a name for themselves by seeking inspiration in its kitsch. But the real problems here are not aesthetic but practical.

The McMansion: independent of its aesthetic qualities, an excellent value

Like its culinary counterpart, the McMansion provides excellent value for its price. American homebuilders are perhaps the best in the world when it comes to providing buyers with the private realm, the insides of the house. Dollar for dollar, no other society approaches the United States in terms of the number of square feet per person, the number of baths per bedroom, the number of appliances in the kitchen, the quality of the climate control, and the convenience of the garage. The American private realm is simply a superior product. The problem is that most suburban residents, the minute they leave this refuge, are confronted by a tawdry and stressful environment. They enter their cars and embark on a journey of banality and hostility that lasts until they arrive at the interior of their next destination. Americans may have the finest private realm in the developed world, but our public realm is brutal. Confronted by repetitive subdivisions, treeless collector roads, and vast parking lots, the citizen finds few public spaces worth visiting. One's role in this environment is primarily as a motorist competing for asphalt.

Outside the McMansion: a depleted public realm

This disjunction between the private and public realm has resulted in a uniquely American form of schizophrenia, suburban Nimbyism. The reason people say, "I like living here, but I don't want any others like me living here," is that new suburban development does not provide them with any more of the satisfying private realm that they love; it only gives them more of the degraded public realm toward which they feel indifferent at best.

While they are known to present environmental arguments, the Nimbys' first concern is rarely ecology. Nor do they care to discuss the link between low-density housing and dependence upon the automobile. All they need to know is that new development, with its wide streets and vast parking lots, will be boring and unpleasant to visit and will, of course, generate more traffic. The exchange of a woodland or farm for a new subdivision is, in terms of the public realm, an uncompensated loss.

This state of affairs contrasts markedly with the way development used to occur. In America's pre–World War II suburbs, the private and public realms were of equal quality, and the prospect of growth was invariably welcomed. Fortunately, many of these places still exist, and most adults have encountered them. Most American cities have at least one turn-of-the-century neighborhood that can provide a powerful example of desirable growth. For this reason, Nimbys with a good memory or some travel experience are not beyond discussing new development in a thoughtful way. If they can be shown that future development will provide them with a gratifying public realm—narrow tree-lined streets, parks, a corner grocery, a café, a small neighborhood school—they may even embrace growth.

THE SEGREGATION OF SOCIETY BY INCOME

There are many characteristics of contemporary suburban housing that distinguish it from its traditional counterpart. Perhaps the strangest and most troubling of these is the way that new housing is distributed. The photo at right shows a typical suburban landscape, this one composed of three different housing pods, or *clusters*. One cluster consists entirely of houses that sell for $350,000 and up. The second cluster contains houses costing about $200,000. The third cluster is made up of apartments priced at less than $100,000. This sort of organization, a suburban invention, represents a relatively recent phenomenon in this country. Our history is fraught with many different types of segregation—by race, by class, by how recently one has immigrated—but for the first time we are now experiencing ruthless segregation by minute gradations of income. There have always been better and worse neighborhoods, and the rich have often taken refuge from the poor, but never with such precision. It would appear that, for many, there is little distinction between someone slightly less wealthy than themselves and a Skid Row bum. To prove this point, one need only to attempt to build a $200,000 house on an empty lot in the $350,000 cluster; the homeowners' association will immediately sue. Certainly, any mention of the word *affordability* is enough to elicit all manner of objections in the new suburbs.

The segregation of housing by "market segment" is a phenomenon that was invented by developers who, lacking a meaningful way to distinguish their mass-produced merchandise, began selling the concept of exclusivity: *If you live within these gates, you can consider yourself a success.* The real estate business caters to this elitism so

The landscape of income segregation: gated homogeneous housing pods

relentlessly that even some mobile home parks are marketed in this way.

In such a Darwinian pecking order—in which each house is sold with bragging rights attached—homeowners are prone to get a bit panicky about the value of the house next door. They fear that if a neighbor chooses the wrong paint color, neglects to mow the lawn, or owns an overweight dog, their own property value will plummet. And, since the average American moves every six years,[1] property value is difficult to ignore.

Moving is a well-established tradition in America, and *moving up* constitutes a significant part of the American dream. Not only is working one's way to a bigger house central to our ethos but it makes sense functionally as families bring children into the world. But why must the move to a larger or more luxurious house bring with it the abandonment of one's neighbors, community groups, and often even schoolmates? Sadly, the suburban pod system causes people to move not just from house to house but from community to community. Only in a traditionally organized neighborhood of varied incomes can a family significantly alter its housing without going very far. In the new suburbs, you can't move up without moving out.•

It doesn't take a sociology degree to predict the sort of culture that this pattern of income-segregated housing creates. There is plenty of evidence in California, Florida, and the other Sun Belt states: the people in the gated pods are the ones consistently voting down necessary taxes. Not one penny more to support the inner city,

---

• The same is true of moving down. Seniors seeking a smaller house are often forced to abandon their familiar community and start over someplace else.

the homeless, schools, parks, or even for the maintenance of the public realm at large. Meanwhile, these people often pay hundreds, sometimes thousands, of dollars a month to their homeowners' association to maintain their personal archipelago. The rest of the world is expected to take care of itself. Robert Reich calls this phenomenon the "secession of the successful."[2]

There has been much discussion recently about gated communities, for they are on their way to becoming the standard American form of settlement. In *Fortress America: Gated Communities in the United States,* Edward Blakely and Mary Gail Snyder placed the number of gated communities at approximately 20,000, holding more than 3 million housing units. They report that "a leading national real estate developer estimates that eight out of every ten new urban projects are gated." This phenomenon is spreading all over the country, but it remains strongest in Southern California, where "a 1990 survey of Southern California home shoppers found that 54 percent wanted a home in a gated, walled development."[3] The repulsion that many citizens feel toward such communities may be justified, but it is important to remember that the problem with gated communities is not the gate itself but what the gate encloses. Nobody objects to the walled towns of Europe and Asia, because they were home to a full cross section of society rather than only a privileged elite. The unity of society is threatened not by the use of gates but by the uniformity and exclusivity of the people behind them.

Unfortunately, the segregationist pattern is self-perpetuating. A child growing up in such a homogeneous environment is less likely to develop a sense of empathy for people from other walks of life and is ill prepared to live in a diverse society. The *other* becomes alien to the child's experience, witnessed only through the sensationalizing eye of the television. The more homogeneous and "safe" the environment, the less understanding there is of all that is different, and the less concern for the world beyond the subdivision walls. It works both ways: the poor also have little understanding of the middle class, whom they consider to be in no way like themselves, and universally insensitive to their hardships.•

How did Americans live before the balkanization created by sprawl? Pictured here is a section of Georgetown, in Washington, D.C. For over a century, these blocks have housed people of widely divergent incomes. There are rental apartment buildings that house schoolteachers, clerks, and recent college graduates. There are town homes that house professionals, young families, and retirees, some of whom may rent out basement apartments to secretaries, day care workers, and students. There are also a number of mansions that are home to some of the great fortunes of the Mid-Atlantic. These have carriage houses and garage apartments on their property that may house artists, architects, and other members of the intentionally poor. In this small part of Georgetown, a large part of American society is represented.

The astute observer will notice that there is a certain form of segregation here: apartments face apartments, town houses face town houses, and mansions face mansions. Housing types are segregated street by street, with the transition always occurring at mid-block, where backyards meet. Like the suburban system, this

The traditional neighborhood as social condenser: a single block in Georgetown provides housing for a wide range of incomes

•This situation is exacerbated by distance. In the contemporary metropolis, the wealthy suburbs typically grow in the opposite direction from the poor side of town, which grows in its own direction. Diverse groups are located miles apart, in an extreme form of spatial inequity.

technique preserves property values and ensures a consistent streetscape. Unlike the suburban system, it does not isolate people from one another. The same sidewalks, the same parks, and the same corner store serve everyone from the C.E.O. to the local librarian. Sharing the same public realm, these people have the opportunity to interact, and thus come to realize that they have little reason to fear each other.

Not only is a society healthier when its diverse members are in daily contact with one another, it is also more convenient. Imagine living just around the corner from your doctor, your child's schoolteacher, and your baby-sitting aunt. Imagine being able to grow old in a neighborhood that can accommodate your changing housing needs while also providing a home for your children and grandchildren. Of course, living in Georgetown does not guarantee that this outcome will occur—but living in Phoenix guarantees that it will not.

Georgetown demonstrates that it is not only due to elitism that suburbia fails to provide mixed-income housing. Making the transition between different housing types at mid-block is only possible within a system of traditional blocks, and this system is often absent in the suburbs. As shown here, the preferred technique of suburban design is to spin the buildings around in search of a pleasantly picturesque effect, rarely achieved. This aesthetic is promulgated by planners and engineers with no aesthetic training and is a far cry from the true discipline of the picturesque, whose intention it is to design spaces that are satisfying not just on paper but perceptually, in three dimensions. Lacking the discipline of building fronts and backs, this kind of suburban planning rules out the possibility of mixing housing type street by street. In fact, there are no streets to speak of, only residual parking lots squeezed between the buildings.

Train wreck: planning in futile pursuit of the picturesque creates buildings without fronts, backs, or street addresses

A typical block in Kentlands: mansions, row houses, and apartments

Planning for diversity: housing on this one block ranges in price from $500,000 homes to $750-per-month apartments

The recently built Kentlands neighborhood in Gaithersburg, Maryland, is a good example of diverse housing. Mansions sit just around the corner from town houses, with garage apartments located on a shared rear lane. Despite its roots in tradition, this design was considered absolutely radical when we proposed it. First, it was against the rules, as it continues to be illegal to mix housing types in most of the United States. Second, and more significant, it contradicted all the accumulated wisdom of the home-building industry, which said that integrating different prices in the same neighborhood would kill sales.

As the ensuing high prices indicated, the experts were mistaken applying conventional wisdom to Kentlands. Variety may be something to fear when selling houses in an isolated pod, but in a real neighborhood, the more housing types the better. In a neighborhood, people buy the community first and the house second. The more a place resembles an authentic community, the more it is valued, and one hallmark of a real place is variety.•

One term that gets a lot of play these days is "cookie cutter." Developers are mortified about the way this term is used to describe their subdivisions, and they expend a good deal of energy—and money—avoiding it. As much as 20 percent of their construction budget goes toward the application of superficial variety—different shapes, colors, window types, different styles of tack-on ornament, French Provincial next door to California Contemporary. But these efforts are in vain, because beneath the surface articulation is a relentless repetition of the same building. The best way to create

---

• Wyndcrest, another Maryland project, also demonstrates that new developments need not conform to the price-point-segregation model. Values vary even more widely, with subsidized town houses at $77,000 facing market-rate houses at $297,000.

real variety is to vary not the architectural style but the building type. Indeed, in places like Georgetown, styles vary only slightly, but one never hears the term *cookie cutter,* thanks to the wide range of building types.

Interestingly, architectural style still plays a key role, but in the opposite way: it is often the consistent use of a single style that makes the integration of different building types possible. In Kentlands, the mid-Atlantic Georgian vocabulary camouflages differences by creating a harmonious streetscape. Any cachet that may be associated with the mansions rubs off on the apartments as well.

In truth, Georgetown and Kentlands only hint at the degree of integration possible among housing types and income levels. Different buildings can be made so compatible in terms of shape, placement, and architectural expression that there may be no need to segregate them, even street by street. This image, from Annapolis, shows two mansions, each worth several hundred thousand dollars, flanking two fourteen-foot-wide town houses. Here affordable housing is not a blight, as it is architecturally compatible with adjacent expensive housing. There is one flaw with housing of this type: the price tends to escalate right out of the affordable-housing market. But in doing so, it can bring the original homeowners along for the ride, into the middle class.•

Affordable housing in a wealthy neighborhood: two row houses sit among mansions in Annapolis

---

• Unfortunately, low-income renters would not participate in this windfall, and might be forced to move. This flaw, an inevitable result of success, should not be allowed to discourage initiatives for neighborhood revitalization. Instead, a responsible local housing policy must be in place to ensure the continued presence of affordable rentals within the neighborhood. Of course, if one wishes to provide new affordable housing that will never appreciate in value, the easiest solution may be to provide it in an incompatible avant-garde style.

TWO ILLEGAL TYPES OF AFFORDABLE HOUSING

The apartment above the store: the most efficient way to provide inexpensive housing is against the law in most of suburbia

In addition to the Annapolis town houses pictured, there are two other models of affordable housing that can be reclaimed from America's older neighborhoods. Both are currently illegal in most suburban zoning codes. One is the timeless custom of living above the store. The lingering memory of industrial pollution blighting residential areas has created a subconscious suburban reflex against providing apartments above commercial space. But since there is no longer any evidence of skyrocketing mortality rates, the arguments for mixed-use buildings become hard to fight. Upstairs apartments provide customers for the shops, activity for the street, and nighttime surveillance for the neighborhood. They also represent one of the most economical ways to provide housing, since the land and infrastructure costs are covered by the shops; the housing can be supplied for the cost of construction alone. The only possible additional expense stems from the local parking requirement, but wise municipalities will waive this rule, since residents need parking primarily when stores and offices are closed, their lots empty.

Not only does the apartment above the store create affordable housing, it also adds population to shopping districts that are otherwise dangerously empty after hours. Additionally, it contributes much-needed height to retail buildings, which with only one story fail to adequately define street space. All of those new Videosmiths, Eckerds, and Boston Markets have parapets that are too low to create a feeling of enclosure on the streets they face. By requiring new stores to be topped by affordable housing, and by subsidizing its implementation, municipalities can create spatial definition for their streets and bring a sense of security back to their downtowns.

Another form of apartment-above-the-store that is witnessing a resurgence is the store-below-the-house, otherwise known as the "live/work unit," which is really just a row house with a ground-floor store or office.• The main advantage of this building type is that it allows a homeowner to finance both a home and a place of business with a single mortgage. At Seaside, these units—which hold shops, artists' studios, and a café with the best espresso in northern Florida—surround the neighborhood's public square. As increasing numbers of Americans choose to work at home, one can imagine that the live/work unit could again become a staple of our communities.

A house and business on a single mortgage: live/work units at Seaside

The second all-but-forgotten form of affordable housing is the outbuilding, also known as the garage apartment or granny flat, which is essentially a bedroom that has migrated out of the body of the house into the rental market.■ The logic is straightforward: there are literally millions of unused bedrooms in this country, but they are not available because renting them out would violate the privacy of the homeowner. As an alternative, the house and the outbuilding create a wonderfully symbiotic system in several ways. The outbuilding provides affordable housing in stable single-family neighborhoods. Additionally, there is a built-in policing mechanism, since the landlord in the principal dwelling is personally responsible for the supervision of the often younger tenant. Also, rental payments from the outbuilding help pay the mortgage on the main house, thus

The backyard granny flat: a bedroom that has been liberated from the confines of the house

---

• The live/work unit can take many other forms as well, such as an office inhabiting the ground floor of a conventional house, or a house set to the rear of its lot, behind a front shop and courtyard.
■ While quite common in older neighborhoods, outbuildings are all but absent from suburbia, primarily because ordinances prohibit them. These ordinances arose mostly from abuse: too many outbuildings were built too large, eating up green space and taxing municipal infrastructure. This outcome can be easily avoided by limiting the size of outbuildings and the amount of plumbing they can hold.

bringing homeownership within closer reach of the middle class. In an interesting twist on this scenario, a young woman in Kentlands lives in her outbuilding and rents out the large house, covering her mortgage entirely. She will one day own a 2,700-square-foot home for the price of the down payment alone.

The final advantage of the outbuilding is the flexibility that it provides to household structure. In our society, which values both community and privacy but provides few alternatives between those two extremes, the outbuilding allows an extended family to live together and apart at the same time. How many middle-aged couples would reconsider opening their house to a widowed in-law or a grown child if they could only give them their own little apartment in the backyard?

In Charleston, South Carolina, the right way to do affordable housing: few in number and stylistically similar to middle-class homes nearby

TWO FORGOTTEN RULES OF AFFORDABLE HOUSING

Affordable housing, while seldom in the headlines, remains a crisis in the United States. Several lessons can be learned from America's long history of housing its poor, and if these lessons are surprisingly obvious, then it is all the more surprising how routinely they are ignored.

Above all, affordable housing should not look different from market-rate housing. The last thing the poor need is a home that stigmatizes them as such, when all they really want is what they perceive the middle class already has. The problem is that the poor, who are presumed to be grateful to have any home at all, have been the object of fifty years of architectural and planning experimentation. With the best intentions, designers have responded to the affordable-housing challenge with the very latest in untested technology and style. The resulting buildings—what the critic Robert

Campbell calls "billboards of indigence"—are often so laden with weird architectural notions that they look ridiculously out of place. This problem is only compounded by the fact that the poor themselves have until recently been largely absent from the design process, and thus unable to exert much influence on the outcome.[*] So, Rule #1: Don't experiment on the poor; they have no choice. Experiment on the rich, who can always move out.

The second rule of affordable housing, so often ignored, is that it should not be concentrated in large quantities. Rather, it should be distributed among market-rate housing as sparsely as possible in order to avoid neighborhood blight and reinforce positive behavior.[■] Probably the most costly error of federal housing policy in the 1960s and '70s was the massive relocation of poor people into terrifying public housing ghettos, many of which still exist today, with disastrous social consequences.

When it comes to the integration of different housing types, there is no established formula, but it seems safe to say that a neighborhood can easily absorb a one-in-ten insertion of affordable housing without adverse effects. In the image of Annapolis pictured earlier, this ratio would place the pair of town houses among twenty larger houses—hardly a threat. Such a distribution provides role models for the poor while mitigating against the close-mindedness

---

[*] There are other contributing factors as well, such as the fact that many municipal housing agencies have imposed institutional standards for construction and ease of maintenance on low-income housing developments, standards that cause these developments to appear even more out of place in their neighborhoods.

[■] Like most monocultures, impoverished neighborhoods are dangerously brittle. One of the manifestations of poverty is the fragility of normalcy. A broken-down car or even a broken window can represent a severe economic hardship. In such an environment, the evidence of small, untoward events can quickly accumulate into a critical mass of blight.

of the wealthy. The one-in-ten approach is gaining favor, but it must overcome a long tradition of government sponsored mega-projects. It is a difficult point to argue when the economies of scale suggest that housing can most efficiently be provided in bulk, like canned peas or paper towels. That may be true, but only in a simplistic analysis. Reducing the cost per unit of affordable housing in this way violates the larger goal of the housing program, which is to provide not just housing but viable places to live. Such places include a social support system; in other words, a community.

The tendency toward dangerous accumulations of affordable housing is unfortunately reinforced by the private development industry, which would prefer to see low-cost homes, especially rental apartments, kept far away from its middle-class subdivisions. Despite some recent examples of successful income-integrated communities, developers remain wary of setting aside their familiar practices. This is a situation in which government policy can make a difference. Since 1974, Montgomery County, Maryland, has let developers build 22 percent more units than they would normally be allowed, with the requirement that 15 percent of the additional units be "moderately priced." This program is not optional. According to Rick Ferrara, the executive director of the Housing Opportunities Commission, "None of the developers would do it if we didn't force them to." But since all developers are subject to the same law, the integration of lower-cost housing has become normal in Maryland's wealthiest county. Similar mandatory but reward-based techniques could be used to produce even higher levels of income integration.

Of the two rules discussed above, it appears that the federal government has learned the first but not the second. By the late nineties, the majority of housing constructed with federal assistance has come to be designed according to traditional models—houses and town houses in a network of streets, a vast improvement over the discredited "tower in the park." The Department of Housing and Urban Development has officially embraced the neighborhood concept, and their newest projects embody many of the planning principles described here. Some of these developments, like Ray Gindroz's redesign of several dysfunctional HUD projects, have received deserved attention for turning around the public housing experience. But, whatever its form, most subsidized housing is still highly concentrated, with only limited integration of market-rate units—well below the 10:1 ratio advocated here. One hopes that these new projects, with their improved architecture and urbanism, will engender good long-term management and not suffer the fate of St. Louis's Pruitt Igoe, Chicago's Cabrini Green, and similar projects that succumbed to social meltdowns so complete that they had to be demolished. But even architects should remain skeptical of the power of well-tested traditional models in the face of extreme social isolation.

Diggstown, in Norfolk, Virginia: a neighborhood-style retrofit of a previously distressed inner-city project that epitomizes HUD's new standards

THE MIDDLE-CLASS HOUSING CRISIS

Virtually all the thought brought to bear on the housing crisis has been directed toward the urban poor, and rightly so, for they inhabit an environment that most would find unbearable. But the housing crisis is a middle-class issue, too. It has become increasingly difficult for the middle class to own satisfactory housing. In 1970, about 50 percent of all families could afford a median-priced home; by 1990, this number had dropped below 25 percent.[4] There are many reasons behind this phenomenon, but the most significant factor is

Two cars per bedroom: investment in mandatory automobiles leaves little money for housing

evident in the image on the left. In what has become a typical sight in suburbia, this family appears to own almost as many square feet of vehicles as it does of housing. Since every single adult in the household must drive a car in order to function, this situation is unavoidable. The impact it has on housing affordability is profound.

According to the American Automobile Association, the average cost of owning a Ford Escort—one of the cheapest cars available—is over $6,000 per year. At conventional mortgage rates, that figure translates into more than $60,000 in home-purchasing power. In other words, two cars will pay for a starter home, and a better one than this photograph portrays.•

This is not just a theory. The banks that qualify mortgages are well aware of the burden that cars can present to homeownership. When qualifying a loan, bankers calculate the "back ratio," which reduces income by the borrower's existing debt, often primarily automotive. Bankers have been known to tell borrowers to sell their car, which the borrowers do, to a friend, from whom they buy it back upon receipt of the loan. And buy it back they must, since they live in an environment where life without it is impossible. In recognition of the burdens imposed by multiple automobile owner-ship, there is now even a new type of loan, a "location-efficient mortgage," that provides special terms to borrowers purchasing housing in pedestrian-friendly neighborhoods.■

• This calculation ignores the fact that most Americans are barraged by advertisements suggesting that their social stature depends on their driving something considerably more expensive than a Ford Escort. American automakers spend almost $40 billion annually promoting their products (Jane Holtz Kay, *Asphalt Nation,* 17).
■ These mortgages are currently available in Chicago, Seattle, and Los Angeles. Vice President Gore took this idea national and created a new $100 million Fannie Mae pro-gram that offers higher-valued loans to families that buy homes near transit. Along with the loan, families receive thirty-year transit passes as well.

The middle-class housing crisis is not new, and there has been no shortage of ideas designed to make the single-family house more affordable. The building industry and generations of architects have dedicated themselves to the task. The results—plastic plumbing, hollow doors, flimsy walls, vinyl cladding—are very clever, but all of them put together do not generate half the savings that can be achieved by allowing a family to own one car fewer. The problem is not one of architecture but of community planning, and as long as we continue to create places where walking, biking, and transit are pointless, we will continue to exacerbate the middle-class housing crisis.

4

THE PHYSICAL CREATION OF SOCIETY

ENVIRONMENTAL CAUSES OF A SOCIAL DECLINE; DRIVERS VERSUS PEDESTRIANS; THE FOUR PREREQUISITES FOR STREET LIFE: MEANINGFUL DESTINATIONS, SAFE STREETS, COMFORTABLE STREETS, AND INTERESTING STREETS

———

The history of a nation is only a history of its villages written large.
— WOODROW WILSON (1900)

———

ENVIRONMENTAL CAUSES OF A SOCIAL DECLINE

Critical writing in recent years has documented a decline in the civic life of our nation. From Richard Sennett's landmark text, *The Fall of Public Man,* to Christopher Lasch's final work, *The Revolt of the Elites and the Betrayal of Democracy,* dozens of books call attention to the same problem: society seems to be evolving in an unhealthy way. Americans are splintering into insular factions, each pursuing an increasingly narrow agenda, with nary a thought for the greater good. Further, more and more citizens seem to be withdrawing from public life into the shelter of their private homes, from which they encounter the world primarily through their television and computer screens. This is hardly a recipe for productive social evolution.

Many factors contribute to this condition, and one must be wary of focusing inordinately on just one, but it is worth investigating the significant role that our changing physical environment may play in that perceived decline. To begin with the obvious, community cannot form in the absence of communal space, without places for people to get together to talk. Just as it is difficult to imagine the concept of *family* independent of the home, it is near-impossible to imagine *community* independent of the town square or the local pub. Christopher Lasch has observed that "civic life requires settings in which people meet as equals. Thanks to the decay of civic institutions ranging from political parties to public parks and informal meeting places, conversation has become almost as specialized as the production of knowledge."[*] In the absence of walkable public places—streets, squares, and parks, the *public realm*—people of diverse ages, races, and beliefs are unlikely to meet and talk. Those who believe that Internet web sites and chat rooms are effective substitutes vastly underestimate the distinction between a computer monitor and the human body.

In the suburbs, time normally spent in the physical public realm is now spent in the automobile, which is a private space as well as a potentially sociopathic device. The average American, when placed behind the wheel of a car, ceases to be a citizen and becomes

---

[*] Christopher Lasch, *The Revolt of the Elites and the Betrayal of Democracy*, 117. Or, as Trevor Boddy adds: "Constitutional guarantees of free speech and of freedom of association and assembly mean much less if there is literally no peopled public space to serve as forum in which to act out these rights" (Boddy, "Underground and Overhead: Building the Analogous City," 125).

instead a *motorist*. As a motorist, you cannot get to know your neighbor, because the prevailing relationship is competitive. You are competing for asphalt, and if you so much as hesitate or make a wrong move, your neighbor immediately punishes you, by honking the horn, taking your space, running into you, or committing some other antisocial act, the most egregious of which have been well documented. Like drinking, driving has become a well-worn excuse for all sorts of rudeness and aggression—"It couldn't be helped; he cut me off." The social contract is voided. Why this is so is worthy of further study. Suffice it to say that only rarely do two pedestrians gesture violently at each other as they pass.

Indeed, there are dissertations on the topic of automobile-induced maladaptive behavior, and no shortage of data. One recent study published in the *Journal of Applied Social Psychology* demonstrated that drivers take 21 percent longer to vacate a parking space if someone else is waiting for it, and 33 percent longer if that person honks.[1] Another interesting phenomenon was described by Jonathan Franzen in *The New Yorker*:

> I'm a recreational walker, and in the past few years I've noticed something odd when I've hit the sidewalks of suburban Missouri and suburban Colorado: a not intangible percentage of men speeding by me in their cars and sport utility vehicles (it's always men) feel moved to yell obscenities at me. It's hard to know why they do this . . . My guess is that they yell at me simply because I'm a stranger, and from the perspective of their glassed-in vehicles I have no more human reality than the coach on their TV screens who has elected to punt on fourth and short.[2]

An *unsurprising occurrence: driving as a generator of pathological behavior*

More serious is the recently documented "road rage disorder." According to the National Highway Traffic Administration, aggressive drivers account for one third of the crashes and two thirds of the deaths on U.S. highways. "Violent, aggressive driving" was a contributing factor in 28,000 traffic deaths in 1996 alone.[*] There is little need to offer anecdotes supporting this figure, since all of us have witnessed road rage firsthand, as either a victim, a perpetrator, or both. Studies show that road rage is directly linked to sprawl: the top five metropolitan areas for aggressive driving deaths—San Bernardino, Tampa, Phoenix, Orlando, and Miami—are all recently designed suburban cities. The same is true of cities six through ten.[*]

DRIVERS VERSUS PEDESTRIANS

Why are people so much friendlier—or at least less sociopathic—when they are walking? The answer may lie in Jonathan Rose's observation that "there is a significant difference between running into someone while strolling down a street and running into someone when driving a car."[3]

Given that most time in public is spent driving around in isolation chambers, it is no surprise that social critics are witnessing a

[*] James Carroll, "All the Rage in Massachusetts," A14–A15. According to *U.S. News & World Report,* the rate of aggressive driving incidents has risen 51 percent since 1990 (Jason Vest, Warren Cohen, and Mike Tharp, "Road Rage," 28).

[*] Michelle Garland and Christopher Bender, "How Bad Transportation Decisions Affect the Quality of People's Lives," 7. "When people have to get behind the wheel to perform every small task in life, driving becomes just another chore to be finished as quickly as possible. It's really no surprise that in such an environment we see more people dying because of . . . aggressive driving behavior." The metropolitan areas ranked sixth through tenth are Las Vegas, Fort Lauderdale, Dallas, Kansas City, and San Antonio, all predominantly suburban.

decline in the civic arts of conversation, politics, and just simply *getting along*. There are those who view suburbanization as merely another symptom of this malaise, rather than a cause, but their arguments ignore the degree to which the atomization of our society into suburban clusters was the result of specific government and industry policies rather than of some popular mandate. It does not seem too optimistic to believe that Americans would spend more of their time on public pursuits if it were only more convenient.

For evidence, consider Disney World, where a disproportionately large number of suburbanites choose to spend their holidays. Why do so many people go there—for the rides? According to one Disney architect, the average visitor spends only 3 percent of his time on rides or at shows. The remaining time is spent enjoying the precise commodity that people so sorely lack in their suburban hometowns: pleasant, pedestrian-friendly, public space and the sociability it engenders.

Social space, now almost exclusively the purview of the Walt Disney Corporation and the mall developers, used to be provided by builders of cities as a matter of course, from ancient Greek fishermen to early American surveyors. It is only since the advent of modern planning that we have witnessed a decline in the inventory of successful public environments. Of the many reasons for this decline, one should not be underestimated: the rules for creating such places may be too simple. While planners have focused on demographics, economics, statistics, and other esoterica appropriate to professional practice, certain commonsense rules may have been considered beneath consideration.

PREREQUISITES FOR STREET LIFE

MEANINGFUL DESTINATIONS

The first rule is that pedestrian life cannot exist in the absence of worthwhile destinations that are easily accessible on foot. This is a condition that modern suburbia fails to satisfy, since it strives to keep all commercial activity well separated from housing. As a result, the only pedestrians to be found in a residential subdivision belong to that limited segment of the population which walks for exercise. Otherwise, there is no reason to walk, and the streets are empty.

There are three other significant factors in the provision of successful pedestrian environments. First, the street space must not only be safe but also feel safe; second, the street space must be comfortable; and third, the street space must be interesting, as safety and comfort alone are not enough to get people out of their cars. Let's examine each of these in turn.

SAFE STREETS VERSUS DANGEROUS STREETS

The problem with current street design standards is not that engineers have forgotten how to make streets feel safe but that they don't even try. Streets that once served vehicles and people equitably are now designed for the sole purpose of moving vehicles through them as quickly as possible. They have become, in effect, traffic sewers. No surprise, then, that they fail to sustain pedestrian life.[*]

---

[*] This is, unfortunately, meant literally as well as figuratively. As the Surface Transportation Policy Project has demonstrated, "Cities which are notorious for their sprawling patterns of land use development [have] the most pedestrian deaths" (Garland and Bender, 4–5). Walking with care—and teaching your children to do the same—is of little

How did this happen? Certainly, the proliferation of automobiles in this century, along with our often blind faith in technology, has led naturally to cars taking priority over pedestrians. But part of the responsibility lies with the modernist architects of the twenties and thirties, who advocated an urbanism without streets. As Le Corbusier put it: "The street wears us out. It is altogether disgusting. Why, then, does it still exist?"[4] The result of the modernists' towers-in-the-park approach was not that streets ceased to exist but that architects stopped designing them. Left to the engineers, streets came to reflect little but engineering criteria.

The desire for increased traffic volume—"unimpeded flow"—has resulted in wider streets. While travel lanes on old streets are often only nine feet wide or less, new streets are usually required to have twelve-foot lanes, which take longer for pedestrians to cross. "Unimpeded flow" also has another name—speeding—adding all the more to pedestrian risk.

There are two other important factors behind the widening of America's streets. The first was the Cold War, and the second was (and still is) the requirements of fire trucks. The influence of the Cold War was profound. In the 1950s, the Civil Defense Committee of AASHTO, the American Association of State Highway Transportation Officials, was a dominant force in the determination of street design criteria. Its prescription was straightforward: street design must facilitate evacuation before, and cleanup after, a major "nuclear event." At the time, this objective may have seemed

---

help. A recent study found that 90 percent of pedestrian deaths were the driver's fault, with 74 percent of such deaths resulting from a traffic violation (Surface Transportation Policy Project, "Campaign Connection," 8).

crucial, so its effect on pedestrian safety was never considered.[•]

Of those streets that have somehow escaped the widening influences of the traffic-flow and Cold War lobbies, many are currently falling prey to the access requirements of the fire departments. Their new standards, which shorten emergency-vehicle response time at the expense of all other criteria, are typically designed to accommodate the most ambitious of maneuvers: the jockeying of a pair of high-rise ladder trucks on a dead-end street. As a result, even single-family suburban cul-de-sacs are now typically paved to a width of thirty feet, often with asphalt circles ninety feet across at the ends, all in order that a large truck can turn around without shifting into reverse.[■] One of the most important aspects of our new towns is being shaped around an extremely unlikely emergency, with the result that they function inadequately in non-emergency situations.

When fire departments are allowed to usurp the role of town

[•] From Chester E. (Rick) Chellman, P.E.'s research into AASHTO committee reports. As with Napoleon's Paris, it may also be likely that the ease of troop movement was a factor. Mr. Chellman is astute in pointing out how architects were equally obsessed with wartime concerns, and how the prospect of an aerial bombardment figured heavily in their designs for the city of the future. In the book *Can Our Cities Survive?*, published by the modernist Congrès Internationaux d'Architecture Moderne, Jose Luis Sert insisted (correctly) that "some districts offer better targets than others." Based upon the likelihood that a bombardment would be more devastating to an old European city—"it is nearly impossible to miss a hit on some overcrowded building"—Sert and his colleagues advocated the two alternatives that became the staple of the suburban city: the single-family house and the "tower in the park" (Sert, 69).

[■] The avoidance of reverse purportedly derives from the fact, now irrelevant, that the earliest fire trucks powered their pumping mechanism with the reverse gear, rendering it inoperable. It is ironic that cul-de-sacs, with their image of small-scale domesticity, must be so wide to satisfy fire trucks, but this comes partly because they provide only a single access point for each destination. In a traditional interconnected network of through streets, there is always an alternate path to the fire, and one truck rarely has to drive past another. Unfortunately, this distinction is never made in suburban zoning codes, and every type of street must meet the cul-de-sac's thirty-foot street-width requirement.

planner, they generally commit two errors. First, they put more weight on fire rescue than on the prevention of injury in general; they try to minimize emergency response time, without considering that the resulting wide streets lead to an increased number of traffic accidents, since people drive faster on them. Fire departments have yet to acknowledge that fire safety is but a small part of a much larger picture that others refer to as *life safety*. The biggest threat to life safety is not fires but car accidents, by a tremendous margin. Since the vast majority of fire department emergencies involve car accidents, it is surprising that fire chiefs have not begun to reconsider response time in this light; if they did, narrow streets would logically become the norm in residential areas. In the meantime, the wider streets that fire departments require are indeed quite effective at providing them with quick access to the accidents they help cause.

The second mistake fire departments make is purchasing oversized trucks, vehicles that have trouble maneuvering through anything but the widest of streets. Sometimes these trucks are required by outdated union regulations, but more often they are simply the result of a town's desire to have the most effective machinery it can afford.* Unfortunately, a part of a truck's effectiveness is its ability to reach the fire in the first place. Once purchased, the truck turns from servant to master, making all but the most wasteful and unpleasant street spaces impossible. When a giant truck is the

---

* This activity may also be the result of what the fire marshals do when they go to their fire marshal conventions, which is to compare the size of their trucks. Never mind that their entire jurisdiction consists of split-level ranches, these chiefs are not about to be outdone in the hook-and-ladder department. One can only hope that the advent of woman-led fire departments will eventually bring this tendency in check.

design template, there is no choice but to build streets that are too wide to support pedestrian life.

Citizens who find themselves pitted against fire departments in road-width battles should focus their arguments on the issue of fire safety versus life safety and arm themselves with the statistical evidence. A recent study in Longmont, Colorado, compared fire and traffic injuries in residential neighborhoods served by both narrow and wide roads. Over eight years, the study found no increased fire injury risk from narrow streets, primarily because there were no fire injuries. One serious fire and several smaller fires resulted in property damage only. Meanwhile, in the same eight years, there were 227 automotive accidents resulting in injuries, 10 of them fatal. These accidents correlated most closely to street width, with new thirty-six-foot-wide streets being about four times as dangerous as traditional twenty-four-foot-wide streets.[*]

One community that has seen beyond the false safety promised by wide streets is Portland, Oregon, whose fire chief helped to initiate a new public program called "Skinny Streets." This program recommends that new local streets in residential areas, with parking on one side, should be only twenty feet wide. These humane streets have their critics, the usual cabal of fearmongers, who would like to enforce standards ten feet wider. They insist that the numbers don't add up—how can two cars pass each other *and* a parked car in a mere twenty feet of pavement? Of course, the founders of the Skinny Streets program have reason for confidence, since they

A city sees the light: Portland, Oregon, promotes its new (old) street standards

---

[*] Peter Swift, "Residential Street Typology and Injury Accident Frequency," 4. Interestingly, traffic volume was not found to be a major factor, except where a lack of volume made speeding easier. Unsurprisingly, the most lethal streets were those that most closely matched the suburban engineering ideal: arrow-straight, long, and wide, with a free flow of light traffic.

derived their measurements from Portland's existing streets, which continue to work perfectly well in the city's most valuable neighborhoods. The Portland firemen have accepted their new standards, admittedly without much enthusiasm.

Narrow streets are necessary but not sufficient to ensure a thriving pedestrian life. Curb radius, the amount a roadway flares at an intersection, has a significant impact as well. The image on the right shows what intersections used to look like: the arc of the curb has a radius of only three or four feet. As a result, this twenty-foot-wide street has a crossing that is also twenty feet wide. The modern standard, however, specifies a curb radius of twenty-five feet or more, which means that the actual crossing distance of a twenty-foot-wide street jumps to about forty feet. More significantly, cars approaching such an intersection need not brake as they turn, as indicated by the dramatic port-side list of the car pictured here. In short, the modern curb radius forces the pedestrian to walk twice as far in the path of a car that is traveling twice as fast.

A similar circumstance surrounds another aspect of street design, the minimum center-line radius, which controls how sharply a street is allowed to bend along its trajectory. Under current standards, streets are allowed only to curve loosely, with the result that one finger on the steering wheel and one foot on the gas pedal are all that it takes to maneuver through a residential neighborhood. The intention is to provide greater safety by allowing drivers to see farther in front of them, but the result is that drivers feel comfortable driving at higher speeds, making walking all the more dangerous.[*]

Pedestrian-friendly geometries: a traditional small curb radius slows cars down and shortens crossing distance

Highway geometries applied to the residential neighborhood: a large curb radius doubles both pedestrian crossing distance and automobile speed

---

[*] Indeed, the design of most traffic-calming devices acknowledges this fact. These devices introduce tighter minimum center-line radii for streets that are too straight and too wide, forcing drivers to slow down.

When it comes to street curvature, like curb radii, what works best for cars hardly works at all for pedestrians.

One would think that, after many years of building such streets and witnessing the results, the engineers—at least some of them—would have added pedestrian- and bicycle-friendly standards to their repertoire. However, Paul Box, the nation's ranking expert on subdivision street design, had this to say when asked how streets might better accommodate bicyclists: ". . . the purpose of the Subdivision Guidelines is to enhance safety and livability. Any statements encouraging bicycle use would not likely address these objectives."[*] Presumably, we should be grateful that bicycles are still legal.

In truth, a number of engineers have accepted more reasonable design standards, but in most cases there is one thing that prevents them from putting those standards into practice: their manuals. Engineers are exposed to substantial liability in their work. The most surefire way for them to avoid losing a lawsuit is to follow the engineering manuals precisely, no questions asked. Because pedestrian-friendly streets are not specified in the manuals, they are simply not possible, despite all the evidence encouraging their use.

The reaction of most municipalities to speeding has been not to question the standards but simply to post hopeful speed-limit signs,

[*] Paul Box, Traffic Engineering Consultant, P.E., Fellow of the Institute of Traffic Engineers (I.T.E.). Mr. Box has been chairman for several decades of the Committee for Guidelines for Residential Subdivision Street Design. His comment is from a September 1991 letter in response to an inquiry from I.T.E. member Chester Chellman, P.E. Given the current standards of residential roadway design, it is not surprising that, according to *Bicycling* magazine, the number of American bike riders has dropped 23 percent over the past seven years (Peter T. Kilborn, "No Work for a Bicycle Thief: Children Pedal Around Less," A21).

resulting in some rather ludicrous scenarios. In Toole, Utah, we have driven on straight streets forty-two feet wide with a posted speed limit of 30 mph. These streets were perfectly navigable at 65 mph, since that was their design speed, and that was indeed the speed at which we drove, even though we were in a quiet residential community. Posting speed limits to slow traffic on high-speed roads is futile, because people drive at the speed at which they feel safe— and teenagers drive at the speed at which they feel dangerous. Generally, the only time that people don't speed in modern suburbia is when they are lost, which is, fortunately, quite often.

In addition to narrow streets, another factor that contributes mightily to pedestrian perceptions of safety is on-street parallel parking. Parked cars create a highly effective steel barrier between the street and the sidewalk, so that walkers feel protected from moving traffic. They also slow traffic, because drivers perceive potential conflict with cars pulling in and out. Additionally, parallel parking supports pedestrian life by delivering people to the sidewalk. Since drivers are seldom able to park directly in front of their destination, they often walk past shops or houses other than the one they are visiting. If on-street parking is, for this reason, slightly less convenient, it is one of those small inconveniences that make life more interesting. While many towns and cities have rediscovered parallel parking, it has been on the decline for decades, frowned upon by the same officials who dismiss trees as Fixed Hazardous Objects. In some states, parallel parking is no longer a required skill on driver's tests.

The misplaced priorities of current traffic engineering criteria are plainly evident in the top image on page 72, taken from the cover of a D.O.T. annual report—a photograph, therefore, that one can

The street as automotive sewer: streamform highway geometries sever walking connections and preclude pedestrian life

The street as a complex, multipurpose social organism: a boulevard, ideal for driving, parking, walking, and sipping coffee

presume represents traffic design at its best. What this photograph depicts is indeed an achievement of sorts: a road of only four lanes that, thanks to highway geometrics, has managed to eat up over 150 feet in right-of-way width while lowering the property value of everything around it. Due to the behavior of the vehicles on this high-speed road, this area will always be the site of the cheapest housing and least prestigious businesses, hiding behind their walls, berms, and sound-attenuation barriers.

To fully grasp this wastefulness, we need only consult the alternative: the traditional boulevard. Instead of an intimidating four-laner, this boulevard is a ten-laner: six lanes of traffic and four of parking. Yet this roadway is so charming and comfortable, thanks to its avoidance of high-speed geometrics, that residents pay good money to sip coffee at curbside cafés—a sight hard to imagine in the preceding photo. The impact of the dumbing down of the engineering manuals could hardly have been more profound. In the early twentieth century, practically every roadway investment resulted in an increase in the value of adjacent properties. But since 1950, roadway investment has often had the opposite effect, robbing neighborhoods of their economic value by degrading the environment.

The engineers' strict adherence to their manuals is actually promising; rather than convincing the engineers to fundamentally rethink their approach, we need only amend the manuals in order to reform the profession. And to their credit, a coalition of forward-thinking engineers is on its way to making this happen. The Institute of Transportation Engineers has recently completed a manual entitled *Traditional Neighborhood Development Street Design Guidelines*, which allows narrower roads, tighter corners, and a number of other once-unthinkable modifications to current design criteria. For the moment, these modified standards are available only as optional alternatives.[*] Clearly, the next step would be to prohibit the conventional high-speed standards in residential neighborhoods, restricting them to long-distance regional roadways, where they belong.

After speeding automobiles, the greatest threat to pedestrian safety is crime, which is what most people have in mind when they clamor for safer streets. It has been the topic of many design books, and the reigning classic remains *Defensible Space,* by Oscar Newman. It is worth elaborating on one of Mr. Newman's subjects as it pertains to suburbia, and that is the concept of "eyes on the street," a phrase originally coined by Jane Jacobs.[■]

In order to discourage crime, a street space must be watched over by buildings with doors and windows facing it. Walls, fences, and padlocks are all less effective at deterring crime than a simple lit window. Interestingly, no one needs to be standing *in* the window, as the window implies a human presence on its own—at any moment, someone could appear. So it is really the windows, not the occupants, that are the *eyes on the street.* Traditional urbanism excels at providing them, as buildings sit close to the sidewalk and plainly face forward. Even residential alleys can be well supervised, by placing granny flats above garages.

[*] In truth, these alternatives are an available option only about half of the time. Even though they have been named a "recommended practice" by the national Institute of Transportation Engineers, they are routinely rejected by local municipal engineers, many of whom still believe that wider is safer.

[■] *Defensible Space* was written in 1969, and the efficacy of many of its ideas has been well demonstrated. These ideas are now promulgated under a new imprimatur, CPTED: Crime Prevention Through Environmental Design. More information on the subject can be found in the book *Safe Cities: Guidelines for Planning, Design, and Management* by Gerda Wekerle and Carolyn Whitzman, or at the National Crime Prevention Institute at the University of Louisville, Kentucky.

Conventional suburbia fails to provide adequate street supervision. Most collector roads aren't fronted by buildings at all. Houses tend to be located far from the street, sometimes behind walls. And, within typical subdivisions, houses often present little to the street but their wide garage doors. With such unsafe conditions, it is no surprise that so many suburban developers feel the need to surround their subdivisions with high walls and hire full-time security.

The suburban development pattern contributes to crime in other ways as well. The single-use zoning system means that many areas are occupied only during certain times of the day. Apparently abandoned, residential subdivisions invite all sorts of misbehavior. Further, the suburban auto orientation means that few people are ever out walking, and nothing undermines the perception of safety more than being alone. It is a vicious circle: the less safe streets feel, the fewer people walk, and the less safe they become.

COMFORTABLE STREETS VERSUS UNPLEASANT STREETS

People don't like to walk where they don't feel safe, nor do they like to walk where they feel uncomfortable, which is slightly different. While many factors contribute to the comfort of a place, the most significant is probably its degree of architectural enclosure—the amount that it makes its inhabitants feel held within a space. The desire for enclosure stems from several sources, among them the fundamental human need for shelter, orientation, and territoriality. Whatever the cause, people are attracted to places with well-defined edges and limited openings, while they tend to flee places that lack clear definition or boundaries.[*] For this reason, the most effective technique for designing successful urban spaces is to think of them as outdoor living rooms.[■] To feel like a room, a street must have relatively continuous walls, whose design calls attention to the space as a whole rather than to individual buildings. That is to say, street walls must be primarily flat and simple.

The California jog: the unpleasant public space that results from wiggling walls

Unfortunately, architects have been working for decades according to the mandate that building walls should not be flat and simple. They were taught that, as much as the budget will allow, walls should stagger up and down and wiggle back and forth so that each house reads as an independent object. However, as pictured above, all that this individuation accomplishes is to remind the residents of how many identical houses there are. More important, the oscillation of the wall plane effectively destroys the roomlike quality of the public space in front, so that the people who live in these units tend to flee indoors soon after cutting their car engines.

The traditional alternative: flat street walls in Georgetown provide an attractive sense of spatial enclosure

The lower image consists of essentially the same housing product as the upper one. They both contain roughly the same size of unit, the same quantity of asphalt, the same cars, even the same gray sky. Yet the dwellings pictured below sell for about three

[*] This has been demonstrated time and again by the disappointing performance of modern housing projects, whose public realm consists of a continuous field of landscape and pavement. The lack of geometric definition of these spaces impedes their residents' ability to develop a sense of ownership for them, and they are inevitably used improperly or not at all, and poorly maintained as a result.

[■] Camillo Sitte's turn-of-the-century treatise, *City Planning According to Artistic Principles,* effectively illustrated techniques for enclosing a full range of urban space types. Sociologists have recently come to recognize the importance of street space in the formation of society. The latest studies on the relationship between human behavior and the physical environment refer to a hierarchy of community ranging from the family to the neighborhood, through something called the *face-block,* which is simply the shared street.

times as much, and that's with spotty wiring, antiquated plumbing, and inconvenient parking—residents consider themselves lucky to find a spot within sight of their house. Why are the inhabitants of Georgetown paying so dearly to live there? Because the *sense of place* is excellent. The continuous flat building wall, with its harmonious and quiet architecture, creates a feeling of enclosure and comfort that is not found in suburbia.

This is not an academic conceit. When Americans pull out their wallets and pay triple the cost for the same commodity, developers should take note. The most irksome aspect of this comparison is that it actually costs less money to provide the more desirable alternative. With their continuous walls, fewer corners, and simple roofline, these buildings are considerably less expensive to build than their hyperactive counterparts.

Homebuilders at the upper end of the market appear to be equally misguided in their approach to building design. Pictured here is what has come to be known as the "North Dallas Special," or, less affectionately, as a "house on steroids." Despite all of its cartoonish qualities—its variety of window types, its overwrought trim—this house represents the industry standard for luxury. The design technique is straightforward: concentrate the budget on extra corners and exaggerated historical references, all in the name of "curb appeal." Never mind that one practically needs a Ph.D. in physics to assemble this roof; this technique is what developers learn at homebuilding conventions, and what realtors have come to call the "twenty-minute house."

Despite the way that it sounds, the "twenty-minute house" is not a derogatory label. Quite the opposite—it refers to the fact that a house has only twenty minutes to win the affection of a potential

The North Dallas Special: a single house attempts to create the skyline of an entire village. It is meant to stand alone

buyer, since that is the average length of a realtor visit. The building industry has responded to this phenomenon by creating a product that is at its best for the first twenty minutes that one is in it. Specifically, the house is usually organized around a tall "great room" from which, immediately upon entering, the potential buyer is astounded by partial views of almost every other room in the house. The disadvantage of this organization is that there is no acoustical privacy for the individual rooms, something that is not discovered until after moving day. Similarly, because so much of the budget is spent on the front of the house (much to the detriment of the street space), the back of the house ends up being a few sliding glass doors in a dead-flat wall, such that the backyard offers no privacy either. You exit the rear door to find yourself completely exposed in a windswept lot, directly visible to the occupants of five other houses identical to your own.•

When houses were designed for more than twenty minutes of occupancy, they looked like this—simple in front, with limited decoration, their beauty derived primarily from excellent proportions. Indeed, it may take extra time for an architect to work out such a façade, but the result can be profoundly satisfying. And like a row of town houses, a simple, flat house façade contributes to the quality of the street space, while leaving some of the budget for rear articulations such as wings and breezeways. These "back buildings" turn the rear yard into an enclosed court, such that complete privacy can be created even on small lots.

A fairly continuous, relatively flat street wall is one of many preconditions to pedestrian comfort. Another is limited street-space

Five plus four and a door: the simplicity of a traditional façade acknowledges the presence of a larger community. Variety occurs not within the single house but among many

• The lack of backyard privacy is largely responsible for the suburban obsession with large lots. In the absence of a well-shaped backyard, size is the only known instrument for achieving privacy. Of course, this approach is futile unless the lot is enormous.

width. If a street is to provide the sense of enclosure that pedestrians desire—if it is to feel like a room—it cannot be too wide. To be precise, the relationship of width to height cannot exceed a certain ratio, generally recognized to be about 6:1. If the distance from building front to building front is more than six times the height of those building fronts, the feeling of enclosure is lost, and with it the sense of place. Even the 6:1 ratio is wider than most successful public spaces. Many theorists locate the ideal ratio at 1:1; above 6:1, streets fail to attract pedestrian life.*

This formula should come as no surprise to observant travelers, many of whom have no doubt used the words *narrow* and *charming* in the same sentence to describe the famously walkable streets of our older cities. Whether it be in Montreal's Old Town, Boston's Beacon Hill, or Elfreth's Alley in Philadelphia, the narrowest streets are typically the ones most cherished by tourists and residents alike. In fact, some statistics suggest that property values are inversely proportional to street width. In other words, the less space and asphalt wasted, the more valuable the real estate. This plainly demonstrates the fundamental economic elegance of traditional urbanism, which developed at a time when Americans were not so absurdly rich as they are now, and they had to be smarter with their resources.

For an example of true inefficiency, look no further than this street, a standard collector road approaching a cluster of housing in suburban Virginia. Large enough to hold eight cars across, it is

The appeal of the narrow street: paradoxically, the less money spent on excessive infrastructure, the more valuable the real estate

Designed for the apocalypse: gold-plated infrastructure built to satisfy exaggerated emergency vehicle requirements

* In high-density downtown situations with skyscrapers flanking a narrow thoroughfare, there is legitimate concern that the violation of this ratio in the opposite direction can result in a dark and unpleasant street space. This problem is best mitigated by requiring buildings to step back from an ideally sized sidewalk-hugging base to a narrower tower above, as was required by the original sunlight code of Manhattan.

as wide as a parking lot. Indifferent to our limited natural and financial resources, this is truly a street that is ready for nuclear attack. Even if it were flanked by buildings—which it is not, adding to its wastefulness—the street space would exceed the 6:1 ratio by a wide margin.

There is one important caveat to this rule, which involves the role played by trees. Even in some old neighborhoods, Americans have had difficulty adhering to the above ratio, because they like their houses low and their front yards deep. When the distance between low houses becomes too great, it is imperative that trees be planted along the street in a disciplined row. These trees are not intended merely to be decorative; rather, they are included to create spatial definition when the buildings fail to do so. The trees narrow the space and provide a natural vault that contributes to the pedestrian's sense of enclosure and comfort. In warmer climates, consistently placed trees are also useful for shade. Skeptics need only tour their own towns to confirm that neighborhoods with healthy trees tend to be highly valued, while neighborhoods with sporadic trees tend to be places to move away from.

Trees as enclosure: orderly rows of street trees compensate for an overly wide street space

This correlation makes clear what should be the first job of landscape architects: to correct the deficiencies they have inherited from the other professionals, who have failed to create comfortable street space. Unfortunately, this is precisely what most landscape architects leave undone. What they do instead is to prettify—to design something that is picturesque and photogenic, clusters of random varieties milling about an entrance gate. Straight lines and the repetition of trees, while beautiful in perspective, look boring on paper and thus are set aside in favor of a creative emulation of nature. The landscaping budget, rather than being spent on necessary remedies, is squandered in an attempt to instill the impression

Landscape architecture as exterior decoration: "naturalistic" tree placement fails to define street space

that the wilderness has somehow wandered into the subdivision. This is why the landscape budget is always the first thing in a project to be cut, and why landscape architects complain of not being taken seriously by their clients. Rather than performing an essential function—correcting for the spatial deficiencies of the urbanism, and complementing the linear relationship between building façades, sidewalks, and street—they have become exterior decorators.

Finally, and perhaps most obviously, streets will not be comfortable for the pedestrian if they are burdened with antipersonnel devices like the eighteen-inch-high curb pictured here. As with gigantic curb radii, this sort of streetscape detail is possible only because the design of the public realm has been left in the hands of technical specialists who place little value on pedestrian access. In this case, in downtown Tampa, it is surface rainwater runoff that has determined the configuration of the street space. Once again, the fundamental question is not how to design a public realm that will work for pedestrians but simply whether or not anyone cares to do so.

The pedestrian as adventurer: engineers add exciting challenges to urban life

INTERESTING STREETS VERSUS BORING STREETS

The upper image on the next page shows a typical streetscape from a successful, not unattractive subdivision in Palm Beach County, Florida. This development contains passable buildings, nice landscaping, and quiet, safe streets. Why, then, do the people who live here drive to the health club in order to use the walking machines? Probably because the wall mirror at the club offers more entertainment value than can be found in twenty blocks of garage doors.

For people to walk, a neighborhood has to be interesting: not terribly so, but enough to convey some notion of human activity. Nothing interests humans more than other humans, and architecture that fails to express the presence of humans is unsatisfying to the pedestrian. This fact accounts for the lack of interest in this image, whose prevailing message is not "People live here," but "Cars live here."

The house pictured below, from Stuart, Florida, is not a skillful piece of architecture. It is neither historic nor modern, and has improperly sized shutters and awkward proportions. Yet it is a pleasure to look at, because everything that this house communicates pertains to human activity. It sits close to the street with windows facing forward, establishing the owner's presence in the house. The picket fence, rather than serving as an unfriendly barrier, represents the owner's care for the small yard it contains. The little front stoop, however weak, dominates the composition, because the garage has been moved to the back of the house, in this case on a rear lane.

The distinction between these two images represents not an architectural flaw but a planning flaw: on a fifty-foot-wide lot, no architect is talented enough to overcome the requirement that two thirds of the façade must be dedicated to garage doors. On narrower lots, the situation is exacerbated. The only way to free narrow-lot houses from the aesthetic burden of the garage is to place it at the rear of the lot, and the most efficient way to access a rear garage is through a rear lane, or alley. Most people who have lived in older communities are familiar with alleys, which contribute significantly to the beauty of places such as Savannah and Boston's Back Bay, as well as a number of suburban neighborhoods from the early twentieth century.

The alley is often criticized for its lack of neatness, but that is its essence: it's where all the messy stuff goes. From garage doors to trash containers, transformers, electrical meters, and telephone

The city of garages: the typical suburban condition of housefronts dominated by car storage

The city of people: placing the garage at the rear allows the housefronts to reflect human habitation

A rear lane at Kentlands: where the garage doors and trash cans should be

equipment, the alley takes them out of public view, something that is all the more necessary these days with the advent of recycling bins and cable TV boxes.[•] Also, by handling many of the neighborhood's underground utilities, alleys allow streets to be narrower and to be planted with trees, which becomes difficult when water, sewer, gas, electricity, cable, and telephone are all placing demands on the front right-of-way. Alleys are also appreciated by the fire chief, since they allow firefighters another path to the building. Alleys may also provide direct access to backyard granny flats, giving them an address independent of the main house.

Like narrow streets, alleys are often illegal in suburban jurisdictions and must be reintroduced with care—and sometimes by stealth. The first time that we designed a neighborhood with alleys, we had to label them "jogging paths" to get them approved.

In addition to the ill effects of the garage door, new subdivisions often fail to generate pedestrian activity because they lack variety. The endless repetition from lot to lot of the same house type makes walking utterly unrewarding. As Jane Jacobs put it: "Almost nobody travels willingly from sameness to sameness and repetition to repetition, even if the physical effort required is trivial."[5] The solution to the cookie-cutter condition, as already mentioned, is to place buildings of different size and type side by side, something that has been taboo for years. One can hope that the financial success of those new neighborhoods that mix housing types will eventually overcome the inertia of the conventional segregationist model.

[•] Of course, despite all of the apparatus of suburban life, alleys need not be ugly. In older suburbs such as Baltimore's Roland Park, the rear lanes are favored as pedestrian ways between backyards, and have been known to become social centers. In Kentlands, the residents have even formed a flower-planting Alley Beautification Committee.

It bears repeating: we shape our cities and then our cities shape us. The choice is ours whether we build subdivisions that debase the human spirit or neighborhoods that nurture sociability and bring out the best in our nature. The techniques for achieving the latter are well known, and available to all who wish to make places worth caring about.

5

THE AMERICAN TRANSPORTATION MESS

The highwayless town and the townless highway;

why adding lanes makes traffic worse;

the automobile subsidy

———

During the height of automania, a zoologist observed that in animal herds excessive mobility was a sure sign of distress and asked whether this might not be true of his fellow human beings. Perhaps it was distress . . . but what historian can list all the causes that led twentieth-century man to race from highway to byway, tunnel to bridge? Suffice to say that he seemed to be constantly going from where he didn't want to be to where he didn't want to stay.

— Percival Goodman, *Communitas* (1960)

———

Redesigning streets and roads for pedestrian viability is a first step toward making our neighborhoods more livable, but there is a larger problem still to be addressed: this country's fundamentally misguided approach to transportation planning as a whole. Because settlement patterns depend more than anything else upon transportation systems,* it is impossible to discuss one without discussing the other.

* Some of the most useful documentation of the relationship between land use and transportation comes from the publications of the Surface Transportation Policy Project in Washington, D.C., and also from LUTRAQ ("Making the Land Use, Transportation,

While we do enjoy the benefits of an effective system for the national distribution of goods—nobody is lining up outside shops with empty shelves—it would still be difficult to overstate the degree to which transportation policy has damaged both our cities and our countryside. This outcome was by no means inevitable; in fact, we knew better all along. By 1940, the rules that should govern the development of a transportation network for the healthy growth of society were well known. They were widely acknowledged, thoroughly disseminated, and, apparently, immediately forgotten.•

THE HIGHWAYLESS TOWN
AND THE TOWNLESS HIGHWAY

The most significant of these rules is illustrated, alongside its violation, in the accompanying diagram. This drawing, more than any other, depicts the greatest failure of American postwar planning, and helps to explain why our country faces both an urban and an environmental crisis. Titled "The Townless Highway and the Highwayless Town," the upper half illustrates the proper relationship between high-speed roadways and places of settlement. Highways connect cities but do not pass through them. Norman Bel Geddes,

---

Air Quality Connection"), a national demonstration project of 1000 Friends of Oregon, comparing the costs and benefits of roadways versus transit.
• Actually, the rules of good transportation planning were not exactly forgotten—they were simply overruled by a government sympathetic to the needs of the automobile, petroleum, and road-building industries. It has been well documented how, at midcentury, these industries were not so much an influence upon the federal government as they *were* the federal government. Jim Kunstler notes how the chairman of President Eisenhower's commission on highway policy was a director at General Motors (James Howard Kunstler, *The Geography of Nowhere*, 106).

the designer of the U.S. Interstate system, declared in 1939, "Motorways must not be allowed to infringe upon the city." Where they do provide access to the city, highways must take on the low-speed geometries of avenues and boulevards. In exchange for this courtesy, the city does not allow itself to grow along the highway. Where high-speed roads pass through the countryside, roadside development is not permitted. The results of these rules are plain to see in much of Western Europe: cities, for the most part, have retained their pedestrian-friendly quality, and most highways provide views of uninterrupted countryside.

This country has allowed the exact opposite to occur. As depicted in the lower half, highways were routed directly through the centers of our cities, eviscerating entire neighborhoods—typically, African American neighborhoods—and splitting downtowns into pieces.[*] Meanwhile, the commercial strip attached itself like a parasite to the highway between cities, impeding through traffic and blighting the countryside in the process. The damage is not yet complete, for we continue to let this happen, with predictable results.[■] How obvious and damaging does an error need to be before it is addressed and corrected? Jane Jacobs may have answered this

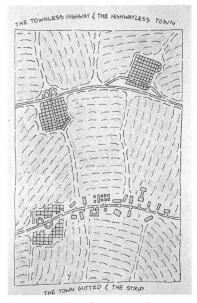

Forgotten wisdom: the proper and improper relationship between highway and town (Drawing by Thomas E. Low, DPZ)

---

[*] The federal highway planners of the fifties actually knew better than to bring highways into center cities, but they were out-lobbied by the big-city mayors, who wanted the U.S. highway money spent in their jurisdictions. As a result, the Federal-Aid Highway Act of 1956 was amended to include over six thousand miles of urban freeways (Witold Rybczynski, *City Life*, 160–61). This pattern continues as local governments, reluctant to leave any federal or state money on the table, build every new road they can get someone else to pay for.

[■] Already a number of highway-intersection-spawned commercial centers have become so congested that a new generation of bypasses are being built around them. One wonders if the malls these intersections serve, like the downtowns they once replaced, will likewise decline as the traffic moves one step farther outward, to the big-box stores located on the new ring.

question in *The Death and Life of Great American Cities*: "The pseudo-science of planning seems almost neurotic in its determination to imitate empiric failure and ignore empiric success."[1]

WHY ADDING LANES MAKES TRAFFIC WORSE

There is, however, a much deeper problem than the way highways are placed and managed. It raises the question of why we are still building highways at all. The simple truth is that building more highways and widening existing roads, almost always motivated by concern over traffic, does nothing to reduce traffic. In the long run, in fact, it increases traffic. This revelation is so counterintuitive that it bears repeating: adding lanes makes traffic worse. This paradox was suspected as early as 1942 by Robert Moses, who noticed that the highways he had built around New York City in 1939 were somehow generating greater traffic problems than had existed previously. Since then, the phenomenon has been well documented, most notably in 1989, when the Southern California Association of Governments concluded that traffic-assistance measures, be they adding lanes, or even double-decking the roadways, would have no more than a cosmetic effect on Los Angeles' traffic problems. The best it could offer was to tell people to work closer to home, which is precisely what highway building mitigates against.

Across the Atlantic, the British government reached a similar conclusion. Its studies showed that increased traffic capacity causes people to drive more—a lot more—such that half of any driving-time savings generated by new roadways are lost in the short run. In the long run, potentially all savings are expected to be lost. In the words of the Transport Minister, "The fact of the matter is that we cannot tackle our traffic problems by building more roads."[2] While the British have responded to this discovery by drastically cutting their road-building budgets, no such thing can be said about Americans.

There is no shortage of hard data. A recent University of California at Berkeley study covering thirty California counties between 1973 and 1990 found that, for every 10 percent increase in roadway capacity, traffic increased 9 percent within four years' time.[3] For anecdotal evidence, one need only look at commuting patterns in those cities with expensive new highway systems. *USA Today* published the following report on Atlanta: "For years, Atlanta tried to ward off traffic problems by building more miles of highways per capita than any other urban area except Kansas City . . . As a result of the area's sprawl, Atlantans now drive an average of 35 miles a day, more than residents of any other city."[•] This phenomenon, which is now well known to those members of the transportation industry who wish to acknowledge it, has come to be called *induced traffic*.

The mechanism at work behind induced traffic is elegantly explained by an aphorism gaining popularity among traffic engineers: "Trying to cure traffic congestion by adding more capacity is like trying to cure obesity by loosening your belt." Increased traffic capacity makes longer commutes less burdensome, and as a result, people are willing to live farther and farther from their workplace.

[•] Carol Jouzatis, "39 Million People Work, Live Outside City Centers," 2A. As a result of its massive highway construction, the Atlanta area is "one of the nation's worst violators of Federal standards for ground-level ozone, with most of the problem caused by motor-vehicle emissions" (Kevin Sack, "Governor Proposes Remedy for Atlanta Sprawl," A14).

As increasing numbers of people make similar decisions, the long-distance commute grows as crowded as the inner city, commuters clamor for additional lanes, and the cycle repeats itself. This problem is compounded by the hierarchical organization of the new roadways, which concentrate through traffic on as few streets as possible.

The phenomenon of induced traffic works in reverse as well. When New York's West Side Highway collapsed in 1973, an NYDOT study showed that 93 percent of the car trips lost did not reappear elsewhere; *people simply stopped driving.* A similar result accompanied the destruction of San Francisco's Embarcadero Freeway in the 1989 earthquake. Citizens voted to remove the freeway entirely despite the apocalyptic warnings of traffic engineers. Surprisingly, a recent British study found that downtown road removals tend to boost local economies, while new roads lead to higher urban unemployment. So much for road-building as a way to spur the economy.[*]

If traffic is to be discussed responsibly, it must first be made clear that the level of traffic which drivers experience daily, and which they bemoan so vehemently, is only as high as they are willing to countenance. If it were not, they would adjust their behavior and move, carpool, take transit, or just stay at home, as some choose to do. How crowded a roadway is at any given moment represents a condition of equilibrium between people's desire to drive and their reluctance to fight traffic. Because people are willing to suffer inordinately in traffic before seeking alternatives—other than clamoring for more highways—the state of equilibrium of all busy roads is to have stop-and-go traffic. The question is not how many lanes must be built to

---

[*] Jill Kruse, "Remove It and They Will Disappear," 5, 7. This study, in analyzing sixty road closures worldwide, found that 20 percent to 60 percent of driving trips disappeared rather than materializing elsewhere.

ease congestion but how many lanes of congestion you want. Do you favor four lanes of bumper-to-bumper traffic at rush hour, or sixteen?

This condition is best explained by what specialists call *latent demand.* Since the real constraint on driving is traffic, not cost, people are always ready to make more trips when the traffic goes away. The number of latent trips is huge—perhaps 30 percent of existing traffic. Because of latent demand, adding lanes is futile, since drivers are already poised to use them up.[4]

While the befuddling fact of induced traffic is well understood by sophisticated traffic engineers, it might as well be a secret, so poorly has it been disseminated. The computer models that transportation consultants use do not even consider it, and most local public works directors have never heard of it at all. As a result, from Maine to Hawaii, city, county, and even state engineering departments continue to build more roadways in anticipation of increased traffic, and, in so doing, create that traffic. The most irksome aspect of this situation is that these road-builders are never proved wrong; in fact, they are always proved right: "You see," they say, "I told you that traffic was coming."

Adding lanes adds traffic: although it is well proven, induced traffic has had little impact on transportation policy

The ramifications are quite unsettling. Almost all of the billions of dollars spent on road-building over the past decades have accomplished only one thing, which is to increase the amount of time that we must spend in our cars each day. Americans now drive twice as many miles per year as they did just twenty years ago. Since 1969, the number of miles cars travel has grown at four times the population rate.[•] And we're just getting started: federal highway officials

---

[•] Jane Holtz Kay, *Asphalt Nation,* 15; and Peter Calthorpe, *The Next American Metropolis,* 27. Since 1983, the number of miles cars travel has grown at eight times the population rate (Urban Land Institute traffic study). The greatest increases in automobile use

predict that over the next twenty years congestion will quadruple. Still, every congressman, it seems, wants a new highway to his credit.[•]

Thankfully, alternatives to road-building *are* being offered, but they are equally misguided. If, as is now clear beyond any reasonable doubt, people maintain an equilibrium of just-bearable traffic, then the traffic engineers are wasting their time—and our money—on a whole new set of stopgap measures that produce temporary results at best. These measures, which include HOV (high-occupancy vehicle) lanes, congestion pricing, timed traffic lights, and "smart streets," serve only to increase highway capacity, which causes more people to drive until the equilibrium condition of crowding returns. While certainly less wasteful than new construction, these measures also do nothing to address the real cause of traffic congestion, which is that people choose to put up with it.

We must admit that, in an ideal world, we would be able to build our way out of traffic congestion. The new construction of 50 percent more highways nationwide would most likely overcome all of the latent demand. However, to provide more than temporary relief,

---

correspond to the greatest concentrations of sprawl. Annual gasoline consumption per person in Phoenix and Houston is over 50 percent higher than in Chicago or Washington, D.C., and over 500 percent higher than in London or Tokyo (Peter Newman and Jeff Kenworthy, *Winning Back the Cities,* 9). Currently, almost 70 percent of urban freeways are clogged during rush hour (Jason Vest, Warren Cohen, and Mike Tharp, "Road Rage," 28). In Los Angeles, congestion has already reduced average freeway speeds to less than 31 mph; by the year 2010, they are projected to fall to 11 mph (James MacKenzie, Roger Dower, and Donald Chen, *The Going Rate,* 17).

[•] Almost any situation seems acceptable to justify more highway spending, even the recent road rage epidemic. Representative Bud Schuster, the chairman of the U.S. Congressional Committee on Transportation and Infrastructure, made this recommendation: "The construction of additional lanes, the widening of roads and the straightening of curves would decrease congestion and reduce the impatience and unsafe habits of some motorists" (Thomas Palmer, "Pacifying Road Warriors," B5).

this huge investment would have to be undertaken hand in hand with a moratorium on suburban growth. Otherwise, the new subdivisions, shopping malls, and office parks made possible by the new roadways would eventually choke them as well. In the real world, such moratoriums are rarely possible, which is why road-building is typically a folly.

Those who are skeptical of the need for a fundamental reconsideration of transportation planning should take note of something we experienced a few years ago. In a large working session on the design of Playa Vista, an urban infill project in Los Angeles, the traffic engineer was presenting a report of current and projected congestion around the development. From our seat by the window, we had an unobstructed rush-hour view of a street he had diagnosed as highly congested and in need of widening. Why, then, was traffic flowing smoothly, with hardly any stacking at the traffic light? When we asked, the traffic engineer offered an answer that should be recorded permanently in the annals of the profession: "The computer model that we use does not necessarily bear any relationship to reality."

But the real question is why so many drivers choose to sit for hours in bumper-to-bumper traffic without seeking alternatives. Is it a manifestation of some deep-seated self-loathing, or are people just stupid? The answer is that people are actually quite smart, and their decision to submit themselves to the misery of suburban commuting is a sophisticated response to a set of circumstances that are as troubling as their result. Automobile use is the intelligent choice for most Americans because it is what economists refer to as a "free good": the consumer pays only a fraction of its true cost. The authors Stanley Hart and Alvin Spivak have explained that:

We learn in first-year economics what happens when products or services become "free" goods. The market functions chaotically; demand goes through the roof. In most American cities, parking spaces, roads and freeways are free goods. Local government services to the motorist and to the trucking industry—traffic engineering, traffic control, traffic lights, police and fire protection, street repair and maintenance—are all free goods.[•]

THE AUTOMOBILE SUBSIDY

To what extent is automobile use a "free" good? According to Hart and Spivak, government subsidies for highways and parking alone amount to between 8 and 10 percent of our gross national product, the equivalent of a fuel tax of approximately $3.50 per gallon. If this tax were to account for "soft" costs such as pollution cleanup and emergency medical treatment, it would be as high as $9.00 per gallon. The cost of these subsidies—approximately $5,000 per car per year—is passed directly on to the American citizen in the form of increased prices for products or, more often, as income, property, and sales taxes. This means that the hidden costs of driving are paid by everyone: not just drivers, but also those too old or too poor to drive a car. And these people suffer doubly, as the very transit

---

[•] Stanley Hart and Alvin Spivak, *The Elephant in the Bedroom: Automobile Dependence and Denial,* 2. Much of the information here on the science and economics of traffic congestion comes from this book, which should be required reading for every professional planner, traffic engineer, and amateur highway activist.

The logic behind the desire to make use of free goods is suggested by an argument overheard at a recent planning conference: "Of course there's never enough parking! If you gave everyone free pizza, would there be enough pizza?"

systems they count on for mobility have gone out of business, unable to compete with the heavily subsidized highways.*

Even more irksome is the fact that spending on transit creates twice as many new jobs as spending on highways. In fact, every billion dollars reallocated from road-building to transit creates seven thousand jobs.[5] Congress's recent $41 billion highway bill, had it been allocated to transit, would have employed an additional quarter-million people nationwide.

Because they do not pay the full price of driving, most car owners choose to drive as much as possible. They are making the correct economic decision, but not in a free-market economy. As Hart and Spivak note, an appropriate analogy is Stalin's Gosplan, a Soviet agency that set arbitrary "correct" prices for many consumer goods, irrespective of their cost of production, with unsurprising results. In the American version of Gosplan, gasoline costs one quarter of what it did in 1929 (in real dollars).■ One need look no further for a reason why American cities continue to sprawl into the countryside. In Europe, where gasoline costs about four times the American price, long-distance automotive commuting is the exclusive privilege of the wealthy, and there is relatively little suburban sprawl.

The American Gosplan pertains to shipping as well. In the current structure of subsidization, trucking is heavily favored over rail transport, even though trucks consume fifteen times the fuel for the

---

* Hart and Spivak, 6. Perhaps the most serious soft cost of driving is pollution. Already, cars and other vehicles are seen as the worst polluters of urban air and the biggest producers of carbon dioxide, the chief suspect in global warming (*The Economist,* "Living with the Car," 4). About half of U.S. air pollution emissions come from motor vehicles (MacKenzie, Dower, and Chen, 14).

■ "Cheap gasoline forever, whatever," is how *The Economist* describes the American approach to transportation planning, adding: "Hence the paradox that the freest market in the world eschews the price mechanism and applies command-and-control regulation to a central portion of its economy" ("Living with the Car," 7).

equivalent job. The government pays a $300 billion subsidy to truckers unthinkingly, while carefully scrutinizing every dollar allocated to transit. Similarly, we try to solve our commuter traffic problems by building highways instead of railways, even though it takes fifteen lanes of highway to move as many people as one lane of track.[6] This predisposition toward automobile use is plainly evident in the prevalent terminology: money spent on roads is called "highway investment," while money spent on rails is called "transit subsidy."

The American Gosplan is not a conspiracy so much as a culture—albeit one strongly supported by pervasive advertising—and it is probably unrealistic to hope that legislators will soon take steps, such as enacting a substantial gasoline tax, to allocate fairly the costs of driving. Pressured by generous automobile industry contributions on the one hand and a car-dependent public on the other, politicians have lately been using gas-tax *elimination* as an election strategy, with some success. But there is encouraging information suggesting that a gas tax may not be the political suicide that most politicians suspect. According to a recent Pew Foundation poll, 60 percent of those asked favored a twenty-five-cent-per-gallon gas tax to slow global warming.•

While there are many supposedly "anti-business" arguments for a higher gas tax—from fighting global warming to supporting public transit—the real justification is economic: subsidized automobile use is the single largest violation of the free-market principle in U.S. fiscal policy. Economic inefficiencies in this country due to auto-

---

• As *The Boston Globe*'s David Nyhan notes, "If that result were an election, we'd call it a landslide . . . Conclusion: the people are way out in front of the politicians again" (Nyhan, "For the Planet's Sake, Hike the Gas Tax," A27).

motive subsidization are estimated at $700 billion annually,[7] which powerfully undermines America's ability to compete in the global economy. Although suburban sprawl is the concern in this book, it is not the only sad result of this fundamental error.

The problems of automobile subsidization have been well documented; this is old news. And yet it is news which few people seem to understand, and which has barely begun to influence government policy in any significant way. So, to all the concerned activists nationwide who are banging their heads against the wall on this issue, we do not have very much to say except "May we join you at the wall?" Fortunately, the automobile subsidy is only one of many forces contributing to sprawl, and there are other avenues along which anti-sprawl efforts are likely to achieve meaningful results.

6

SPRAWL AND THE DEVELOPER

THE DECLINE OF THE AMERICAN DEVELOPER;

THE INSIDIOUS INFLUENCE OF THE MARKET EXPERTS;

QUESTIONABLE CONVENTIONAL WISDOM; STRUGGLES WITH THE

HOMEBUILDERS; A VISIT TO THE NATIONAL ASSOCIATION OF

HOME BUILDERS' ANNUAL CONVENTION

———

If what you are selling is privacy and exclusivity, then every new house is a degradation of the amenity. However, if what you are selling is community, then every new house is an enhancement of the asset.
—VINCE GRAHAM, ADDRESSING THE NATIONAL
ASSOCIATION OF HOME BUILDERS, 1997

———

THE DECLINE OF THE AMERICAN DEVELOPER

Of all those who suffer from suburban sprawl, who is the greatest victim? It could be argued that the distinction belongs to that former pillar of society, the real estate developer. Certainly, over the past quarter century, few members of American society have experienced as drastic a fall from grace as he has. While entire segments of the population have been forced by suburbia to significantly compromise their quality of life, the developer has been victimized in a different way: he has become persona non grata.

It was not always thus. When George Merrick built Florida's

The town founder: George Merrick, beloved developer of Coral Gables

Coral Gables, only seventy years ago, he was regarded not as a developer but as a town founder. A bust in his likeness still presides proudly over City Hall. He is hailed, appropriately, as the city father, a visionary, and mentioned regularly in the public discourse, not unlike the framers of the U.S. Constitution. The same is true of J. C. Nichols in Kansas City, James Oglethorpe in Savannah, Mary Emery in Mariemont, Ohio, and myriad other developers nationwide who were lucky enough to go about their business prior to 1945.

Since then, developers somehow have devolved from admired figures into reviled characters, challenging drug dealers and pimps for position in the public's esteem. How could this have happened? Are they of no use to society? In fact, developers provide the nation with products that it needs: they build houses, shops, offices, even streets and roads, and they often do so at great financial risk. But they are resented, because they are unable to provide these things in the form of towns, places that people care about. Instead, they can provide only sprawl, toward which most people feel indifferent at best. As long as the conventions of real estate development effectively outlaw the construction of mixed-use neighborhoods, developers will find it very difficult to build anything that provides residents with a sense of community. Similarly, as long as zoning codes favor low-density development over the creation of compact communities, developers will not be able to shake their reputation as land rapists, as they turn farm after farm into cookie-cutter sprawl. This is why one can buy a bumper sticker that reads: LEAVING TOWN? TAKE A DEVELOPER WITH YOU.

Essentially, the demonization of the developer arises from the relationship in people's minds between nature and culture. Any new

The modern developer: snake-oil salesman

construction on undeveloped land replaces nature, typically farm-land or forest, and few would claim that this is not a loss. However, if what replaces nature is a town or a village—a place of culture—then perhaps that transaction could be considered a fair trade. After all, even the most ardent environmentalist wouldn't want to level Nantucket, Charleston, or Santa Fe so that nature could reclaim that territory. On the other hand, were the typical citizen offered the opportunity to remove a subdivision, a strip center, or an office park for, say, an orchard, one might expect an enthusiastic response. The public knows that these single-use pods are not places of culture, and that trading nature for sprawl was not a fair transaction—and they know that it was the real estate developer who brought them the lousy deal.

THE INSIDIOUS INFLUENCE
OF THE MARKET EXPERTS

But the hapless developer deserves only part of the blame, for the deck was already stacked against healthy growth by municipal regulations and engineering conventions. Perhaps even more culpable in this scenario are those surprisingly powerful advisers to the development industry, the *market experts,* who have been unrelentingly spreading the same message for over thirty years: build sprawl or lose your shirt. Specifically: do not mix uses; do not mix incomes; build walls and security gates; put the garages up front; and assume that nobody will walk. Thanks to the market experts, most developers are still trying to sell the equivalent of a 1972 Chevy in a world that is anxiously awaiting the next Toyota Camry.

Selling the image: suburban developers' commitment to the traditional neighborhood typically runs no deeper than their marketing departments

Perhaps the most frustrating thing about the market gurus is that they are well aware of the popularity of the traditional neighborhood concept. Much of their literature, their imagery, and their sales technique pays homage to the idea of neighborhood, village, and small town. They know that the small town sells—preferred by a 3:2 ratio over the suburb in a recent Gallup poll[*]—and they tell their developer clients to label their products as such, whatever form they may actually take. They have co-opted much of the original vocabulary of traditional town planning in their efforts, from the village green to the corner store. Unfortunately, by doing so, they discredit those terms and debase the neighborhood concept. The result is subdivisions that advertise "the feeling of a great hometown"—and may even go so far as to stock the firehouse with a pair of Dalmatians—while the "corner store" sits isolated in a sea of parking, and walking to work or school remains a memory.

The marketing profession skillfully misleads the development industry because it has thoroughly managed to mislead itself. In considering what "building product" to recommend to developers, the market experts study and compare *recent* product only. These studies are concerned solely with what sells the most—by definition, the newly built and mass-marketed houses—rather than what sells *for* the most, the houses located in the healthy older neighborhoods. If they were to cast the net a bit further, beyond the successes of the past five years to the successes of the past hundred years, they would show that the neighborhoods built before World

[*] Philip Langdon, *A Better Place to Live,* 119. In 1989, the Gallup Organization asked people whether they preferred to live in a city, suburb, small town, or farm: 34 percent chose a small town, compared to 24 percent who chose a suburb; 22 percent chose a farm; and 19 percent chose a city (Dirk Johnson, "Population Decline in Rural America," A20).

War II—the ones that developers evoke in their sales pitches—are the ones that dramatically outperform all of their recent product. These older neighborhoods do not register on the marketing radar screen, because the houses in them come up for sale only one at a time, and are often snatched up immediately, sometimes without advertising. As a result, these precedents are usually ignored, as are the lessons they teach us.

In addition, experts often mislead themselves and their clients by conducting opinion polls that are poorly targeted, badly worded, or simply biased. For example, how can a homeowner who has just purchased a conventional suburban tract house—the most common survey participant—be expected to express a preference for something different? To do so would be to acknowledge committing a grievous error in a major investment. Similarly, certain terms, taken out of context, can be counted on to evoke certain responses. One erstwhile client of ours backed out of a traditional neighborhood project in Ames, Iowa, after conducting a survey that asked questions like, "Would you like to live on a cul-de-sac?" and "Do you like alleys?" The results were unsurprising. Home buyers will almost always choose a cul-de-sac over a through street when asked. But if you show them the two different *systems*—how the cul-de-sac's very existence presupposes a high-volume collector road nearby—they tend to prefer the pedestrian-friendly network of through streets. Similarly, few people express any fondness for alleys when asked, but the question prompts a vastly different response when phrased more carefully: "Would you prefer a streetscape fronted by garage doors, or one in which porches face the street because garages are placed on a rear alley?" Even more accurate, and gaining acceptance among developers, are photo comparisons such as the Visual

Too valuable to ignore: built in the 1920s, Mariemont is one of many successful new towns that have escaped the notice of market experts (Drawing by Felix Pereira, student, University of Miami)

Preference Survey.* But standard market surveys, when written carelessly—or with a desire to endorse the status quo, as we suspect was the case in Ames—can kill a well-meaning developer's initiative quickly.

What happens when surveys really address the significant distinctions between conventional and traditional development? Conventional market advisers inform their developer clients that their purchasers are attracted to clubhouses, entry features, and security walls. But one comprehensive study found that a "private country club" was requested by only 18 percent of respondents, while 64 percent preferred a "small cluster of convenience stores nearby." A "dramatic entrance" appealed to 8 percent of respondents, while 45 percent asked for a "small neighborhood library." Only 12 percent requested "walls around the subdivision," compared to 46 percent who wanted "little parks nearby." In question after question, respondents expressed a greater desire for the conveniences of neighborhood life than for the amenities of middle-class suburbia.[1]

Another fundamental problem with market advice is that it comes from so few sources.■ Every month, two nationally circulated builders' magazines tell developers what buyers want. The underly-

---

* Created by Anton Nelessen, a professor at Rutgers University, the Visual Preference Survey has become the tool of choice for municipalities fighting sprawl to demonstrate a public desire for traditional development, and to generate political will for revised development standards.
■ One venerable and powerful source of real estate market information is the Urban Land Institute, or ULI. Long considered an advocate of the development industry, fortifying the hegemony of conventional building practice—and, for that reason, fondly referred to as the United Lemmings Institute—the ULI has recently begun to advocate traditional town planning, albeit as one of several development alternatives worth considering. Interestingly, the ULI was founded in 1936 by J. C. Nichols, the developer of Kansas City's wonderful Country Club District, a series of neighborhoods that exemplify most of the principles advocated here.

ing message is inescapable: "Diverge from these conventions at your peril!" The danger of marketing advice, good or bad, being collected and disseminated in such a concentrated way—momentarily ignoring the stupefying monotony of the result—is that those designs which are endorsed become overbuilt almost immediately. We often lecture to developers, and we always tease them: "You all listen to the same advice, and you all build the same thing. No wonder you periodically overbuild and go bankrupt!"

A final reason behind the undue influence of the market experts has to do with how developments are financed. Few real estate projects are funded entirely by their own developers; most depend on huge loans from banks, pension funds, and other institutions looking for safe investments. Such investors, before financing a development, typically require market surveys demonstrating the success of previous similar projects, called "comparables." To qualify for funding, projects have to be presented as *not materially different from* the comparables—with unsurprisingly repetitive results. Developers that possess the initiative to try something different—such as creating a mixed-use community—find themselves unable to move forward without the blessing of a market analysis advocating their proposal. This is something that most market experts are unable to provide, as their data is collected from the subdivisions recently built by their conventional clients.

QUESTIONABLE CONVENTIONAL WISDOM

With or without the advice of the market experts, the development industry is also led astray by its own conventional wisdom, most

The value of design: two houses with similar statistics but vastly different prices

Seaside: a holiday resort designed on the model of a traditional town

significantly its well-worn mantra of "location, location, location." This is true enough, but the evidence suggests that good design, generally discounted by developers, can have an impact equal to or greater than location on the value of a property. Two houses in Coral Gables provide an instructive example. They are located across from each other on the same street and are served by the same schools. Both contain about 3,000 square feet of air-conditioned space on a 10,000-square-foot lot. But the house above recently sold for $370,000, while the house below sold in the same year for $1.4 million. What is the difference between the two properties? Design. One is classically inspired, is carefully detailed, and sits toward the front of its lot, creating a large interior yard of uncompromised privacy. The other is a standard one-story ranch house sitting smack-dab in the middle of its lot, with residual yards all around, none of which is particularly usable.

An important point to make here—which helps explain the higher value of both traditional houses and traditional communities—is that expensive older real estate owes its price to more than just its history, its mature trees, or what the art historian Alois Riegl referred to as "age value." There is no doubt that historical significance can also contribute to property values, and the age of Georgetown and Boston certainly plays some role in those cities' vertiginous housing markets. But age value does not explain the neotraditional developments of Seaside and Kentlands, both built in the 1980s, in which houses and homesites sell at a significant premium over similar properties nearby. At Seaside, which is located in the middle of nowhere, a small house a quarter mile from the water sells for twice the price of a twice-as-large oceanfront lot in a nearby subdivision.[2] At Kentlands, houses sell for a $30,000 to $40,000 premium over comparable units on larger lots in neighboring subdivisions.[3] The difference is not age, or location, but design: the fact that the properties at Seaside and Kentlands are part of a town, a place where people want to be.

The same phenomenon can be seen in the new village of Windsor, in Vero Beach, Florida, where home lots overlooking the golf course and the ocean—a conventional developer's fantasy—are being outsold by lots in the village core. These lots, like the older Coral Gables house, offer both privacy *and community* to their owners. These and other recent projects—both restorations and new construction—demonstrate that, when offered true community, buyers require no other amenity, not even location.

Windsor: small lots that offer privacy as well as community

There is one other crippling misunderstanding that prevails in the development industry regarding traditional versus conventional design. Some developers who are unschooled in the details argue that traditional neighborhoods are more expensive to build than conventional subdivisions—"Who's going to pay for the alleys?" they ask. That gripe is easy to refute on a macroscopic level; few people would claim that, on the regional scale, it is cheaper to produce a sprawling, automobile-dependent environment than one that is compact and pedestrian- and transit-friendly. But, since the macro-scale costs of sprawling infrastructure are often absorbed by an unwitting government, developers must also be convinced that traditional development is cheaper at the smaller scale of the individual neighborhood infrastructure, which they must pay for.

Take this typical subdivision layout, from an advertisement in the *Detroit Free Press.* In traditional neighborhoods, all streets except highways are "fronted" by salable lots on both sides; none

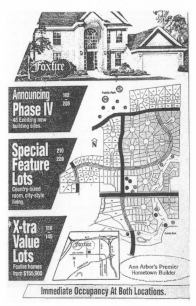

Infrastructure wasted by the cul-de-sac system: gray streets have only 50 percent salable frontage. Black streets have no salable frontage at all

of the infrastructure is wasted on transportation alone. But in this development by "Ann Arbor's Premier Hometown Builder," the roads marked in gray are fronted only on one side. Those marked in black have no building frontage at all; they are the automobile-only collector roads mandated by the dendritic cul-de-sac system. Not only is one third of the asphalt therefore redundant, but when one accounts for the fact that these roads are one-third wider than those found in traditional development, the cost of alleys becomes negligible. Further, since rear alleys eliminate the need for driveways, traditional urbanism provides savings there as well. In fact, alleys, if they are not overengineered, cost no more than the driveways they replace.

There is another way in which traditional neighborhoods offer savings over sprawl: they can be built in much smaller phases. Smart developers do their best to serve many different market segments at once—"starter," "move-up," "family," "retirement," and so on—but in suburbia they must build an independent pod for each market segment, since different incomes must never mix. In a traditional neighborhood, every market segment can be served through the construction of a single mixed-use area, thus limiting the infrastructure. Finally, there are the efficiencies that result from building at slightly higher densities, something that is viable within a traditional street network but is rarely achieved gracefully in sprawl.•

To be fair, some developers of new traditional neighborhoods are

---

• The ability of new traditional neighborhoods to handle higher densities attractively is often due to the presence of the rear lane, which allows row houses and apartments to be parked from the back. Row houses are often only about twenty feet wide, such that a two-car garage eclipses the entire façade if no alley is provided. Apartment houses typically require large parking lots, which are a visual blight unless hidden behind the buildings.

quick to attest that they achieved no savings over conventional development. The reason is usually that these projects are hybrids: traditionally organized street networks that have been burdened with gold-plated infrastructure such as unnecessary collector roads, conventional street widths, and fully engineered curbs in alleys that are as thickly paved as streets. These compromises are typically required by old-school public works departments with no sympathy for different standards. It is only this sort of engineer-imposed hybridization that threatens to bring the costs of traditional neighborhood development within the lofty realm of suburban sprawl.

STRUGGLES WITH THE HOMEBUILDERS

Even as land developers become aware of the true economy of traditional neighborhood design, there remains one other group that requires conversion if sprawl is to be overcome: the homebuilders. As already described, there is a considerable difference between conventional and traditional development at both the urban scale and the scale of the individual building. Even the best traditional neighborhood plan will achieve only limited success without the appropriate architecture, which requires the active cooperation of the people who build the houses.

What does traditional neighborhood design require of homebuilders? First, that they adjust their house plans so that the garages are located on a rear alley, or at least set back behind the house fronts, to avoid dominating the street. It also asks them to calm down the architecture: to simplify roofs and to limit the amount of variety within the house façade, recognizing that variety should instead occur at the urban scale, among different houses. In some cases, it demands that they supply front porches, stoops, and picket fences, to better define the transition between the public and the private realms. None of these requirements is particularly onerous, but there is no denying that traditional neighborhood design requires the builder to take a risk: specifically, to take the house plans that have been selling successfully for years, and to change them more than slightly.

Fortunately, the reasons for doing so are becoming apparent. In those few instances in which new traditional product has competed head-to-head against new conventional product, the popular preference is quite clear. In Belmont, a new village we designed in northern Virginia, three separate homebuilders were active: two local firms and a national conglomerate, a veritable 800-pound gorilla. The smaller builders were content to follow our urban regulations, which required front porches, picket fences, and alley-served garages. The national builder, too successful to listen, threw out the code, and insisted on building a standard garage-front product. After eighteen months on the market, sales figures were as follows: Local Builder A: 30 homes; Local Builder B: 14 homes; Gorilla: 1 home. There was little interest in the conventional product when buyers were presented with equal access to its alternative.

Aside from the general conservatism that it shares with land developers, the homebuilding industry finds its reform inhibited by a more deeply rooted problem, one which can be traced to the name of the industry itself. The term *homebuilder* describes the house as a product that exists independent of its context. This approach would be appropriate if houses floated freely in space, or in some other environment where actual interaction between neighbors was neither possible nor desired. But houses are not meant to exist in isolation, so to think of the individual house as the ultimate outcome of the builder's craft robs that craft of its broader significance. This point becomes more meaningful when one considers that most subdivision developers are simply ambitious homebuilders, general contractors whose businesses have grown to the point where they are taking on larger and larger parcels of land. For these people to continue thinking of themselves as homebuilders only is like Stradivarius thinking of himself as a string purveyor, ignoring the fact that the string has a much greater value when stretched across a violin. But this misperception persists and is no doubt partially responsible for the fact that most American subdivisions feel like collections of individual homes rather than true neighborhoods.

A VISIT TO THE NATIONAL ASSOCIATION OF HOME BUILDERS' ANNUAL CONVENTION

If one wishes to understand the homebuilding industry, there is probably no event more eye-opening than the annual convention of the National Association of Home Builders. The NAHB convention can be an unsettling experience for those who have never witnessed it. The typical conventioneer is a skilled no-nonsense small businessman who removed his tool belt only moments before boarding the airplane. Sixty-five thousand people, mostly men, all eat lunch under large tents pitched on parking lots, where the choice of entree ranges from beef barbecue to pork barbecue. This is not a place for idle chatter about community.

The convention floor itself is an astounding sight, a collection of building products that together could serve as a compelling argument against increased GNP: refrigerators disguised as walnut wardrobes, Jacuzzis the size of sports utility vehicles, and home entertainment centers worthy of a film producer. Entertainment abounds. Two talented performers juggle Craftsman tools while extolling the virtues of Sears' Buyer Protection Program. Showgirls dance in front of a fifty-foot-high Koehler display while lab-coated actors demonstrate the latest in high-tech toilets. Amid this circus atmosphere, consultants offer hundreds of seminars intended to give the builders an advantage over their competition. Typical courses are "Designing and Marketing Homes for Aging Baby Boomers" and "Fifty Great and Zany Ideas Guaranteed to Jump-Start Your Sales."

Year after year, homebuilders return to the NAHB convention in search of those new concepts and appliances that will give their houses *product differentiation,* that will somehow distinguish their output from everyone else's. They design and market their houses like cars, characterized primarily by their factory options: will the gimmick be a path-oriented lighting control panel or an integrated garage door opener/burglar alarm deactivator? Meanwhile, by ignoring the issue of context—the quality of the environment surrounding the houses—they miss out on their best opportunity to provide something truly desired: community. Community is the amenity most cherished by those looking for a place to live. According to Fannie Mae, Americans prefer a good community to a good house by a margin of three to one. This fact is the key to the emancipation

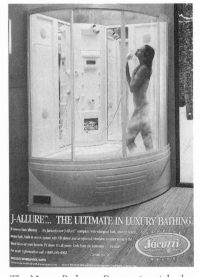

The Master Bedroom Resort: gimmicks that homebuilders offer to fill the spiritual void created by the absence of community

of the homebuilder from his slavery to the gadgets and doohickeys of the NAHB convention.

Unfortunately, the homebuilders have yet to get this message. Only two or three presentations and panels out of literally hundreds at each convention address the concept of traditional neighborhood development. These seminars are well attended and feature speakers on both sides of the issue, but they make little impact on the bulk of convention attendees. The primary goal of the industry remains to build and sell individual houses as quickly and profitably as possible, to "blow and go," as they put it. A pro-community panelist at the NAHB convention can't help but feel like a flower child at boot camp.

Homebuilders, land developers, and marketing advisers are all constituencies that must be won over if the campaign against suburban sprawl is to succeed. Their participation will be meaningful in the long run only if it is driven by the profit motive, because in America at the millennium, ideas live or die based upon their performance in the marketplace. While there are ways in which government intervention is necessary—most obviously in rolling back the federal, state, and municipal policies that continue to promote sprawl—sprawl will not become obsolete by changing laws alone. A higher standard of development will become commonplace only if it offers greater profits to those who practice it.

The generation of developers that pioneered neotraditional town planning—Robert Davis (Seaside), Joe Alfandre (Kentlands), Phil Angelides (Laguna West), Vince Graham (Newpoint), Henry Turley (Harbortown), and even Michael Eisner (Celebration)—were all motivated primarily by a desire to provide a better place to live, and only secondarily by profit. Since then, a second generation of developers, many of them large corporations, are copying these techniques, primarily because they want to duplicate the financial success of these pioneers. If this generation finds traditional neighborhood development to be a better investment than sprawl—as it has so far—it is reasonable to expect that the development industry as a whole will learn to change its ways.

7

THE VICTIMS OF SPRAWL

CUL-DE-SAC KIDS; SOCCER MOMS; BORED TEENAGERS;

STRANDED ELDERLY; WEARY COMMUTERS;

BANKRUPT MUNICIPALITIES; THE IMMOBILE POOR

———

Surplus wealth enables people to persist in building wasteful, inadequate communities and then compensate for the communities' failings by buying private vehicles and driving all over the metropolitan area in search of what ought to be available close to home.

— PHILIP LANGDON, *A BETTER PLACE TO LIVE* (1994)

———

Aside from the real estate developer, who else is victimized by suburban sprawl? To some degree, almost everyone is. Most obvious are the 80 million Americans who are either too young, too old, or too poor to drive. But it doesn't stop there. Upon investigation, it is difficult to identify a segment of the population that does not suffer in some way from the lifestyle imposed by contemporary suburban development.

Perhaps most worrisome is the situation facing the children of suburbia. In one of the great ironies of our era, the cul-de-sac suburbs, originally conceived as youth's great playground, are proving to be less than ideal for America's young.

That suburban life may be bad for children comes as a surprise. After all, most families move to the suburbs precisely because they think it will be "good for the children." What do they mean by that? Better suburban schools—a phenomenon peculiar to the United States—are good for children. Big, safe, grassy fields to play on are also good for them. What is not so good for children, however, is the complete loss of autonomy they suffer in suburbia. In this environment where all activities are segregated and distances are measured on the odometer, a child's personal mobility extends no farther than the edge of the subdivision. Even the local softball field often exists beyond the child's independent reach.

The result is a new phenomenon: the "cul-de-sac kid," the child who lives as a prisoner of a thoroughly safe and unchallenging environment. While this state of affairs may be acceptable, even desirable, through about age five, what of the next ten or twelve years? Dependent always on some adult to drive them around, children and adolescents are unable to practice at becoming adults. They cannot run so simple a household errand as picking up a carton of milk. They cannot bicycle to the toy store and spend their money on their own. They cannot drop in on their mother at work. Most cannot walk to school. Even pickup baseball games are a thing of the past, with parents now required to arrange car-pooling with near-military precision, to transport the children at the appointed times.

Out of reach: clustered baseball fields that few children can access without parental transport

Children are frozen in a form of infancy, utterly dependent on others, bereft of the ability to introduce variety into their own lives, robbed of the opportunity to make choices and exercise judgment. Typical suburban parents give their children an allowance, in order to empower them and encourage independence. "Feel free to spend it any way you like," they say. The child then says, "Thanks, Mom. When can you drive me to the mall?"

SOCCER MOMS

Another word for *dependent* is *burden,* and that term better describes these parents' perception of the children who rely upon them for mobility. Mothers often derail their careers so that their children can experience a life beyond the backyard. The role of journalist, banker, or marketing director is exchanged for that of chauffeur, with the vague hope that their career will resume when the last child turns sixteen; thus the term *soccer mom*—a distinctly suburban euphemism. The plight of the suburban housewife was powerfully conveyed in a letter we received in 1990 from a woman living outside of Tulsa:

Dear Architects:

I am a mother of four children who are not able to leave the yard because of our city's design. Ever since we have moved here I have felt like a caged animal only let out for a ride in the car. It is impossible to walk even to the grocery store two blocks away. If our family wants to go for a ride we need to load two cars with four bikes and a baby cart and drive four miles to the only bike path in this city of over a quarter million people. I cannot exercise unless I drive to a health club that I had to pay $300 to, and that is four and a half miles away. There is no sense of community here on my street, either, because we all have to drive around in our own little worlds that take us fifty miles a day to every corner of the surrounding five miles.

I want to walk somewhere so badly that I could cry. I miss walking! I want the kids to walk to school. I want to walk to the store for a pound of butter. I want to take the kids on a neighborhood stroll or bike. My husband wants to walk to work because it is so close, but none of these things is possible . . . And if you saw my neighborhood, you would think that I had it all according to the great American dream.

BORED TEENAGERS

Those who have experienced adolescence in modern suburbia have their own stories of boredom and frustration. Eric Bogosian's play *Suburbia,* set in a 7-Eleven parking lot, depicts the culture that develops in a public realm devoid of decent public gathering places. In an interview, Bogosian noted:

There's nothing wrong with these kids. The landscape around and within their own minds isn't providing them with the tools to get around in the world beyond the suburbs. Meanwhile, T.V. is bombarding them with so much stuff that all they can feel is frustration. No wonder they think there's no point in doing anything . . . The people who designed the suburbs were married couples with children, who wanted a sedate place to grill burgers in the backyard. Young people didn't have a say in it, and they get into a lot of trouble there because they're bored. Driving around, driving drunk, drowning in frozen ponds. The suburbs can be a dangerous place at a certain age.[1]

It seems odd to say that the suburbs are dangerous, since many families relocate to suburbia precisely to find a safer environment. In terms of crime, this motivation seems justified, but suburbs are hardly free from violent crime, and recent examples of suburban gang activity call the assumption into question. It is fair to say that the suburbs are no more crime-free than their higher-income demographics would suggest.

But there is more to protecting life than avoiding crime, as any parent of a sixteen-year-old driver will attest. Far and away, car crashes are the largest killer of American teenagers, accounting for more than one third of all deaths.[2] Yet all the suburban parents who can afford it will readily buy the additional cars that provide independence for their children, often in order to regain their own freedom.

When they get behind the wheel, teenagers automatically join the most dangerous gang in America. Automobile accidents kill over 45,000 people annually in this country, almost a Vietnam War of casualties every year.• A child is twenty times more likely to die from

Crashes Kill 37 in Texas In Single Day

Deaths on Highways Are Close to Record

WEATHERFORD, Tex., July 3 (AP) — In one of the deadliest days ever on Texas highways, 31 people died in three crashes today, including 14 people killed when a tractor-trailer hit the back of a family's van.

Eleven people, many of them children, died in a collision involving a tractor-trailer near the West town of Snyder, and six were

Highway carnage: an accepted outgrowth of an automobile-dependent society

---

• In 1988, 14.8 million accidents involving motor vehicles led to 47,000 deaths and almost 5 million injuries (MacKenzie, Dower, Chen, 19). Taken out of context, the amount of carnage on America's highways is absolutely shocking, as is the degree to which we have come to accept it as a fact of life. Jane Holtz Kay asks, "Where else do we

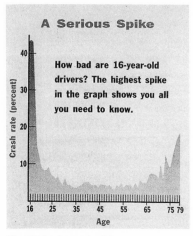

A Serious Spike

How bad are 16-year-old drivers? The highest spike in the graph shows you all you need to know.

The Triple-A rates its drivers

an automobile mishap than from gang activity, as most young drivers are involved in *at least* one serious auto accident between ages sixteen and twenty. In their first year of driving, over 40 percent of teenagers have an accident bad enough to be reported to the police.[3] For this reason, it is more dangerous, statistically, to grow up in the suburbs of Seattle than in that city's most urban neighborhoods.•

The second most likely cause of death among teenagers, suicide, is also correlated with the growth of sprawl. Teenage suicide, almost unheard of before 1950, had nearly tripled by 1980 and now accounts for over 12 percent of youth mortalities. Sociologists, who cite "teen isolation and boredom" as a contributing factor, confirm that national rates of teenage suicide are much higher in suburbs than in cities.[4] This "isolation and boredom" is the outcome of an environment that fails to provide teenagers with the ordinary challenges of maturing, developing useful skills, and gaining a sense of self.

Much has been made of recent suburban high school shootings, and even *The New York Times* has suggested that suburban design

---

accept some 120 deaths a day so offhandedly? Imagine a plane crash each afternoon . . . An engineer recorded it in military terms: during the same forty days of the Persian Gulf War in which 146 men and women were lost fighting to keep the world safe for petroleum, 4,900 died with equal violence on our country's highways" (Kay, *Asphalt Nation,* 103). By 1994, car crashes had killed over three million Americans in total (Andrew Kimbrell, "Steering Toward Ecological Disaster," *The Green Lifestyle Handbook,* 35). Internationally, car crashes cause an estimated 250,000 deaths and 3,000,000 injuries annually (Wolfgang Zuckermann, *The End of the Road,* 64).

• James Gerstenzang, "Cars Make Suburbs Riskier Than Cities, Study Says," A20. A study of the Pacific Northwest by Alan Thein Durning found that 1.6 percent of city residents were likely to be killed or injured by traffic accidents or crime, versus 1.9 percent of suburban residents. "Tragically, people often flee crime-ridden cities for the perceived safety of the suburbs—only to increase the risks they expose themselves to," Mr. Durning notes.

may be to blame.[5] It is unwarranted, however, to automatically presume a causal relationship. Since suburbia houses most of America's teenagers, it is bound to have its share of violent ones. Yet it is easy to imagine how a homogeneous and unstimulating environment might lead thrill-seeking teenagers to inhabit an alternative reality, whether it be computer games or psychosis. And one might speculate that the sterility of the suburbs—their very *unreality*—could make the leap to fantasy more possible.

There are other ways in which suburban sprawl victimizes America's youth. The building pictured here is not, as it may appear, a refugee relocation center or a storage depot, although it could be considered a storage depot of sorts: it's the place where we store our children while earning the money to pay for their cars. The reason that so many new schools look as dismal as this one is that there is not enough money left over after the road-building budgets are allocated. Even while we fret about the sorry state of our schools, our government spends the greater part of our public wealth on horizontal infrastructure: asphalt surfaces for cars.

At the bottom of the public funding hierarchy: our schools

It is true that the United States has the most luxurious road system in the world. We build magnificent new highways at a cost of $30 million per mile,* and every cloverleaf is more generous than the last. We happily spend twice as much per capita on transportation as do other developed nations.▪ Nothing seems too good for our

At the top of the public funding hierarchy: our roadways

* Tri-State Transportation Campaign conference, "Beyond the Open Road," at New York University. In addition, the cost of operating and maintaining the United States' primary highway system has been estimated at $500,000 per mile per year (Wolfgang Zuckermann, *The End of the Road,* 86).
▪ Michael Replogle, *Transportation Conformity and Demand Management,* 22. While the Japanese spend 9 percent of their gross national product on transportation, Americans spend 15 to 18 percent. Our excessive family expenditure on automobiles is matched by tremendous corporate spending on parking lots and garages.

cars. Meanwhile, more and more of our children attend school in fields of prefabricated portable barracks with air-conditioning backpacks, surrounded by chain-link fencing. It is difficult to be encouraged by what this says about our national priorities.

It would clarify matters if Americans would think about schools, town halls, libraries, and other civic buildings as *vertical infrastructure,* to be financed out of the same purse as our horizontal infrastructure. Such buildings are not mere luxuries but investments in community-making that evoke identity, pride, and participation in public life. A society's civic buildings are ultimately as important as its roads, and we should not use the table scraps of public funding to construct them. Most Americans would tolerate aging asphalt and fewer new lanes if they knew that their children would not be educated in the equivalent of trailer parks. Unfortunately, this choice is not offered.

STRANDED ELDERLY

Whether or not the suburbs work as promised for children, they are intended to benefit families, especially young ones. As families age and disperse, however, parents begin to find themselves in an environment that is no longer organized to serve their needs. As driving skills diminish with age, parents become increasingly dependent upon others for mobility, just as their children were once dependent upon them. This situation may represent some form of divine justice, but hardly a satisfying one, since being forced to drive and being forced to ride are equally unpleasant.

Many seniors choose to retire to a house in the suburbs, especially in the Sun Belt—at least, they *think* that's what they're doing.

But they would be mistaken, because, as soon as they lose their driver's licenses, the location of that house puts them out of reach of their physical and social needs. They become, in effect, nonviable members of society. Unless they are wealthy enough to have a chauffeur, or are willing to burden a relative, they have no choice but to *re*-retire into a specialized home for the elderly. Then, having left a second community behind, they spend the rest of their days quarantined with their fellow nonviable members of society. The retirement community is really just a way station for the assisted-care facility.

Most elderly are neither infirm nor senile; they are healthy and able citizens who simply can no longer operate two tons of heavy machinery. The phenomenon of suburban auto dependency is not just a theory for these people. It is the reason why we see otherwise reasonable men and women falsifying eye exams and terrorizing their fellow motorists. They know that the minute they lose their license, they will revert from adulthood to infancy and be warehoused in an institution where their only source of freedom is the van that takes them to the mall on Monday and Thursday afternoons.

It should not be surprising that contemporary suburbia, with its strict separation of land uses, has inadvertently segregated the elderly from the rest of society. Prior to 1950, there were few if any retirement communities in the United States; they did not exist, because they were not needed. The elderly would almost always stay in their old neighborhoods after retiring. Once they lost their ability to drive, they could still maintain a viable lifestyle by walking, even if slowly. The ladies pictured here have the good fortune of living in Winter Park, Florida, a small city built in the late nineteenth century. In such a place, where housing and shopping are in

Winter Park, Florida, a NORC (Naturally Occurring Retirement Community): senior citizens can remain self-sufficient when their environment does not force them to drive

close pedestrian proximity, they can remain independent until they become infirm. This option is simply not available in today's suburbs.

Acknowledging the conveniences that traditional urbanism offers the elderly, sociologists have recently identified what they call a NORC: a Naturally Occurring Retirement Community. Amateur observers have another name for it: a neighborhood full of older people. Winter Park, Florida, is one such community, as is the Upper East Side of Manhattan. Many American cities have their NORCs, where a disproportionate number of the better-off elderly have moved in order to realize the benefits of retiring in a mixed-use, pedestrian-friendly environment. One hopes that this sort of self-sufficiency does not become the exclusive privilege of the upper classes.

WEARY COMMUTERS

How Americans must spend their free time

Suburbia clearly is not an empowering environment for that third of the population that cannot drive. What of the two thirds that can, and the lucky minority that can afford multiple cars—has their lot improved? For people who do not particularly enjoy driving in traffic, the answer is probably no.

The largest segment of the population inconvenienced by sprawl is undoubtedly the middle-class commuter. Here, the degradation may not be as severe as it is with the young or the elderly, but the statistics can be quite unsettling. Say you live an hour's drive from your job. You would be spending a minimum of 500 hours per year in your car, the equivalent of twelve work weeks. In a society that provides its citizens only two to three weeks' annual vacation, that is a dismaying figure.

Early in the twentieth century, the labor movement secured for Americans the eight-hour day, an idea that was embraced as a powerful contribution to the quality of life of the average citizen. What the eight-hour day accomplished, essentially, was to liberate about two hours daily for the pursuit of happiness. These hours meant different things to different people. Some spent them on family or community activity, others at sport or in a café, others reading, or in recent years—for better or for worse—watching television. In any case, these two hours provided middle-class workers with the opportunity to experience leisure on a daily basis.

Now, largely because of suburban land-use patterns, the eight-hour day has once again become the ten-hour day. These two hours, once the most interesting, varied, socially productive hours of the day, have become some of the most stressful and unpleasant. They were not so bad when spent on a commuter train—at least it was possible to sleep, read the news, or do the crossword—but these activities are not possible behind the wheel. Some people insist that they enjoy their hour-long drive, and they may be telling the truth. But wouldn't they rather, if given the chance, take those twelve work weeks, take the $6,000 annual cost of an inexpensive second car, and spend it all on a magnificent vacation?

The tragedy of this situation is that these hours were time that parents used to spend productively with their children. Instead, the parents are stuck in their cars, and the children are warehoused in front of the television, since they don't have independent access to much else. Our locus of civic activity has become the highway, and theirs has become the TV.[•]

Of course, time squandered in traffic extends well beyond the wasteful commute. Eighty percent of all suburban automobile trips have nothing to do with work at all,[6] but are short drives to places that used to be accessible on foot, such as shops, schools, parks, and friends' houses. With the disappearance of that once common activity, the useful walk, the weight of the average American adult has risen eight pounds in ten years. Nearly 60 percent of Americans are overweight.[■]

Suburbia victimizes the middle-class commuter not only in terms of time and health but also economically. The typical American family spends four times as much on transportation as its European counterpart, even though gasoline costs four times as much in Europe. The economic plight of the suburban American family was summed up in a note from Peter Brown of Houston:

> There are five of us in our family, and I am sad to say that we own five cars. This costs us over $27,000 a year. I have a car

---

[•] In considering a move to suburbia, parents must ask themselves such fundamental questions as how much television they want their children to watch. A study comparing ten-year-olds in suburban California and small-town Vermont found that the Vermont children had three times the mobility—independent access to desired destinations—while the Orange County children watched four times as much television (Peter Calthorpe, *The Next American Metropolis,* 9). No wonder Philip Langdon feels compelled to say that "A modern subdivision is an instrument for making people stupid" (Langdon, *A Better Place to Live,* 49). Some have even argued that a modern subdivision is a place for making people unhappy. In ultra-suburban Santa Clara County, California, there were more divorces in the early eighties than marriages (Langdon Winner, "Silicon Valley Mystery House," 46).

[■] "Most Americans Are Overweight," *The New York Times,* October 16, 1996, C9. According to the Centers for Disease Control, 22 percent of American children are obese, twice the level of ten years ago (Kilborn, A21).

for business and pleasure. My ex-wife works; she has a car. Our son, away at college in Fort Worth, has a car; our eldest daughter has to have a car for college and her part-time job. Our youngest daughter recently got her driver's license and has a car to drive to school and to her music lessons. Cars are essential to my children's social lives. Neither I nor my ex-wife can afford to take time off from work to chauffeur the children, which they don't want or expect anyway. Even more horrifying, we can't afford to buy collision insurance for our children's cars. So if one has a wreck and is at fault, the repair bills will be astronomical; if a car is totaled, it will need to be replaced somehow.

Recognizing the tremendous cost of the auto-dependent lifestyle, the author Philip Langdon has proposed a new national holiday: "Automobile Independence Day." It would take place on that date each year by which we have earned one quarter of our salaries, the amount that it takes to support our cars.[7] How appropriate that it is April Fool's Day.

BANKRUPT MUNICIPALITIES

Other victims of sprawl include the organizations that suffer economically from the inherent inefficiency of an automobile-oriented environment. The most obvious of these are the local suburban municipalities that must provide services to far-flung houses, houses that do not begin to pay for themselves with their taxes. One such municipality, the city of Franklin, a Milwaukee suburb of

25,000, conducted a careful cost analysis in 1992. It found that a new single-family home pays less than $5,000 in property taxes but costs the city more than $10,000 to service.[8] The inefficiency of new sprawling development had to be covered by a general tax hike paid by all residents, even those in more efficient older neighborhoods.

Fearful of red ink, governments respond to the costs of sprawl in a variety of ways, many of them shortsighted. Rather than insisting upon dense, efficient development patterns that pay for themselves, beleaguered municipalities embark upon stopgap measures such as prohibiting new development that houses schoolchildren, or simply refusing to enlarge their sewage facilities—a strategy that typically leads to land-hungry septic-tank sprawl. Some municipalities, and even some states, require that developers pay up front for the anticipated cost of servicing their subdivisions, which passes these costs on to the new-home consumer. This solves the municipal cash shortfall but does nothing to remedy the fundamental wastefulness of a sprawling development pattern. It also aggravates income-based segregation, as houses in suburban subdivisions become too expensive for all but the rich.

Another organization that has had difficulty coping with sprawl is the U.S. Postal Service. An ex–Postmaster General once explained to us where most of the postage money goes: to those little Jeeps and vans delivering mail on the suburban fringe. These vehicles are the main reason why the post office is perennially hiking its rates, and why aluminum gang mailboxes at subdivision entries have replaced door-to-door delivery on foot. The main-street post office as social center has also become an endangered species, as large-scale vehicle-storage requirements lead toward the consolidation of services into regional mega-offices on the suburban fringe.

Crime prevention has suffered as well. The most successful technique in reducing crime has proven to be community policing: getting the police officers out of anonymous patrol cars and onto the street, where they become part of the neighborhood. But, like the walking letter carrier, the community policeman is only effective at certain densities, and it is hard to imagine the community officer marching in and out of the cul-de-sacs of a modern subdivision. Even patrol cars have difficulty doing their job in suburbia, with its long distances and single-entry subdivisions. The response time in some suburban municipalities is often twenty minutes or more.

Subdivision residents are already aware of the ineffectiveness of suburban policing, which is why many of them pay substantial sums to employ their own security forces. Indeed, such private security is often necessary, as the suburbs have begun to experience the same social pathologies—crime, vandalism, drugs, and gangs—that helped trigger the flight to the suburbs in the first place. Unlike the real police, whose primary duty is to maintain law and order, these guns-for-hire are not public servants and need only enforce the objectives of their employers. Sadly, these objectives often lead to the harassment of visitors who fail to match the proper socioeconomic or racial profile—unless they are carrying mops or pushing lawn mowers.

THE IMMOBILE POOR

Suburbia's most helpless victims do not live in the suburbs at all. They are left behind in the cities, on the bottom tier of our increasingly polarized society. The exclusion of the poor from the gated enclaves of the wealthy may be the most obvious inequity of suburbia, but it is hardly the most significant. The rich have often contrived to separate themselves from those less fortunate, and the new suburbs are remarkable only for the thoroughness with which they accomplish this task. Far more troubling, though, is the concentrated poverty that remains in our inner cities. While this radical segregation of haves and have-nots seems natural to most American observers, it was by no means an inevitable outcome of our national evolution. Government policy might have prevented it, but it didn't try. To the contrary, our suburban expansion was largely government-driven, and completely lacking in incentives to integrate different housing types or incomes among the new construction. In a sense, our government did half its job: it provided the means of escape from the city—highways and cheap home loans—while neglecting to allocate those means fairly. The resulting social stratification of suburban development—compounded by racially based white flight—continues today.

Inevitable or not, the fact remains that the inner city is now where America's least privileged are most concentrated, a condition exacerbated by sprawl. Two aspects of suburbanization contribute dramatically to the plight of the urban poor: government investment in suburb-serving highways has left many inner-city neighborhoods sundered by high-speed traffic, and disinvestment by fleeing corporations robs city residents of adequate access to jobs.

The new highways of the sixties and seventies, designed to provide suburbanites with better access to downtown, were located on the cheapest land available, land usually confiscated from poor neighborhoods. The devastation wrought by such inner-city highways was, in retrospect, so extreme that one cannot rule out a nefarious social intention. Less obvious, but almost as damaging, are the many streets in low-income neighborhoods that were widened and relieved of on-street parking to facilitate through traffic to distant destinations. While the era of the community-killing highway may be over, such roadway widenings continue unchecked. These regular investments in automotive infrastructure—too small to be noticed by anti-highway protesters—can subject a community to a death by a thousand cuts. Previously pedestrian- and business-friendly streets in almost every large city continue to expand at the expense of their host communities, primarily so that suburban commuters can get through them more quickly. Bringing suburbanites into the city is a worthwhile goal, but not when it means turning local streets into dangerous speedways.

Of greater concern to the urban poor has been the gradual disappearance of many of the jobs that the working classes rely upon for survival. Corporate flight to the metropolitan fringe would be less damaging if adequate public transportation existed to bring the urban poor to and from exurban jobs. Unfortunately, most new jobs in the suburbs are accessible only to people with cars, and automobile ownership is a hurdle that the would-be working poor are often unable to surmount.

While waiting for a taxi recently in the outskirts of Washington, we saw a black hotel worker likewise trying to hail a cab. After watching several pass him by, we hailed the next taxi, invited him to ride along, and then learned that he spends $25 a day on the only form of transit available to his suburban minimum-wage job. The inaccessibility of suburban work has become such a dominant factor in the cycle of poverty that it was recognized as a key policy issue in the Clinton Administration's welfare reform proposals, which asked Congress for $600 million to fund welfare-related transport programs.•

One oft-suggested solution to this predicament is government-supplied job-chasing vans, but these have inflexible schedules and often involve multiple-hour commutes, since the suburban employers are too dispersed to be reached by mass transit. It might be more effective simply to give free jalopies to the poor, as several philanthropic organizations are now doing. Once again, it is clear that the fundamental inefficiency of the suburban model—its organization around the automobile—is its most ruthless quality, victimizing those who can't drive even more than those who can.•

A final problem emanating from the separation of rich and poor exists at the level of municipal government: there are now rich cities and poor cities. The rich cities have good infrastructure, good services, good schools, and good management, all supported by ample taxes from high-end commercial and residential real estate. The poor cities have a deteriorating physical environment, woefully inadequate services, and a severely limited tax base, compounded by an inability to attract jobs, commerce, or real estate investment. The federal government's largesse in subsidized housing and other forms of assisted development—halfway houses, rehabilitation centers, homeless shelters—congregates the needy in needy places, further institutionalizing their character of poverty.

• Michael Phillips, "Welfare's Urban Poor Need a Lift—to Suburban Jobs," B1. According to a U.S. Congress study, two thirds of all new jobs are in the suburbs, while three quarters of welfare recipients live in the center city or rural areas. In addition, 95 percent of welfare recipients do not own cars (Hank Dittmar, "Congressional Findings in Tea-21," 10).
• A better policy would be to require that new workplaces be located within walking distance of transit. This solution is within the power of local zoning ordinances, but could be further encouraged by making it a precondition to federal transit funding.

This situation is exacerbated by the costs of sprawl. Everyone's taxes—from rich and poor cities alike—fund the construction of new far-flung infrastructure. Minnesota State Representative Myron Orfield has effectively demonstrated how the poor in deteriorating cities subsidize the new suburban enclaves of the wealthy. In Minneapolis–St. Paul, the central city pays $6 million more in annual sewer fees than it incurs in costs, so that the Metropolitan Council can finance the expansion of sewer lines in the shrinking farm belt.• It seems fundamentally unjust that these struggling communities are forced to help build the very suburbs that rob them of their population, jobs, and vitality.

The American tendency toward building ever anew is most damaging to the poor because it is inextricably linked to the abandonment of the old. As we neglect our older neighborhoods, we also neglect their residents. Those who can leave the deteriorating city behind are quick to do so; those who can't are stuck, without the support or inspiration of success around them, doomed to the generational cycle of poverty. The disposable city will thus continue to dispose of its citizens until we embrace a healthier form of growth, one that treasures existing places more than imagined ones.

• Myron Orfield, *Metropolitics,* 71. Moreover, inner-city households pay subsidies 50 percent higher than the regional average. To add insult to injury, this infrastructure is unnecessary, as nearly one quarter of the Minneapolis–St. Paul urban area served by sewers remains undeveloped (72). Why, then, were these new sewers built? The answer is complicated, but is likely to include the fact that they made privately owned farmland much more valuable.

8

THE CITY AND THE REGION

THE POSSIBILITY OF GOOD SUBURBS; SUBURBS THAT HELP
THE CITY; THE EIGHT STEPS OF REGIONAL PLANNING;
THE ENVIRONMENTAL MOVEMENT AS A MODEL

———

There can be no doubt . . . that, in all our modern civilization, as in that of the ancients, there is a strong drift townward.
— FREDERICK LAW OLMSTED (1877)

. . . we shall solve the City Problem by leaving the City.
— HENRY FORD (1922)

———

THE POSSIBILITY OF GOOD SUBURBS

We have discussed the evolution of cities and the two contrasting models for growth, focusing thus far on the design of new places rather than the improvement of existing places. Insofar as new places are being built at an astonishing rate—and are also influencing the rebuilding of older places—this approach has been useful. But it raises some important questions: Can suburban growth be organized in a way that is not detrimental to existing cities? What are we learning from new developments that can help make our

The suburban city: acre for acre, most American cities are composed primarily of freestanding houses

Traditional planning in the traditional city: new low-cost homes (81 in all) blend in with existing houses in central Cleveland

cities better places to live? What can be done to refocus development from the rural edge back to our neglected center cities?

We can begin to answer these questions by noting that most of the old neighborhoods within America's cities and towns are made up of elements that could be described as suburban. With the exception of the core business districts, almost all of the land within urban America is covered with the very same components discussed in this book, foremost among them the single-family house. With a few notable exceptions, a tour of any American city, be it Boston, Chicago, Minneapolis, St. Louis, or Seattle, would confirm that the typical American urban street is lined with buildings one to three stories tall, most of them freestanding.

Evidently, in the right form, suburban-scale growth is a healthy and natural way for cities to develop, as we will show. In Chapter 9, we will argue that many of the principles already described for making new places apply equally well to the improvement of existing neighborhoods. This cross-fertilization has proven effective in the best inner-city work of the past ten years. From the revitalization of downtown West Palm Beach to the rebuilding of low-cost housing in central Cleveland, the rules of neighborhood design are the most effective tool for bringing life back to older neighborhoods. Furthermore, since most American cities evolved from small towns, and since most American downtowns began as common main streets, many of the principles that apply to smaller neighborhoods also apply to the inner city. The difference is one of density, not of organization; in fact, one of the great virtues of traditional urbanism is that increased density only makes it work better. Of course, some problems and conditions are unique to the inner city, and these, too, will be addressed in the next chapter.

SUBURBS THAT HELP THE CITY

Many of America's cities include their suburbs, which contribute in no small way to the health of the city centers. Because these suburbs are usually quite close to downtown, their residents participate in the life of the city, working or shopping downtown. As a part of a larger municipality, they contribute tax revenues that can benefit the inevitable troubled areas. Because of this, the presence of suburbs within the city limits is perhaps the single most significant determinant of economic health in urban America. The cities that continued to annex their suburbs well into the twentieth century, such as Minneapolis, Seattle, and Phoenix, are generally successful financially, while those cities that missed annexation, such as Washington, D.C., Philadelphia, and Miami, are much more likely to be undermined by suburban competition.•

But the case of Phoenix reminds us that there is more to urban health than economic viability, because it is precisely places such as Phoenix—and its cohort of Sun Belt cities—where civic life has almost ceased to exist, and where residents complain about their quality of life. This brings up a second factor determining a city's health: whether the suburbs take a form that will accommodate public transit. The failure of Phoenix to maintain a pedestrian-scale downtown that supports civic life stems directly from the fact that

---

• David Rusk has confirmed this point statistically in his book *Cities Without Suburbs.* But the focus on keeping all revenue within the municipal boundary still begs the question of how long an urban organism can sustain itself as it sprawls inefficiently outward while abandoning its own center. David Petersen of Price Waterhouse has gone one step further and demonstrated that a sustainable urban area requires a critical mass of residential, shopping, and entertainment uses within one mile of the downtown (David Petersen, "Smart Growth for Center Cities," 51).

very few people can get there without their cars. It is virtually impossible to generate urban density under the tyranny of today's excessive roadway and parking requirements. Between one third and one half of urban America's land is typically dedicated to the driving and parking of vehicles. In Los Angeles, that ratio jumps to two thirds. Houston provides the equivalent of 30 asphalt parking spaces per resident.[1] The suburban-scale carscape that constitutes the vast majority of downtown Phoenix is the inevitable outcome of the fact that its suburbs cannot efficiently accommodate transit. The same shortcoming is also why, when one asks to see the social center of Houston, one is taken to a mall.*

As we've already made clear, the only urban form that efficiently accommodates mass transit is the neighborhood, with its mixed-use center and its five-minute-walk radius. Only within a neighborhood structure will residents readily walk to a bus stop or tram station. The sole alternative to neighborhood-based transit is the park-and-ride, which could bring suburbanites into the city on transit, if it only worked. Unfortunately, park-and-ride is just another way of saying "intermodal shift"—switching from one form of transportation to another. This is a transit engineering bugaboo, since most commuters, once they've settled into the driver's seat, will tend to cruise all the way to their final destination. If transit is to work, its users must start as pedestrians. While park-and-ride has been effective along old established rail corridors such as Philadelphia's Main Line and the Long Island Railroad, it has not had much success

---

*This may not last, as a nascent back-to-the-city movement could soon give Houston a downtown that can compete against its fabled Galleria. Interestingly, unlike in most East Coast cities, in Houston the urban settlers are less brash pioneers than disgruntled suburbanites who have given up on a failed freeway system. The recent huge investment in downtown housing should improve this situation quickly.

elsewhere. If driving and parking downtown are anything other than a nuisance, park-and-ride will never be a popular alternative.

Besides placing transit stops within walking distance of most houses, how can suburbs contribute to the well-being of a city? The first step must be to acknowledge that the two are interdependent. An entire discipline called *regional planning*—about which very much is known and very little is put into practice—has emerged to address this reality. The few cities that have begun to plan region-ally, such as Portland, Oregon, are already becoming popular reloca-tion destinations.

Regional planning manages urban growth at the scale of people's daily lives. Planning at the scale of a single town or city is rarely effective, because working and shopping patterns routinely take most people across municipal lines. What good is it for a New En-gland village to outlaw Wal-Mart to save its main street when the suburb down the highway welcomes it with open arms? Any munic-ipality that tries to limit sprawl typically risks the loss of its tax base to surrounding towns. Only at the regional scale can planning have a meaningful impact.

The absence of regional vision plagues neighborhood-oriented planners, especially in sprawling cities like Atlanta. They move heaven and earth to secure dozens of zoning variances and rewrite the engineering regulations, all in order to build walkable mixed-use neighborhoods. Yet, even with the improved lifestyle offered by these communities, it is impossible to go anywhere else without a car. Only when these neighborhoods are linked to a regional transit system will the broader world become truly accessible. Meanwhile, all of the surrounding subdivisions are designed in a way that makes public transit too expensive to provide.

The difficulty in establishing a regional planning authority derives primarily from the fact that few municipal bodies exist at the regional scale. Cities are too small, states are too big, and county lines are ignored under the creep of sprawl. Of the few significant regional planning authorities, most were put together to address single problems—environmental crises, usually—that are only incidentally of regional concern. For example, the South Florida Water Management District, organized to preserve the Everglades, is the only authority with a jurisdiction large enough to plan the megalopolis that stretches from Palm Beach past Miami. Similarly, metropolitan Los Angeles is fighting air pollution at the regional level through the Southern California Association of Governments. Where such organizations can be found, they have come to recognize their relevance beyond their original mandate and have joined the battle against sprawl. But there are few of them, and there is little demand for more.

At the federal level, it is generally understood that municipalities are interdependent with regard to a few obvious issues like transportation, which is why there is a new regional Metropolitan Planning Organization to coordinate transportation funding. But regional-scale social and economic problems are less quantifiable and have yet to receive recognition, let alone resources. And the idea of establishing an additional layer of government within the federal/state/county/town hierarchy is hardly popular.*

---

* Less formal versions of regional consolidation may be easier to institute, such as the New York Regional Planning Association, an influential nonprofit agency established in 1929 to provide more coordinated growth across the political boundaries of the Tri-State area. The RPA continues to evolve in its guidance; one of its most recent initiatives is the promotion of suburban-ring transit connections. One indication of how difficult formal regional planning can be is Kansas City Mayor Emmanuel Cleaver's recent

Regional planning is also made more difficult because, by definition, it often runs up against local concerns. The best plans are usually degraded by the short-term concerns of local residents and business interests. For example, there is a highly visible civic initiative in South Florida called *Eastward Ho!,* which encourages urban infill projects to counter the area's westward sprawl into the Everglades. In response to that initiative, in one city in one year, twenty-seven separate projects were proposed by developers, all bucking the tide and trying to do the right thing. Of those, not a single one was approved, thanks to a local government unwilling to stand up to a few noisy neighbors. Twenty-seven well-intentioned developers wasted a full year, and are now convinced that doing the right thing does not pay.

Another example: In 1985, Miami built its elevated Metro-Rail transit system at a cost of $1.3 billion. Visitors often ask why it serves neither Miami International Airport nor Miami Beach, two of the city's most common destinations. It turns out that Metro-Rail's ultimate trajectory was strongly influenced by the city's taxi lobby, which had everything to gain from making the transit system as useless as possible. Obviously, effective regional planning is not possible in the absence of effective regional political leadership.

Given the difficulty of implementation, it is of some comfort that at least the principles of regional planning are straightforward. Their primary purpose is to organize the growth of metropolitan areas on behalf of environmental health, social equity, and eco-

---

signing of what has been called a "Non-Aggression Treaty" with his surrounding suburban governments. Of course, even the smallest first step toward regional-scale thinking deserves commendation.

nomic sustainability. Recognizing that it sounds easier than it really is, we present below an eight-step process for Regional Planning, admittedly in its ideal form.

THE EIGHT STEPS OF REGIONAL PLANNING

1. Admit that growth will occur. The first step of any recovery program is to acknowledge that a problem exists. In regional planning as well, it is a form of denial to presume that urban expansion can be stopped. No-growth movements, when successful, last for only one or two political generations, and often serve as an excuse to avoid planning entirely. When they are eventually reversed, as they inevitably are, growth quickly resumes in its worst form.

The reasons behind this common sequence of events are economic. Growth moratoriums eventually create such a scarcity of real estate that prices become severely inflated. Meanwhile, the potential profit to be made on new development grows so high that the building industry is motivated to mount a huge lobbying effort, which seems justified by the housing shortage. Such political pressure is difficult for public servants to ignore.

Acknowledging the inevitability of growth leads to a further admission, that growth is a problem whose solution must be shared by multiple jurisdictions. Metropolitan growth nowadays is typically accompanied by the loss of population, jobs, and tax income in the core city. The social inequity that results from separating new development from old deterioration can be addressed only by governments working in concert. Since governments prefer absolute political autonomy, there is little motivation for them to do so.

2. Establish a permanent Countryside Preserve. One of the most disastrous consequences of sprawl is the way that it consumes the farmlands and wilderness surrounding populated areas. Cities and towns that were once able to satisfy their food needs locally no longer can; indeed, a brief breakdown in our transportation infrastructure would quickly demonstrate how far we have drifted from self-sufficiency. Similarly, most American cities once provided their citizens with easy access to nature, but ever-greater efforts are becoming necessary to escape the urban envelope. In his books of near-future science fiction, William Gibson refers to BAMA, the Boston–Atlanta Metropolitan Axis, an uninterrupted carpet of sprawl. Trends suggest that such an outcome is quite possible.

The preferred technique for preserving countryside is the Urban Growth Boundary: a line defining the edge of the metropolis, most famously employed in Portland, Oregon. While these boundaries have sometimes proved effective, they are rarely a long-term solution. Political pressure forces them outward eventually—even Portland's lauded boundary faces constant legislative challenges.[*] A more realistic technique is the Countryside Preserve, which sets aside multiple parcels of conservation land independent of their relationship to the center city. Unlike the Urban Growth Boundary, the Countryside Preserve is drawn using objective environmental

---

[*] Actually, Portland's growth boundary does not deserve to be accepted uncritically as an unqualified success. It was originally drawn not at the edge of urbanization but at a distance many miles out, anticipating and effectively sanctioning twenty years of bad growth. Currently, thanks to the removal of a highway, the introduction of light rail, and considerable wise investment, the downtown is indeed in excellent shape. But the growth boundary contains *within it* thousands of acres of the most mundane sprawl. And now that the edge has finally been reached, Portland's suburban developers—who have never been told "no" before and are thus particularly unruly—fight relentlessly for its expansion.

criteria, and therefore is not as susceptible to the development pressure straining against a typically arbitrary edge. It is effectively a *rural* boundary, drawn on the basis of criteria that can stand up in a court of law. Areas to be designated as permanent countryside include waterways and other wetlands, habitat for endangered species and communities of species, forests and large woodlots, steep slopes, cultural resources, scenic areas, view-sheds for highways, agricultural land,* and current and future parks. If at all possible, the Countryside Preserve should form continuous greenbelts to best accommodate wildlife mobility requirements. A Countryside Preserve line will probably end up looking different from an Urban Growth Boundary line, since it will be drawn according to the demands of the terrain. The environmentalist Benton MacKaye described such countryside preserves as "dams and levees for controlling the metropolitan flood,"[2] and argued that these green areas should penetrate deeply into the city to be integrated with its urban park system, as they do in Washington's Rock Creek Park.

3. Establish a temporary Countryside Reserve. Unlike the permanent countryside, the Countryside Reserve is available for future high-quality development, when such development is justified. It

---

* A gloomy discussion is currently making the rounds about how to preserve agricultural land in the face of development pressures. While it is said that we are approaching a population crisis in which the planet will fail to feed its inhabitants, fear of that crisis has yet to raise the value of farmland. It is fair to say that many American farmers in suburban locations are seriously considering the "developer sellout retirement plan." Since the loss of farmland to development is, for all practical purposes, permanent, it would seem wise to create a program for mothballing a certain percentage of this land until it becomes valued for its production capacity alone. Similarly, an acknowledgment of limited resources would recommend an approach to farmland distribution that allocates a minimum local agriculture reserve around each city, so that it can meet its food needs without excessive transportation or energy costs. This approach was plainly articulated by Ebenezer Howard over one hundred years ago.

consists largely of fields, pastures, and small woodlots within easy reach of existing infrastructure. Reserving this land for *high-quality* development means compact communities based on the neighborhood model, not luxury houses on two-acre lots. Incredibly, many municipalities attempt to preserve open space by mandating large-lot development only, which of course only ensures that the landscape will disappear all the more quickly.

4. Designate the Corridors. Corridors are the regional-scale elements that serve both to connect and to separate different areas. They can be natural or man-made, and include waterways, wildlife corridors, continuous greenways for pedestrians and bicycles, parkways for cars and trucks, and rights-of-way for rail lines. Rail corridor designations are particularly significant, as they provide an opportunity for transit-based development, the ideal way to organize growth. Whenever possible, future development should be organized along a transit corridor, in the manner of our historic streetcar suburbs.

5. Establish Priority Development Sectors, and an incentive program that eases development within them. The obvious goal here is to counteract the existing government and market forces that make it less profitable for developers to work in the city ("urban infill") than on the rural "greenfield" fringe. Priority areas include, in order of preference: urban infill sites, suburban infill sites, existing and future rail stops, urban extensions adjacent to existing neighborhoods, and major roadway intersections. Ideally, approval agencies would accept development applications following this order. For example, any applications for urban extension should be put on hold until all applications for urban infill are processed.

6. Establish a proactive permitting process for development that follows the neighborhood model, such that developers proposing

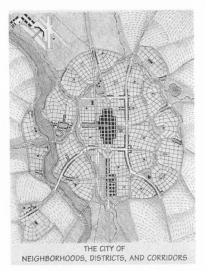

THE CITY OF
NEIGHBORHOODS, DISTRICTS, AND CORRIDORS

A healthy city as the basis for a healthy region: expansion occurs in the form of complete neighborhoods (Drawing by Thomas E. Low, DPZ)

complete neighborhoods—or completions of existing neighborhoods—within the developable area are assigned a municipal regulator. This official, rather than creating bureaucratic friction, would be charged with walking the project through an accelerated process. Getting permits for neighborhoods must be understood to be considerably easier, quicker, more predictable than getting permits for sprawl. These neighborhoods must comply with an eligibility review based upon an objective instrument such as the Traditional Neighborhood Development Checklist, included in Appendix A. Or better yet, they should be permitted according to a new zoning ordinance specially written to encourage mixed-use neighborhoods, such as the Traditional Neighborhood Development Ordinance, discussed in the final chapter. This pro-neighborhood policy must apply to all sites, whether in a Priority Development Sector or in the temporary Countryside Reserve.

7. Designate all other types of development as districts, to be permitted only through a rigorous public process of documentation and justification. Districts are sectors where a single use dominates, typically because a thorough mix of uses is not practical. Acceptable districts focus on civic, medical, or educational campuses; large or noxious agricultural or industrial facilities; depots or terminals; and entertainment zones. Undesirable districts include the components of sprawl: housing subdivisions, shopping centers, and office parks; such unjustified single uses should ideally be prohibited, but designating them as districts would at least make them more difficult to develop than neighborhoods.

8. Fairly distribute the Lulus. Locally Undesirable Land Uses range from the dramatic (garbage dumps and power plants) to the mundane (the large high school made noxious by the traffic it generates). Affordable housing, homeless shelters, and other facilities serving the poor are often the most hotly contested of Lulus; everyone agrees that they are necessary, and they also agree where to put them: in *someone else's* neighborhood. Responsible regional planning recognizes that even the most privileged—especially the most privileged—must carry their fair share of community service facilities regardless of how unpopular they may be. Lulus must be distributed independent of the pressures of local politics, or they are likely to end up in the wrong places. For example, without a regional distribution mandate, affordable housing is typically rejected by middle-class neighborhoods, even though it is precisely in such neighborhoods that affordable housing has the best chances for success. Responsible regional planning is based on a foundation of spatial equity.

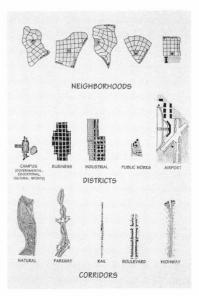

The components of a healthy region: neighborhoods, districts, and corridors (Drawing by Thomas E. Low, DPZ)

This eight-step program, unlike some of the wishful thinking currently being promulgated by anti-growth groups, accepts the realities of the American real estate business. The most practical—and popular—aspect of the program is that it encourages good development rather than attempting to outlaw all development, which is tantamount to political suicide in most jurisdictions. This process recognizes and capitalizes on the one resource readily available to bureaucracies: time. Because most permitting agencies have trained their local developers to wait months or even years for a permit—in a business in which time is money—they essentially have the opportunity to grant large monetary awards by offering quicker permitting to the appropriate projects. In such an environment, bad development need not be outlawed; it need only remain subject to the same drawn-out process it currently follows, a process that becomes all the more painful in comparison to that which is available to neighborhood development.

Of the eight steps, the sixth one—encouraging the construction of true neighborhoods—is perhaps the most important. But it is also the most easily forgotten. In the absence of a neighborhood structure for new development, even the best planning efforts can be fruitless. Miami once again proves an instructive example. By any common measure of planning wisdom, the city has done a stellar job. It has had a single regional government (Miami–Dade County) since 1957. It has a consolidated school district serving the entire county, so that school quality will not cause relocations. It has an urban boundary that was drawn tight to the edge of existing growth in 1976. And it has a top-of-the-line regional transit system, including a downtown People-Mover tram, a complete bus network serving locations many miles away, and the already mentioned twenty-seven-stop elevated Metro-Rail.

Yet, by any common measure of planning success—environmental quality, social equity, or quality of life—Miami is far from where it should be. One need not marshal statistics to support this assertion; a single afternoon driving in the city's western suburbs will convince anyone. What is missing in the Miami plan is neighborhoods: the organization of growth into mixed-use, pedestrian-friendly, transit-ready communities. Without neighborhoods, the city could double its rail service and still not lessen its harsh traffic.

While the above eight-step program is open to dispute, the fundamentals are well accepted. As growing pains become severe, the problem lies not just in agreeing on a course of action but in developing the regional-scale coordination necessary to implement it. The will to do so seems to be mounting, thanks to some well-publicized examples, both good and bad. Cities are looking with envy at the success of Portland's regional plan, and with fear at Atlanta, where decades of laissez-faire construction have led to a traffic and air-quality crisis. Indeed, Atlanta recently created a regional transportation authority to confront this crisis, proof that regional planning cannot be avoided, only postponed.•

It is wise to be suspicious of any solution that implies *more government,* but this is not one of them. Regional governance can best be achieved not by adding more bureaucracy but by redistributing existing responsibilities.▪ Those towns and cities that are reluctant to think regionally would be wise to consider how many of their problems, from crime to traffic, are generated from outside their municipal boundaries. These problems will never be solved in the absence of regional coordination.

THE ENVIRONMENTAL MOVEMENT AS A MODEL

While bemoaning the current confusion surrounding the American landscape, we take some solace from the words of Winston Churchill: "The American people can be counted on to do the right thing, after

---

• On the day of this writing, the Atlanta government has advised all of the city's residents—not just asthmatics—to stay indoors because of a severe air-quality crisis.
▪ The regional-scale issues of environmental conservation and restoration, transportation, social services, affordable housing, the location of Lulus, and economic development, to name a few, should be managed by a single regional jurisdiction, or by existing regional agencies working in close coordination. Meanwhile, middle-scale issues such as local planning and zoning, policing, and maintenance should remain in the hands of municipal government, while local issues such as community enhancement and redevelopment, quality of life, and tourism should be attended to by neighborhood organizations. This redistribution recognizes that the success of governance at every scale depends on the assignment of responsibilities to the smallest jurisdiction that can handle it comprehensively.

The natural habitat: after only thirty years, near the top of the political agenda

The human habitat: also in dire need of protection

they have exhausted all the alternatives." Indeed, this country has shown an uncanny affinity for self-correction, and it seems reasonable to expect that this ability will eventually make itself felt in the design of the built environment. Still in question is how long this will take, but there are reasons to be hopeful.

In 1962, Rachel Carson published *Silent Spring,* sparking the environmental movement. Less than two decades later, the Environmental Protection Agency had become the largest regulatory body in the United States government. Environmental consultants now take a prominent place at the table in planning sessions, equal in stature to traffic engineers and fire chiefs. A typical large project in Florida has to secure approval from six overlapping agencies on the subject of wetlands alone. While such drawn-out processes can be a nightmare, we are encouraged by the speed with which America has placed the environmental movement near the top of its political agenda.

While environmentalists had to overcome centuries of misunderstanding of the natural world, the urbanists' task is not so daunting. After an aberrant period of only fifty years, America should not find it particularly difficult to return to its tradition of community-making. Many Americans still live in real neighborhoods, and even more remember them vividly from childhood. Here, unlike environmentalism, no sacrifices are necessary—no shorter showers, no sorting through rubbish—only a willingness to lead a more varied and convenient life, in the kind of urban environment that has successfully housed the human species without interruption for thousands of years.

Environmentalists are beginning to understand the compatibility of these two agendas. Now that they have achieved some significant victories in the protection of flora and fauna, they are extending their purview a bit higher up the evolutionary tree, to the protection and projection of the traditional human habitat: the neighborhood. Environmentalists have already begun to mount an attack against sprawl, as they recognize the dangers posed to farms and forests by low-density, automobile-oriented growth. The Sierra Club has launched an official anti-sprawl campaign, producing such publications as *Sprawl Costs Us All: How uncontrolled sprawl increases your property taxes and threatens your quality of life.* As *The New York Times* put it, "Sprawl, in sum, is the new language of environmentalism."[3] Of course, environmentalists have always been concerned with the survival of the human species, but only lately have they recognized that the neighborhood itself is a part of the ecosystem, an organic outgrowth of human needs. If all the energy and goodwill of the environmental movement can now be applied within the urban boundary, the results will be dramatic.

9

THE INNER CITY

THINKING OF THE CITY IN TERMS OF ITS SUBURBAN COMPETITION; CATEGORIES IN WHICH THE SUBURBS TYPICALLY OUTPERFORM THE CITY: THE AMENITY PACKAGE, CIVIC DECORUM, PHYSICAL DESIGN, RETAIL MANAGEMENT, MARKETING, INVESTMENT SECURITY, AND THE PERMITTING PROCESS

———

Anybody who travels back and forth across the Atlantic has to be impressed with the differences between European cities and ours, which make it appear as if World War Two actually took place in Detroit and Washington rather than Berlin and Rotterdam.

— JAMES HOWARD KUNSTLER, *HOME FROM NOWHERE* (1996)

———

In turning from the region to the city, it is important to remember that America's inner cities did not wither all at once, or by chance. For much of the twentieth century, they have suffered from the unanticipated consequences of government policy and urban planning. The availability of the massive interstate system for daily commuting made it easy to abandon the city for houses on the periphery. The widespread construction of parking lots downtown further eased the automotive commute while turning the city into a paved no-man's-land. Racism, redlining, and the concentration of subsidized housing projects destabilized and isolated the poor, while federal home-loan programs, targeting new construction exclusively, encouraged the deterioration and abandonment of urban housing. Worse yet, the application in the city of suburban zoning standards, with their deeper setbacks and higher parking requirements, prevented the renovation of existing buildings, which became illegal under the new code.

THINKING OF THE CITY IN TERMS OF ITS SUBURBAN COMPETITION

The fact that policy and planning can be blamed for our cities' problems is actually encouraging—it implies that better policy and better planning can produce better cities. But that is not enough. To be effective today, urban leaders must stop thinking of their cities strictly from the inside out, only from the point of view of their own citizens. That approach may seem virtuous, but it ignores the reality of regional competition in an open market. Urban leaders must borrow a page from the suburban developers' handbook and look at their communities from the outside in, through the eyes of a customer who is comparison-shopping. A family or company moving to a metropolitan area has a choice between the city and the suburb, both of which are competing for its business. Will it be a house on Maple Street, or one in a gated subdivision? Will it be an office suite downtown, or a glass box in the business park? Often the greatest disadvantage of the city is not its own problems per se but the extreme competence and ingenuity of the suburban developers, who are constantly raising the expectations of consumers.

A few years ago, for example, we were riding through a California subdivision in the Jaguar of a successful developer. Without warning, he stopped, jumped out, crouched to inspect the lawn, and then returned to the car to dial his cell phone. "Sprinkler head sixty-seven is crooked." Before we had finished our tour, a maintenance man was working on it. Imagine such a thing happening in downtown Los Angeles.

Suburban development is a well-honed science. New subdivisions outperform the city in category after category—in their amenity package, civic decorum, physical health; in their retail management, marketing techniques, investment security, their permitting process, and so on. Exploring each of these categories in turn helps show how the city can once again become competitive. Of course, the following discussion of what cities can learn from the suburbs should not overshadow the important physical distinctions between suburban and urban places, differences that are to be celebrated and reinforced. The greatest mistake the planners of the sixties and seventies made was to try to save the city by turning it into the suburb. Their approach could not have been worse. The future of the city lies in becoming more citylike, more pedestrian-friendly, more intense, more urban, more urbane.

THE AMENITY PACKAGE

The new suburbs are known for their private yards, their tennis clubs, their golf courses, and their guardhouses. The city does not offer these amenities in abundance, nor should it attempt to. Perhaps the best-known urban amenities are cultural and sports events.

These are indeed an advantage of city life, but they are not the most effective way to renew a downtown, as some suggest. These events may periodically attract suburban visitors, but they are not sufficient to persuade people to live or work in the city. Instead, the most significant amenity that the city can offer potential residents is a *public realm,* with the vibrant street life that phrase implies. Such an environment is the compensation the city offers its customers for forgoing the suburban amenity package. If it exists, it can be enough, as downtowns from Manhattan to Portland show.•

The key to active street life is creating a twenty-four-hour city, with neighborhoods so diverse in their use that they are inhabited around the clock. Eating, shopping, working, socializing—no one activity can flourish in the absence of any other, since they are all mutually reinforcing. As Jane Jacobs observed, a business district such as Wall Street normally cannot support fine restaurants, as there are not enough local residents to generate adequate dinner traffic; the restaurants are forced to make all their money between 12 and 2 p.m. The same is true of other businesses, such as health clubs, which rely on both daytime and evening clientele. Urban revitalization must begin, then, by reinstating the balance among the widest range of local uses.

• This is not to denigrate the positive influence of organized group activities, and downtown is certainly the best location for the stadium and the performing arts center—especially given its ready access to transit—as well as for the fairs and street festivals simply not possible in the suburban hinterland. But all the festivals in the world will not overcome the lack of a pedestrian-friendly physical environment in getting people to come downtown. Convincing evidence of the power of successful urbanity can be seen in the many downtown destinations to which suburbanites will drive two to three hours for the experience of strolling, shopping, and dining in a lively public place. Greenwich Village, Coconut Grove, and Georgetown have even spawned a new real estate industry classification: the "urban entertainment center." Most of us would prefer to call it a city.

CIVIC DECORUM

The first job of city government, as any resident or business owner will tell you, is to "keep it clean and safe." Suburban developers have taught prospective home buyers to expect both scrupulous security and excellent maintenance. When it comes to security, customers demand not just safety but the perception of safety, which means that all potential signs of danger must be eliminated, including graffiti and litter. These are not truly difficult to eliminate, but they must be specifically targeted and assigned a dedicated staff member, since they often slip through the cracks of city bureaucracy.

Reuben Greenberg, the much-admired police chief of Charleston, South Carolina, has an effective method of dealing with graffiti. When an officer or a citizen spots new graffiti, he calls the police station, where forty-two colors of paint are stocked, including one called "old concrete." At four-thirty the same day, an officer drives by with a state prisoner, who paints over the graffiti in minutes with a perfectly matching color. "We can cover it faster than they can put it up," says Chief Greenberg, who has gone so far as to stage a public *graffiti artist versus painting convict* race to prove his point. No graffiti, be they on public or private property, stay visible for more than twenty-four hours, even in the poorest part of town.

Chief Greenberg, more than just an aesthete, is acting in accordance with the best crime-fighting intelligence. It has been demonstrated that graffiti, litter, broken glass, and other seemingly innocuous transgressions create an environment of civic demoralization in which serious crime is much more likely to occur. In recent years, concerted attention paid to the little things has proved to have a significant impact on the big things.

Suburban maintenance derives much of its effectiveness from providing management in small increments, through homeowners' associations (HOAs). The willingness of tax-averse citizens to pay considerable monthly fees to these associations demonstrates that elective taxation is viable if the revenues are spent in proximity, where residents feel they have some control over the outcome. The same technique can be applied to the city, and has been used with success. There are over one hundred private management districts in New York City alone, the most notorious of them focusing on Times Square. Many have complained about the sanitized, tourist-oriented outcome, but few will suggest that it has not achieved its aim.

Whether or not it implies the creation of private management districts, the success of the suburban HOA has a lot to teach the city regarding the appropriate scale of governance. The faceless bureaucracy of a large city tends to become accessible and responsive if it is broken down into neighborhood-scale increments. Indeed, some issues that seem irresolvable at the citywide level, such as parking policy, are best addressed street by street.

PHYSICAL HEALTH

Fifty years ago, America's cities provided a pedestrian environment that compared favorably with the world's best cities. What has happened in the intervening decades has been sheer lunacy: in an attempt to lure auto-dependent suburbanites downtown, consultants of every ilk turned our cities into freeways. Interstate highways were welcomed into the city core, streets were widened and made one-way, street trees were cut down, sidewalks were narrowed or eliminated, and on-street parking was replaced by massive parking lots, often on the sites of demolished historic buildings. The result was the evisceration of the public realm.

In some cities, the street was relegated entirely to the poor and the homeless in favor of underground malls and pedestrian bridges, which continue to sap vitality from the street. Cities such as Dallas and Minneapolis built these stratified systems not because of the weather but to allow cars free rein of the terra firma. Dallas justified its system with the following explanation: "One of the chief contributing factors to traffic congestion is crowds of pedestrians interrupting the flow of traffic at intersections."● What some cities would now give to regain those pedestrian crowds!

It is difficult to count the number of cities that have been extensively damaged by kowtowing to the demands of the automobile. So many come to mind—Detroit, Hartford, Des Moines, Kansas City, Syracuse, Tampa—that it has to be considered the standard American urban condition. The typical result is a downtown where nobody walks, a no-man's-land brutalized by traffic. In the apotheosis of this condition—in which the mixed-use street has been replaced by an "analogous city" of pedestrian bridges and tunnels,

A stratified public realm for a stratified society: pedestrian bridges abandon the street to the underclass

An appropriate fate for the Motor City: freeways and parking lots paved the way for Detroit's decline (shown in 1950 and 1990)

● Planner Vincent Ponte, in William Whyte, *City: Rediscovering the Center,* 198. Only in the most extreme conditions has bad weather proved capable of eliminating pedestrian traffic along a properly designed street. There is more sidewalk-fronting retail space in Toronto than in all the cities of the Sun Belt combined.

Many authors have commented on the social implications of the privatization of street life; Trevor Boddy sums up the situation as follows: "Precisely because downtown streets are the last preserve of something approaching a mixing of all sectors of society, their replacement by the sealed realm overhead and underground has enormous implications for all aspects of political life. Constitutional guarantees of free speech and of freedom of association and assembly mean much less if there is literally no peopled public space to serve as forum in which to act out these rights" (Trevor Boddy, "Underground and Overhead," 125).

the outcome approaches the condition of a suburban mall. But the city cannot compete with the suburb by becoming more suburban, since it has no hope of providing the same amount of convenient parking and open space.

Designing the city around automobiles has yet to be widely recognized as misguided, and pedestrians are losing the battle against the car on a daily basis. New York City has recently made it an infraction for pedestrians to cross certain midtown streets where vehicles turn onto one-way avenues.[1] Meanwhile, in the name of pedestrian safety, traffic engineers in Los Angeles are erasing the city's crosswalks. They are taking this approach because "more pedestrians are killed in crosswalks than in unmarked intersections," ignoring that the streets with crosswalks are wider and faster. It is troubling that most efforts meant to "improve" pedestrian safety end up limiting pedestrian access.

That said, the solution is not the removal of cars from the city—far from it. The most vital American public spaces are full of cars. But these cars move slowly, due to the appropriate design of the thoroughfares. Just as in residential neighborhoods, city streets must be narrow—lanes should be ten feet wide, not twelve—with on-street parallel parking to protect the pedestrian. To make life easier for both walkers and drivers, streets should be two-way (typically one lane in each direction), since one-way streets contribute to speeding and make it difficult to find one's way around.* Traffic lights must have short cycles, to avert both driver and pedestrian frustration.

---

* People speed on multiple-lane one-way streets because there is less friction from opposing traffic, and because of the temptation to jockey from lane to lane. Whichever lane you are in, the other seems faster. In contrast, when two-way traffic makes passing impossible, the driver is less likely to slip into the "road racer" frame of mind.

The taming of the automobile is a necessary but not sufficient precondition to pedestrian life. Sidewalks must be lined with continuous building frontage, with few blank walls, parking lots, or other gaps that undermine the spatial definition of the street.[•] Because there are never enough high-quality frontages for all streets to satisfy these criteria, the city may need to engage in what could be called *urban triage*. In pedestrian crises, as in battle, the worst-off must sometimes be sacrificed for the greater good. In the city, this means designating an "A/B" street grid. "A" streets must maintain a high standard of spatial definition and pedestrian interest, while "B" streets can be assigned to the lower-grade uses—the parking lots, garages, muffler shops, and fast-food drive-throughs. The A streets must be organized in a continuous network so that the pedestrian experience is uninterrupted. A pedestrian will cross unattractive side streets when walking on a street that provides an otherwise continuous urban fabric of buildings fronting the sidewalk with doors and windows.

The need for a clear A/B hierarchy is particularly evident in newer cities such as Dallas. Its downtown has at least a dozen city blocks of excellent pedestrian quality. Unfortunately, no two are

---

One-way streets should generally be avoided in retail areas because they distribute vitality unevenly. For example, traffic planners in Miami turned two streets in Little Havana into a one-way pair, such that people drive to work on SW Eighth Street—"Calle Ocho," the retail heart of the district—and drive home from work on SW Seventh Street, which is entirely residential. The problem with this configuration, in addition to the fact that drivers are always jockeying for the fastest lane, is that people don't shop on their way to work; they shop on their way home. Unsurprisingly, merchants on Calle Ocho were devastated. Decades later, city leaders are still scratching their heads over why this once vibrant main street continues to struggle.
[•] There is an observable hierarchy of pedestrian streetscapes as follows, best to worst: shopfront, porch, stoop, yard, blank wall, parking lot, parking structure.

adjacent to each other. A person cannot walk more than four hundred feet in any direction without being confronted by automobile-dominated banality. By attempting to be universally excellent, most cities are universally mediocre. The A/B grid is eminently practical because it recognizes that many cities are beggars. Desperate for the twenty-five jobs, they will accept onto their Main Street a McDonald's with an iridescent plastic jungle gym in front and a drive-through at the side. With an A/B grid, a city can give McDonald's a choice: behave in a responsible way—with doors and windows on the sidewalk and the drive-through to the rear—and you get a site on Main Street; behave in your standard boorish suburban way, and it's off to the access road with you.

One of the most compelling reasons for an A/B grid is the demand for parking lots and garages, which must not be allowed to erode the network of A streets. But even well-placed parking, in excess, can be a bad thing. Like automobile use, parking rarely costs the driver as much as it should, and is thus a *free good*. For this reason, there is always an outcry for more parking, just as there is always a demand for more lanes of traffic. Building additional parking lots causes more people to drive downtown, which requires the construction of more roadway, creating demand for yet more parking lots. The question is not how much parking is enough but how many of its buildings a city must level before it gives up trying to meet the demand.•

When it comes to parking, every city must eventually answer

•Actually, there is indeed a point at which a city can satisfy its parking needs. This situation can be found in many small, older American cities and is almost always the result of the same history: at mid-century, with automobile ownership on the rise, a charming old downtown with a wonderful pedestrian realm finds itself in need of more parking spaces. It tears down a few historic buildings and replaces them with surface parking lots, making the downtown both easier to park in and less pleasant to walk through. As

two questions: Do new buildings have to provide their own parking, and where should that parking go? Most cities answer both of these questions incorrectly. A commitment to suburban standards of parking is a commitment to a second-class transit system used by virtually no one but the poor, since everyone else will drive. Further, most cities require new and renovated buildings to provide their own parking on site. This is probably the single greatest killer of urbanism in the United States today. It prevents the renovation of old buildings, since there is inadequate room on their sites for new parking;• it encourages the construction of anti-pedestrian building types in which the building sits behind or hovers above a parking lot; it eliminates street life, since everyone parks immediately adjacent to their destination and has no reason to use the sidewalk; finally, it results in a low density of development that can keep a downtown from achieving critical mass. All told, there is nothing to be said in favor of the on-site parking requirement. Cities that wish to be pedestrian-friendly and fully developed should eliminate this ordinance immediately and provide public parking in carefully located municipal garages and lots. Parking must be considered a part of the public infrastructure, just like streets and sewers.

Consideration of the pedestrian scale must also play a role in the provision of transit. Diesel-belching buses are a poor substitute for

---

more people drive, it tears down a few more buildings, with the same result. Eventually, what remains of the old downtown becomes unpleasant enough to undermine the desire to visit, and the demand for parking is easily satisfied by the supply. This phenomenon could be called the Pensacola Parking Syndrome, in honor of one of its victims.
• One of the more unusual aspects of our master plan for Stuart, Florida, was our categorical elimination of the on-site parking requirement, which was preventing local developers from renovating existing buildings. Four years after the completion of the plan, the number of downtown businesses had risen by 348 percent and the town was able to lower its tax rate (Eric Staats, "The Renewal of Stuart," 10a).

benevolent streetcars, trolleys, and jitneys. Where laying track is not affordable, the city should consider small electric trams, which have brought new life to cities such as Chattanooga and Santa Barbara.

The reader will notice that, in discussing the physical form of the city, we have not once advocated the use of brick sidewalks, festive banners, bandstands, decorative bollards, or grassy berms ("the Five B's"). The quick fix of the eighties, the Five B's now decorate many an abandoned downtown, along with the latest-model light poles, trash cans, and decorative tree grates. There is nothing wrong with any of the Five B's, except for the fact that, alone, they can do little to bring a downtown back to life. Actually, some retail consultants argue that decorative streetscapes are counterproductive because they distract shoppers from what they really should be looking at: the store windows. The average shopfront has only eight seconds to catch the attention of a passing pedestrian, so no competition is needed from flashy sidewalks or decorative planters.

RETAIL MANAGEMENT

The sad fact is that the newest, most spectacular suburban shopping center would fail within a few months if it were managed as haphazardly as the typical main street. In order for Main Street to compete against the mall, it must be run with all the expertise lavished on the mall.

Suburban retailers are predatory by definition. Most new malls, big-box outlets, and other shopping centers are built not to satisfy unmet demand but to steal demand from existing retailers.[•] Since malls survive by undermining other malls (and main streets), they have refined the techniques of merchandising to a science. Mall designers know that, upon entering, people tend to turn right, and walk counterclockwise. They know that visitors will most likely purchase sunglasses if they are near the rest rooms. They know that women's clothing stores will fare badly if placed near the food court. How can Main Street possibly compete? Fortunately, many of the concepts and techniques that mall designers use can be easily adapted for the benefit of the city core:[■]

Centralized Management: While centralized ownership of real estate may be the ideal, as in a mall, a central management agency can be nearly as effective.[▲] In its weakest form, this would be nothing more than an interested chamber of commerce. In its strongest form—which may not be necessary—it would be an agency legally empowered to coordinate hours of operation, security, maintenance, landscape, storefront design, and even the location and mix of

---

[•] More precisely, they are built to attract investors as much as shoppers, which means that their developers focus on absorbing a large market share of an already existing market. In this scenario, something, somewhere, has to give. Unlike housing, which benefits from being located in a stable physical environment, retail has a history of constant change that grows out of its competitive nature. It is worth noting that Main Street's demise began long before the advent of the suburban shopping center. The department stores of the late-nineteenth century were in fact quite destructive to small merchants. The twentieth century has witnessed an iterative history of retail cannibalism, even though certain organizational principles have carried from one generation of retail to the next. For more information on the predatory approaches of retail developers, we recommend Margaret Crawford's article "The World in a Shopping Mall" in *Variations on a Theme Park.*

[■] Many of these techniques were learned from Robert Gibbs, a former mall planner for the Taubman Companies, who now specializes in teaching Main Street merchants the secrets of the mall.

[▲] The list of downtowns that have succeeded over the decades includes many that are wholly owned by a single company, such as Kansas City's Country Club Plaza; Shaker Heights, Ohio; Lake Street, Chicago; and downtown Nantucket.

stores. The following techniques can only be implemented effectively under unified management.

Joint Advertising and Merchandizing: Shoppers are attracted to malls by an advertising strategy that emphasizes the variety of merchandise available at a single location—what experts call a "park-once environment." Inside the mall, directories and "You Are Here" maps help customers find their way. Further incentive to shop is offered through coordinated sales and festival days, as well as concerts, celebrity appearances, and the like. In many ways, Main Street provides a public atmosphere that is much more natural than the mall for festival-oriented marketing. Instead of offering *mall events* for shoppers, downtown merchants can organize *town events* for all.

Anchors: Almost every mall gives away locations rent-free to the so-called anchor tenants that will bring shoppers from a distance. Downtowns should also be prepared to offer subsidies—even free leases or land—in order to secure a major retail draw. Many national retailers and cinema chains have "rediscovered downtown," but they may still need enticement. Of course, existing anchors should be handled with great care and, in some cases, given incentives to stay in place, as the cinemas are in Portland. This should not be thought of as socialism for capitalists, or even as a subsidy, but rather as the city operating competitively within the reality of a cutthroat marketplace.

Strategic Relation of Anchors and Parking: All malls place anchor department stores at the extremities and cluster the small stores in the middle. In Miami's Cocowalk, the cinema is located on the third floor, the ticket booth on the ground floor, and dozens of shops and restaurants in between, where they are practically unavoidable to the impulse buyer. Meanwhile, most cities that attempt to revitalize their downtowns with a convention center, sports arena, or movie theater unthinkingly place all parking immediately adjacent to the site. This strategy robs the city's merchants of potential customers passing by. For this reason, the self-sufficient Astrodomes of the sixties and seventies did nothing for their cities; the promised neighborhood revitalizations never occurred.[*] Any new anchor downtown must be designed to maximize street activity, with parking at least a block away, the exact opposite of what most zoning codes require. Downtowns must be arranged cunningly, with a strategic separation of origins and destinations. The only caveat here is that the gap between anchor and parking must be lined with continuous pedestrian-quality street frontage, so that the walk is pleasurable.

Proactive Leasing and Retail Mix: When a mall first opens, or when a vacancy occurs, space is not simply leased to the first qualified applicant that comes along. Rather, the management carefully determines what type of store will best contribute to the mall's retail mix and seeks it out, often offering incentives for relocation. In addition, mall management recognizes that certain stores fare better or worse in proximity to certain other stores, and arranges shops according to a careful merchandising plan. Mutually supportive stores are clustered to form such places as fashion districts and entertainment districts. We've watched retail consultants sit in a closed room for hours on end, painstakingly assembling stores like the pieces of a Chinese puzzle. While this approach may seem

---

[*] The same is true for large office facilities. When we were working in Trenton, New Jersey, we were surprised to learn that sixteen thousand state office workers were located in that seemingly unpopulated downtown. They were largely invisible, thanks to their being able to park in garages immediately adjacent to their buildings. Not only did their daily trajectories never leave state property but any desire to venture to nearby shops and restaurants was immediately discouraged by the no-man's-land of surrounding parking.

unwieldy on Main Street, with its patchwork of ownership interests, an effective merchants' association can monitor the store mix and actively seek the ideal businesses to fill vacancies as they arise.

Dimensions: Whether indoors or out, the best retail street has certain dimensions, related to complex physical and social predilections. Although commercial corridors may stretch uninterrupted for miles in some cities, the most successful shopping streets restrict their length to a reasonable walking distance, usually less than half a mile. Their width is similarly constrained in order to ensure visibility from one side to the other, so that when exiting one store you are looking straight at the display of another. For this reason, malls usually keep their corridors less than fifty feet wide, a dimension that is, of course, easier to achieve in the absence of cars. Since the best main streets have two-way driving, parallel parking, and wide sidewalks, about sixty feet is a workable standard. Sidewalks should be at least twelve feet wide, which is ample enough for passage and for outdoor dining, something the malls cannot provide.[*]

Retail Continuity: The American shopper has an attention span surpassed in brevity only by that of the American adolescent television viewer. Experience suggests that most strolling shoppers will not walk down dead-end streets—thus the need for big stores at the ends of malls. In addition, they will turn around and head back to their cars rather than walk past fifty feet of blank wall. This explains why malls generally do not include post offices: stamp posters are simply too boring to endure. While malls turn down the U.S. Mail, Main Street

---

[*] In Miami Beach, sidewalk dining is subject to a number of wise regulations: All tablecloths and napkins must be real cloth rather than blow-away paper. Instead of cheap plastic, all glasses must be real glass, all plates must be ceramic, and all flatware must be metal. These rules provide a more elegant dining and pedestrian environment, discourage bad food, and reduce litter.

has to incorporate banks, brokerage houses, travel bureaus, and real-estate offices, with their plain walls and boring displays. These must be located so as not to interrupt retail continuity for more than the shortest stretches: either dispersed in small increments, or collected in a harmless location off the main shopping trajectory.

Incubators: Pushcarts serve a purpose in suburban malls, which is to incubate new businesses until they do well enough to afford their own storefront space. The same process can occur on Main Street, supplemented by additional incubators such as live/work units and artists' cooperatives. The Torpedo Factory in Alexandria is one such example of an industrial-loft-turned-arts-incubator that has become a tourist anchor. Often, for such ventures to be successful, fledgling businesses must be allowed to occupy older buildings without upgrading fully to code. Farmers' markets located in old or temporary quarters, such as in West Hollywood or Philadelphia's Reading Terminal, are almost always effective in energizing their downtowns.

All of the above techniques depend to some degree upon managed retail, a concept that causes some to bristle. "Whatever happened to a natural diversity?" they ask. "Are there any *real* places left?" The surprising answer to that question is that a *lack* of management has proven to be the enemy of diversity. It is why Key West has become an emporium of T-shirt shops, and why the only lunch available on Rodeo Drive for under ten dollars consists of potato chips and a soda. When left alone, retailers tend to repeat easy successes and entire sectors become homogeneous. Variety is achieved not through natural selection but through careful programming. Thanks to management, the main street of Disney's Celebration provides not only restaurants for four different price ranges but a bar that is required to stay open until the last movie gets out. Even if there are only two customers, martinis are available at midnight. Does this make Celebration any worse, or any less real?

MARKETING

Suburban developers have lapsed into a bigger-is-better, "build it and they will come" mentality. Typically, they direct their efforts at the largest market segments only, providing huge tracts of housing and big-box retail. This approach may make sense in the urban periphery, where a critical mass is necessary to attract customers, and where homogeneity is considered a virtue. But in the city, where a diversity of form and activity already exists—and is cherished—development must be approached on a smaller scale, and with a thorough understanding of the customer base.

One of the most effective ways to revitalize an underbuilt city core is to subdivide undeveloped superblocks into smaller increments affordable to individual investors. This technique opens the door for local stakeholders to become small-scale developers, lessening the city's dependence on the few national-scale real-estate corporations. The town house lot, usually no more than twenty-four feet wide, is an ideal increment of development, as it can hold a home, a business, or both. Many superblocks now lie fallow, thanks to the unsuccessful mega-projects of the eighties, "quick fix" solutions that failed owing to their reliance on unrealistically large increments of investment.

In addition to operating at the correct scale, renewal efforts must proceed with realistic expectations about who will move downtown, and market accordingly. According to William Kraus, the market segment that pioneers difficult areas is the "risk-oblivious": artists and recent college graduates. These are followed by the "risk-aware": yuppies; and finally by the "risk-averse": the middle class. City developers must anticipate this often inevitable sequence, and provide the appropriate housing at the appropriate time. For example, the risk-oblivious are not well served by finished units with separate bedrooms but by lofts, which are large, tough, inexpensive, yet easily converted to yuppie housing upon the arrival of the risk-aware.

Developers often fail to recognize this. In Providence, when we advocated new housing construction downtown, we were confronted by a local developer who said, "It doesn't work—I tried it." Skeptical, we asked to see his building. Sure enough, it was outfitted with dishwashers, carpeting, and frilly curtains, like a garden apartment in suburban New Jersey. He had forgotten that urban pioneers, in addition to wanting to save money, cherish their edgy self-image and eschew iconography that smacks of middle-class contentment. Their taste for roughness cannot be overestimated. If the walls of the elevator are covered with Formica paneling, better to rip it off and just leave the glue.

To encourage urban pioneers, cities must be prepared to bend the rules a little. Zoning that prohibits housing in commercial and industrial areas—often largely empty and therefore affordable— must be replaced with a mixed-use classification. The on-site parking requirement can be waived, as pioneers can be expected to park on the street, if they own cars at all. In addition, a number of antiquated laws, introduced to fight the tenement houses of the turn of the century, can make urban pioneering prohibitively expensive. For example, the BYOS (bring your own sheetrock) unit should be legalized, and developers should be able to get certificates of occupancy for apartments that are habitable but as yet unfinished. Otherwise, urban living will be affordable only to those who have no desire to live there.

Any proper urban marketing analysis must also include families with children, the market segment that is hardest for the city to serve. Bringing families downtown is possible only with good schools, and good city schools rarely occur without a consolidated regional school district. Only if city schools are able to share the resources of those in the wealthier suburbs can large numbers of parents be convinced to locate their families downtown.[*] When a consolidated school district is not a realistic possibility, cities should take measures to encourage parochial and charter schools downtown, giving them land and other special incentives. It is important to be realistic: revitalization efforts should not focus unduly on bringing families back to the inner city. In truth, many urban neighborhoods do quite well in the absence of children. Of course, the long-term health and diversity of a city is ultimately tied closely to the quality of its schools.

A more difficult issue to tackle is gentrification. At the macroscopic level, activists are justified in their fight against gentrification if it is likely to result in the displacement of tenants. But at the microscopic level of the neighborhood, fighting gentrification is tantamount to fighting *improvement*; revitalization will not occur

---

[*] An important catalyst in the revival of West Palm Beach has been the county's performing arts magnet high school, established on an abandoned school site downtown.

without it. Indeed, the challenge faced by most center cities today is not to provide affordable housing—which they typically supply at alarming ratios, thanks to public subsidies—but to create a market for middle-class housing. Cities, after all, cannot flourish without taxpaying residents. For this reason, city planners charged with the task of revitalizing a downtown have little choice but to encourage gentrification or resign from their job. It is sometimes helpful to investigate the source of the complaint: the cry of "gentrification" is less often sounded by citizens who fear displacement than by politicians who suspect that racial and economic integration will undermine their power base.

One technique that has been used to stop gentrification is to limit the rise in tax assessments. But keeping real estate assessments down can be a real problem, as this can prevent home and business owners from obtaining building improvement loans. Once again, fighting gentrification proves counterproductive to the improvement efforts of existing residents. For this reason, governments and activists must turn their attention from stopping gentrification to mitigating its negative impact. Gentrification became a dirty word because it used to occur in the absence of a safety net, and many a displaced tenant in the sixties had nowhere to go. Nowadays, that need not be the case.*

---

* There is, however, a form of gentrification that should always be fought: government-imposed speculative gentrification, in which cities attempt to stimulate rebuilding downtown areas by raising their zoning capacity. This technique results in an *increased* tax assessment, which more often than not forces existing residents and businesses to depart. Meanwhile, the resulting higher land values actually end up impeding development, because the large-scale projects suggested by the new zoning present a risk that often can be undertaken only by the large developer. As a result, only one project may get built every five years, with that project singlehandedly absorbing all the real-estate demand of the next five years. While Americans seem to accept this form of develop-

The above discussion of urban marketing and development implies something that many might find surprising: a proactive municipal government acting in the role of the developer. Rather than waiting for Gerald Hines or Hyatt to come to town, civic leaders must develop a physical vision for their city which they commit to and then actively promote. Rather than being victimized by the self-interests of the private sector, they must determine the type, scale, and quality of new growth and then act as the lead booster for that growth.

This approach seems inescapable when one considers the greater expense and difficulty that developers face when they try to work downtown. As the developer Henry Turley puts it, "It costs $1.25 to build downtown what it costs $1.00 to build in the suburbs, and that's ignoring all the hassles." For this reason and others, developers operate on an extremely tilted playing field, one that discourages inner-city investment in favor of exurban greenfield development. Thus, while it is the first rule of regional planning to concentrate growth in existing urban centers, many factors conspire against doing so, including fragmented property ownership, title problems, inappropriate zoning, higher land costs, deteriorating or inadequate infrastructure, environmental contamination, historic preservation limitations,* complex regulatory frameworks, unwieldy

---

ment as inevitable—half of the city sitting empty while huge projects land in isolated locations like spaceships—a quick look across our northern border shows that this need not be the case. In Vancouver or Toronto it is not uncommon to see big new buildings inserted among old two- and three-story buildings. The difference is a tax policy that allows large-scale development without penalizing existing small property owners with higher taxes.

* Historic preservation ordinances are essential to maintaining the quality of our cities. Although such laws are often regarded as anti-business, many a troubled neighborhood has experienced a dramatic economic resurgence as a result of preservation-induced

permitting processes, neighborhood politics, opposition to gentrification, and higher taxes, to name a few. As a result of these disincentives, inner-city development tends to attract only those investors who are either altruistically motivated or efficient manipulators of government subsidies. Until the disincentives are eliminated, the inner city will continue to be outperformed by the outer suburbs.

INVESTMENT SECURITY

Owing to single-use zoning and deed restrictions, suburbia offers developers and purchasers enormous predictability regarding their investment. If a family buys a single-family house in a new subdivision, it can be certain that it will never be surrounded by anything but single-family houses. Similar assurance can be found in an office park. Whether or not the result is something to celebrate, it is certainly comforting.

In contrast, the risk associated with urban development can be summed up in a single word: *dingbat*. A dingbat is a type of small apartment building, popular throughout the Sun Belt, which sits on

---

tourism, Miami's Art Deco South Beach being an obvious example. However, as currently enforced, historic preservation can also undermine an area's urban quality. This is due to the U.S. Department of the Interior guidelines which, inspired by the early modernist writings of the *Congrès Internationaux d'Architecture Moderne*, do not allow building additions to blend in. Specifically, they recommend that additions to older structures "always be clearly differentiated from the historic building," in order to avoid any confusion of the different eras represented (The Secretary of the Interior's Standards, pp. 58–59). In many cities this recommendation has been expanded beyond just additions, such that even entirely new buildings may not emulate their surroundings. This attitude, bred from the modernists' hatred of historic styles, is now only useful to architectural historians who hate being fooled.

Invasion of the Dingbats: apartment buildings atop parking lots bring down property values

URBAN CODE · THE TOWN OF SEASIDE

A physically based zoning code: addressing a building's form in terms of look and feel, not legalese and numbers

stilts over a parking lot—a direct outcome of the ubiquitous American on-site parking requirement. The construction of a single dingbat on a street of row houses is all that is necessary to bring down the real estate value of the entire block. Yet, in many cities, there is nothing to stop this from occurring. Zoning has a history of changing over time with little regard to building compatibility. Moreover, most zoning codes, focused on numbers and ratios rather than on physical form, can't tell the difference between a dingbat and a block of row houses, as they may be statistically identical. For better or worse, the city will not be able to compete against the suburb for risk-averse investors until it can provide the same level of protection against dingbats and their ilk. Without physical predictability, there can be no investment security.

The best way to ensure predictability in downtown neighborhoods is with an *urban code.* This cannot be a conventional words-and-numbers zoning code, focusing only on uses and square feet, but must instead be a physically based code that visually describes the building's volume, articulation, and relationship to the street—in other words, its *building type.*[*] This code should ensure that all building types are pedestrian-friendly, and that buildings are located

---

[*] This code looks different from a standard zoning code because it is about physical form. For example, it addresses building height instead of F.A.R. (Floor Area Ratio), the measure used by most municipalities nationwide. (F.A.R. is the ratio of allowable building area to lot size; a two-story building covering half its lot would have an F.A.R. of 1.0.) F.A.R. is a zoning tool that makes it easy to calculate the value of a property based on its development capacity, but it says nothing about whether that property will hold a row house or a dingbat—it's only a number. In contrast, a height limit—given in stories rather than feet, to encourage generous ceiling heights—gives priority to a specific physical result. As with most distinctions outlined here, the objective of these new codes is to complement planning—the cause of surprisingly unpredictable results—with something more effective, something called *design.* Interestingly, F.A.R. presents an additional problem in that, in combination with a standardized setback requirement, it

nearby buildings of similar type. It should also specify the building's alignment, in order to shape public spaces. This discipline is especially important in areas of mixed use, as it is a consistent streetscape that makes different uses compatible. Such a code is not difficult to write, but it requires an approach to city planning that has fallen out of use in recent years. Rather than specifying what it doesn't want, this code specifies what it does want, which implies a degree of proactive physical vision that is currently rare among urban planning and zoning boards.[•] One such urban code is the Traditional Neighborhood Development Ordinance, described later, which is currently being used and imitated by municipalities nationwide.

In certain instances, it makes sense to complement the urban code with a second document, an *architectural code*. Cities and neighborhoods hoping to achieve a high degree of harmony in building style—either to protect and enhance their historic character or to develop a new character of their own—can benefit from a code that addresses building materials, proportions, colors, and other surface design issues. Charleston, Santa Barbara, Nantucket, and Santa Fe are well-known places that owe their success in part to architectural coding.

---

privileges large-lot development. Two 5,000-square-foot lots are inferior to a single 10,000-square-foot lot in terms of their resulting F.A.R. capacity, which discourages the involvement of small-scale developers downtown. This scenario leads cities to become dependent upon a few large speculative developers rather than on a diversity of local property owners.
[•] Specifically, physically based zoning codes such as these require a well-articulated vision of what the city is to be, rather than an acquiescence to the ad hoc results of laissez faire. Fortunately, some cities are beginning to emerge from a prolonged crisis of confidence in which they abdicated initiative to market forces rather than providing a predictable environment for the market to thrive in.

The good news about these codes is that once they are evolved and enacted, processing can be simplified dramatically. Because these codes are prescriptive rather than proscriptive, buildings that correspond to their specific physical criteria can be permitted automatically and allowed to move forward immediately. To assist in this process, city planning and building departments must be encouraged to see themselves as an enabling staff rather than a regulatory staff.* Instead of fighting bad development, they can concentrate on supporting good development, which is a much more rewarding job. The implementation of such a process would be an important step in leveling the playing field between suburban and urban development, so that suburban developers could be enticed back into the inner city.

THE PERMITTING PROCESS

There is a general perception that it is difficult to get projects permitted in the suburbs. This is often true, but only as it refers to *projects:* not to buildings, but to entire office parks and subdivisions, which are often the size of towns. In the suburbs, there are two types of developer: the master developer, who must secure the initial site permits, and the building developer, who then constructs individual buildings within the project. While an office park developer may have to endure a painful permitting process, the builder

---

* Ideally, each developer submittal should be handled by a single contact, and all of the necessary approvals should be integrated into a single process, such that zoning, architectural, historic preservation, public works, environmental, and all other reviews occur simultaneously.

who subsequently wishes to place an office building within that park faces no hassles whatsoever. He is given a site, a building footprint, and perhaps some rules regarding construction quality, and he's ready to go. Only a routine building permit stands between him and construction.

The problem with developing individual buildings in the inner city is that there are no master developers running interference for the building developers. Instead, the would-be builder must weed through a complicated and confusing zoning code and then prepare for a series of confrontations with permitting authorities, local organizations, and resistant neighbors. If the city is to compete against the suburb, someone must play the role of the master developer, and in most cases this someone can only be the city government itself. As discussed above, the city can best achieve true predictability by replacing its zoning ordinances with a physical plan, one with as much precision as that of a new office park, in which every projected building is given shape. This plan must be created through a public process in which citizens participate with the understanding that the outcome will become the law. Once completed and enacted, this plan will control future growth, such that potential developers know exactly what they can build and when they can start construction. Under such a system—currently active in West Palm Beach, Florida, and Providence, Rhode Island—the city can begin to offer building developers a permitting environment that does not make them flee to the suburbs in frustration.

There are many benefits to creating a physically prescriptive master plan for a city, not the least of which is that it allows government to return to the business of governing. Currently, city commission agendas are overwhelmed by a disproportionate number of contests over individual real estate projects, as if real estate were more important than schooling, public safety, economic development, or quality of life. These battles are fought precisely because there is no master plan in place to guide development. Completing and enacting a new city master plan can often seem like a war, but isn't it better to wage one big war and get it over with, rather than fighting new battles every week?

One wonders why more cities have not completed effective master plans, and why some cities create master plans but fail to enact them. As with the perpetuation of any patently unworkable system, the answer lies in the fact that certain powerful people benefit from the status quo. In the case of real estate permitting, the situation is clear. Most cities currently have on the books a vast collection of land-use ordinances so vague, confusing, and negotiable that few developers even try to follow them. In such an environment, the developers know that the most important design decision they can make is to retain the right attorney or planner. There is no shortage of such experts, who essentially tell developers, "I'll get you the best deal in town."

These consultants thrive in the swamp of unpredictability. A master plan that offers clarity is their mortal enemy, as it immediately diminishes the value of their services. When such a plan is completed, they begin to stir, warning their developer clients, "Watch out—if that plan is passed, you'll lose your flexibility!" Eventually, the master plan is rejected, and the status quo prevails. For this reason, master plans must be enacted in principle as quickly as possible. The record still belongs to our plan for Stuart, Florida, which was presented at 4 p.m. one day and was law four hours later.

Any realistic master plan will include an implementation component with a schedule for its passage.

It is natural to be cautious, even pessimistic, when addressing the subject of master plans. So many "shelf plans" have been completed—plans that do nothing but gather dust—that wise municipalities do not jump into the planning process without trepidation. Why spend the time and money, when so many plans have failed? The obvious answer to this question is to study the plans that have been successful and to find out what made them so. While it is dangerous to generalize, most successful plans seem to share two qualities: first, they were completed through a fully open, interactive, public involvement process; and second, they include a physically based urban code that was passed into law. As such, they are not dependent on the future goodwill of individuals who may not even be there in the long term.[*]

Thanks to changing demographics and a strong economy, America's cities have already begun to experience a renaissance. More and more people are finding suburbia poorly suited to their needs, especially the bored young and the non-driving old. It is not unreasonable to expect that the early years of the twenty-first century will be a time of reinvestment in our older downtown cores. As it occurs, it is essential that growth follow traditional neighborhood principles rather than being simply a higher-density version of auto-dependent sprawl. This latter outcome is by no means unlikely, since so many

[*] Of course, with enough popular support, even officially unsuccessful plans can have a powerful impact. Consensus-driven master plans, supported by an activist citizenry, have been known to be effective development guides even without gaining official status. Such was the case in the historic district of Miami's South Beach, where a preservation master plan that was never passed by the City Commission nevertheless served as an effective guide for two decades of Art Deco restoration.

developers are experienced in suburban building and nothing else. It will fall to the cities to protect themselves from a watered-down future of isolated towers and parking lots. If they are successful, not only will their own citizens benefit but so will the many residents of nearby suburbia, who will again be given the opportunity to experience authentic urbanity on a regular basis.

10

HOW TO MAKE A TOWN

REASONS NOT TO, AND REASONS TO DO SO ANYWAY;

REGIONAL CONSIDERATIONS, INCLUDING MIXED USE AND

CONNECTIVITY; MAKING THE MOST OF A SITE; THE DISCIPLINE

OF THE NEIGHBORHOOD; MAKING TRANSIT WORK; STREETS,

BUILDINGS, AND PARKING; THE INEVITABLE QUESTION OF STYLE;

A NOTE FOR ARCHITECTS

———

To affect the quality of the day, that is the highest of arts.
— HENRY DAVID THOREAU, *WALDEN* (1854)

———

As badly as we have been shaping our built environment, we still possess the ability to do it right. The principles and techniques of true urban design may have been forgotten, but they are not lost; they can be relearned from the many wonderful older places that still exist. By emulating the past, a number of recent projects have demonstrated that designers can make new places that are as impressive as the towns which inspired them. Many of the principles of successful town-making have already been discussed. This chapter will elaborate on the particulars of designing new communities from scratch.

REASONS NOT TO, AND REASONS TO DO SO ANYWAY

About once a week we receive a call from someone who has read about one of the new towns we've designed, and is prepared to move almost anywhere to experience the sense of community described. Our first response is to ask the caller to consider one of the older towns that has served as our inspiration. Frankly, as residents of traditional communities ourselves, we wonder why someone would want to live in a brand-new development rather than a neighborhood that has matured over generations of use. Why live in Seaside instead of Key West, or Kentlands instead of Georgetown? The short answer to this question has to do with people's desire for new houses without surprises, and the lower prices available in communities that have yet to experience the appreciation that beautiful old neighborhoods have already undergone. Whatever the reason, it is troubling that people are happily moving into new communities when there are still many old communities that could benefit from new arrivals.

New towns are not always the answer. The appropriateness of a greenfield development depends on the particular characteristics of the surrounding region. Certain facts must be accepted as given. If a region is not growing statistically—in population or wealth—it should not be growing geographically. The result of such unwarranted dispersal is the draining of the inner city and the wasteful distribution of new infrastructure. Even in regions that *are* growing, the objectives of economic efficiency and social justice suggest that growth be focused in areas that are already at least partially developed.

Why create new places at all when existing places are underutilized? It must be clearly stated that many social and environmental ills would best be solved, at least temporarily, by a moratorium on greenfield development. There is a ready supply of vacant land available for infill projects, both in the inner city and in existing suburbs. But, as already described, forces conspire to make exurban investment more attractive to developers than infill work. For the time being, as we fight these incentives for suburban growth, we must admit that it is still occurring, and in the worst possible form: automobile-based sprawl.

Conscientious designers are faced with a difficult choice: to allow sprawl to continue without intervention, or to reshape new growth into the most benevolent form possible. Given those options, a growing number of designers feel compelled to choose the ambiguous risk of engagement over the easy moral purity of inaction. Distancing oneself from the problem may be easier, but it implies that nothing good can come from the current circumstances. Unless unjustified greenfield development is stopped—an unlikely prospect[*]—designers should endeavor to ensure that what gets built on the urban fringe is as environmentally sound, economically efficient, and socially just as possible.[■]

[*] Recent Supreme Court decisions have made it clear that property rights are held in greater esteem than good planning. While limiting the development of certain private lands may be in the public interest, many attempts to do so have been labeled as "takings," entitling the landowner to reimbursement equal to lost revenue.

[■] Lessening the negative impacts of growth is reason enough to do suburban work, but, happily, this work has produced some unintended positive consequences in the inner city as well. Two stories are fairly typical: In central Cleveland, an old African American neighborhood that was largely abandoned—and had been slated for demolition—was considering how it might rebuild. The local Neighborhood Progress Foundation visited us and told us about their vision for their community: Seaside. Clearly, Seaside was not appropriate to the local climate or building tradition, and what they ended up with was Cleveland. But their enthusiasm for the traditional organizational principles that Seaside embodies motivated them to build eighty-one new houses that were compatible in scale and style to the neighborhood's remaining building fabric.

In Gaithersburg, Maryland, Mayor Ed Bohrer, who had presided over the growth of

The pages that follow outline the design principles that underlie our practice, principles that should inform any conscientious attempt at healthy suburban growth. These principles are also presented in simplified form in the Traditional Neighborhood Development Checklist provided in Appendix A.

REGIONAL CONSIDERATIONS

The most important design criteria of any new village or town—and the least often satisfied—are regional. Currently, most development occurs not according to geographical logic but according to the random disposition of resources: the first parcels to be developed are often those whose owners have the financing, rather than the ones that are the best located or the least environmentally sensitive. This is a good argument for regional planning authorities, if Europe is any evidence. There, the government typically designates and executes the land development, while private developers focus on individual buildings, with vastly superior results.* Ideally, parcels under con-

---

Kentlands and insisted that it be built to the highest standard, asked his community why its old downtown was not of equal quality. At his recommendation, the city commissioned a master plan for its main street that is guiding a revitalization of downtown Gaithersburg. Perhaps unsurprisingly, much new urban inner-city work is completed for municipalities that have witnessed the popularity of neotraditional greenfield projects.
* In many German cities, the local city government historically has determined the location and rate of new growth, rather than leaving it up to the private sector. When expansion was desired, the city would condemn farmland at farmland prices, design the new neighborhood, lay the infrastructure, subdivide the land, and sell it off at market rate. The value generated in preparing the land for building would accrue to the city. This technique not only ensures wise development but also explains why the city of Berlin can afford an arts budget larger than America's entire National Endowment for the Arts.

sideration for growth should be rationally located within a comprehensive regional plan that seeks to limit automobile dependence and preserve open space. If not immediately adjacent to existing development, the new development should be at a concentration of infrastructure and, if possible, at a likely transit stop. In the best regional plans, existing and future rail lines serve as a basis for locating new neighborhoods and town centers.

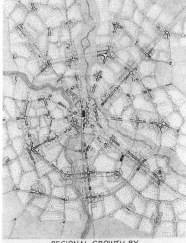

REGIONAL GROWTH BY
TRADITIONAL NEIGHBORHOODS

The region idealized: new developments take the form of complete neighborhoods, either within the city or along existing transportation corridors (Drawing by Thomas E. Low, DPZ)

MIXED-USE DEVELOPMENT

Regardless of location, a new neighborhood can avoid unduly contributing to sprawl by being of mixed use. At the bare minimum, every residential neighborhood must include a corner store to provide its residents with their daily needs, from orange juice to cat food. While it is only a start, a small corner store does wonders to limit automobile trips out of the development, and does more than a social club to build the bonds of community.

The corner store should be constructed in an early building phase. It will not, at first, be economically self-sufficient, due to the small number of houses around it. It should not be expected to turn a profit until the neighborhood matures, and for that reason the retail space should be provided rent-free by the developer as an

---

In the current American system, which supposedly reflects a repulsion for big government's interference in free enterprise, it must be stressed that city government is still a partner in the land development process—albeit a silent one. It typically finances the roads, the infrastructure, the schools, the libraries, the police and fire stations, just as in Europe. The only real difference is that, in America, city governments exercise little control over the enormous taxpayer investment in these facilities.

amenity, much in the way a conventional developer would construct an elaborate entry feature or a clubhouse. Since it can be very effective in marketing real estate—if properly staffed with a gregarious busybody—the corner store is a fairly easy concept for enlightened developers to understand.

To witness the range of possibilities, one might consider corner stores in two recent developments. In Middleton Hills, a new neighborhood just outside Madison, Wisconsin, the developer—a protégé of Frank Lloyd Wright—built a sophisticated Prairie Style structure that houses a corner store, a community center, a post office, and a walk-in medical clinic, which helps pay the rent. The corner store/café contains an espresso machine and a wide selection of gourmet specialty items. If anything, it errs in being too upscale for its middle-class clientele, but that situation will surely change as the neighborhood grows and the shopkeeper responds to demand for everyday items.

At the other end of the spectrum is the corner store in Belmont, Virginia, which is simply an expanded single-family house, in the age-old tradition. The shopkeepers live upstairs and have not required a developer subsidy. The store is stocked with touching precision to match the neighborhood's needs, so much so that it buys seven PowerBars each week to satisfy one resident's daily habit—a small-scale exemplar of "just in time" inventory. Each child in the neighborhood holds a five-dollar charge account, to be used at will, thanks to the autonomy they gain from living in a pedestrian-scale community. Complete with a television and sleeping dogs, the store may not be an architectural masterpiece, but it serves its purpose.

The corner store is, of course, only the first step toward a true mix of uses. A neighborhood-scale shopping center may be appro-

Up-market: the corner store / office building in the new village of Middleton Hills, Wisconsin

Down home: the corner store / shopkeeper's house in the new village of Belmont, Virginia

priate for a larger population or when adjacent to through traffic. Such a concentration of retail—around 20,000 square feet, including groceries, dry cleaner, video rental, and other daily needs—should be designed as part of any large development in anticipation of future demand. Any town plan with two neighborhoods or more should include such a town center, which is built when there are enough citizens to make it viable.

A mixed-use neighborhood also includes places to work, the more the better. Perhaps the smallest, aside from the home office, is the neighborhood work center, a place where residents can share the costs of a secretary, office equipment, and meeting rooms. Such neighborhood work centers are emerging in a for-profit form as the local Kinko's, a business that is flourishing as more people choose to work at home.

Ideally, every neighborhood should be designed with an even balance of residents and jobs. While this flies in the face of convention, it is not impossible to implement. All that is needed is for the housing and commercial developers to agree to work in the same location with a coordinated plan. When there is only one developer for both, it is even easier. Riverside is a new Atlanta neighborhood recently built by Post Properties, a company large enough to develop housing and office space at the same time. Their first phase of construction included a quarter-million square feet of office space and two hundred apartments, all of which were rented immediately at rates 40 percent above the market average. Pictured at right is the main street, which terminates on a square fronted by street-level shops and cafés. The immediate success of this experiment has convinced Post to stop building suburban sprawl, and to focus its efforts on high-density mixed-use developments, including projects in the inner city.[1]

Shops, offices, and apartments: the Main Street in the new neighborhood of Riverside, Georgia

A common criticism of "forcing" the workplace into residential areas is that, even though the workplace is near the homes, it is not near the homes of the people who work there. This assertion may be true at first, but not over the long run. There is no doubt that most of the workplace in new towns will be staffed initially by people who commute from some distance away, just as most of the new houses will be occupied by people with steady jobs elsewhere. But the study of older communities shows that this relationship improves within a generation. When they can, people will relocate their home or business to be near their business or home. It is the planner's imperative to offer them the opportunity to do so.•

Criticism of traditional town planning can be shortsighted, as it presumes that fully integrated communities can be conjured up overnight. True towns take time; a designer can only provide the ingredients and conditions most likely to lead to a mixed-use future. Eighteen years after it was planned, Seaside just built its first school, but has yet to build its town hall. Those critics who question whether Seaside should bother continuing to reserve space for a town hall are the same people who initially scoffed at the idea that it should also include a school. But the developer Robert Davis ignored the nay-sayers, and now the children of Seaside can walk to school.

Which brings up the final component of mixed use: civic buildings. After housing, shops, and workplaces, civic buildings are a required element for any new community. Indeed, land should be reserved for them at the most prominent locations, such as a high

Plan it and they will come: eighteen years in the making, the school at Seaside

---

• In the meantime, many of the evils of commuting can be mitigated by concentrating the workplace at transportation nodes—town centers—in order that the jobs be transit-accessible, no matter where the workers live.

ground, a main intersection, or the town square. Larger civic buildings—city halls, libraries, and the like—require the most patience, as they are typically the last to get built, but they must be planned for if they are to exist at all. In the meantime, smaller civic buildings such as the neighborhood recreation center or the bandstand on the town green square can serve as social centers and contribute to a sense of community identity.

The most important civic building is the neighborhood elementary school, which should never be more than a fifteen-minute walk from any home. This may seem a radical proposition these days, when schools seem to be sized primarily for the efficiency of the janitorial service, but there are many arguments in its favor. It has become clear that small schools are key to effective learning. Recent studies have demonstrated that schools with fewer than four hundred students have better attendance rates, fewer problem children and dropouts, and often higher test scores. In response to such data, progressive school boards nationwide are replacing the mega-schools of the eighties with smaller neighborhood-based schools.[*] Walking to school rather than being bused or driven can contribute significantly to a child's physical and emotional development. Moreover, busing costs over $400 per student annually, an expense that is not always considered when school boards decide to consolidate elementary schools into mega-facilities. Like housing projects and shopping malls, schools have fallen prey to a "bigger is better" strategy that simplistically champions economies of scale while ignoring the myriad secondary costs involved.

True neighborhoods mix different uses within individual

---

[*] Susan Chira, "Is Smaller Better?," A1. The most comprehensive of these conversions are taking place in Philadelphia and New York City.

The "city building": Steve Holl's contribution to downtown Seaside contains housing over offices over shops, a combination rarely found in suburbia

buildings as well. Many mixed-use buildings containing apartments, offices, and shops have been constructed in new traditional towns such as Seaside. The most progressive of these, by Stephen Holl, has received considerable praise in the architectural press. Most non-architects consider it ugly, but that doesn't stop them from shopping there, and its presence on the town square contributes tremendously to the vitality of the community.

CONNECTIVITY

If a new neighborhood is to contribute more to its region than traffic, it must do more than just mix uses. Its relationship to its neighbors is important as well. In order to avoid the inefficient hierarchical street pattern of sprawl, in which virtually every trip uses the same few collector roads, the new neighborhood must connect wherever practical to everything around it, even if its neighbors are nothing but single-use pods.[*] One must say "wherever practical," because it is obviously not possible to connect across superhighways or riverbeds, nor is it advisable to connect to oil refineries or trucking depots. But all compatible land uses should be connected, especially between residential areas, the most common adjacency.

This is easier said than done. Whenever we design a new neighborhood, we make every effort to convince the adjacent subdivisions

---

[*] In fact, a well-placed town center can even mitigate the traffic problems of surrounding suburban subdivisions by providing walkable destinations such as workplace, convenience retail, and a transit stop, and also by intercepting automobile trips that would otherwise be longer.

to allow us to connect to them. We'll go so far as to place the most luxurious housing directly abutting the neighbors, whatever the quality of their housing. We hand them photographs and testimonials from our other developments, and appraisals demonstrating their impressive financial performance.

For example: Seaside is connected in no fewer than three places to preexisting Seagrove, to its east. There is almost no perceptible seam between the two communities. As a result, lots in Seagrove have shared in Seaside's 25 percent average annual appreciation since 1980, rising in value approximately 10 percent each year. On the other hand, there is The Orchards, a town house development adjacent to the new town of Kentlands, which was not allowed to connect. While lots at Kentlands have been appreciating at 12 percent since 1991, The Orchards has hardly kept pace with inflation.[2]

Rejecting the gate: Seaside connects directly into the Seagrove street grid to its east

Even when presented with the evidence, subdivision residents rarely want to associate with us. In a recent project in Warwick, New York, a woman went so far as to drag her six-year-old daughter to the microphone to wail about the suffering she would endure from the proposed development. At the hearing for another project, in suburban Utah, a neighbor circulated this letter:

[The planner] states, with deliberate intent to deceive, that "The lives of kids are enriched with narrow streets; kids are everywhere, they can play in the streets and alleys." Street play is mindful of tenements in the big eastern cities, where yards are absent. When kids are not in your yard, but are away from your supervision and out where kids govern, the gang culture prevails. Might and fear will rule the street. We will experience the drive-by shootings that are gang-member initiations. Children away from home are far more susceptible to being kidnaped, daughters and sons to being attacked and raped at the playground some blocks away.

Whether or not they are justified, Nimbys can be effective barriers to community connectivity, which explains why many new town plans have relatively few entrances and exits. When refused access to neighboring subdivisions, we instead try to place a few road easements or pedestrian paths in strategic locations, so that the neighbors have the option of changing their minds later.

Connectivity is also an important issue as it concerns highways and arterials. As discussed in Chapter 5, the concept of the highwayless town implies two basic rules: highways and arterials approaching neighborhoods should skirt them rather than split them; and when they do come into contact with a neighborhood, they should take on low-speed geometries. Unfortunately, this contradicts current conventions. We battle over these rules in almost every development we work on, thanks to public works directors who prioritize traffic volume over neighborhood viability. Two of our projects in the Midwest alone ran up against the same problem: a municipal plan that jammed a major arterial straight through the middle of a new neighborhood to connect low-density suburbia to empty farmland. In anticipation of future traffic—traffic that will be generated only by this new roadway construction—we were forced to rend these neighborhoods in two. In Middleton Hills, Wisconsin, the result is a main street that is much too wide, an unpleasant sea of asphalt. In Ames, Iowa, a planned four-lane arterial was converted to two lanes at our request, and switched back again to four the minute we left town.

A skirmish lost to outdated standards: the Middleton Hills store, seen across its oversized street

When faced with a major road, how should a neighborhood respond? That depends on whether the road is designed as a civic thoroughfare or as an automotive sewer. When it is properly detailed as an avenue or a main street—as is appropriate within the neighborhood—or as a parkway or boulevard at the neighborhood edge, the thoroughfare becomes a worthy setting for buildings and will benefit aesthetically from their presence. Princeton, New Jersey, has just such a main street—a delightful collection of shops fronting a major regional arterial—and in Kansas City's Country Club District, expensive estates directly face a heavily trafficked roadway. Seen to best advantage across deep lawns, these houses provide motorists with a grand entry into the city.

Only when noxious, high-speed traffic is inevitable should a road face the backs of houses. If a developer resorts to this solution, he must build a wall as well, or the backyards become uninhabitable. Since most major roads are designed to create high-speed traffic, the "sound wall" is the standard solution in the new suburbs.

The ruling principle is that as long as the road is designed with low-speed geometries, traffic generally treats the neighborhood the way that the neighborhood treats it. Friendly house fronts tell drivers to slow down, while blank walls and house backs tell them to speed up. An intermediate solution, appropriate for roads of moderate speed, is to face the road with the short ends of the blocks, so that it is met with the sides of houses, with a deep lawn as an additional buffer. Sunset Boulevard in Beverly Hills is configured this way. Every block ends on the boulevard, resulting in an intersection every 300 feet or less. Such frequent spacing can raise the hackles of the traffic engineers, who tend to want much wider spacing between intersections, so that cars can travel at higher speeds. These engineers must be reminded of the difference between a boulevard and a highway, and that the latter has no place in residential areas.●

MAKING THE MOST OF A SITE

Modern development is notorious for its unique approach to nature, typically: *level the site first, design it later.* This attitude has been the rule rather than the exception since the 1800s, when Jefferson laid his perfect grid across the continent.■ It comes as no surprise, then, that the typical American builder would rather spend $100,000 on bulldozers and artificial drainage than on a sensitive site plan.

We know better now, and there are many justifications for preserving a site's natural qualities, aside from the obvious ecological benefits. First, natural features—not just waterfront and hillsides, but wetlands and trees—can add significantly to property value. Second, the character of the landscape can help people understand and negotiate their environment. It is much easier to give directions, even in cul-de-sac suburbia, if one can say "take a left at the pond." Finally, for planners, varied and idiosyncratic sites are actually easier to design, and much more interesting. While flat and featureless

●This argument becomes a bit easier when one mentions—as the engineering manuals demonstrate statistically—that roads carry more traffic at 30 mph than they do at higher speeds. As cars breach 30 mph, they begin to spread apart, and this increased vehicle spacing results in a drop in roadway capacity.
■ In the Northwest Ordinance of 1787, Thomas Jefferson and his colleagues applied a regular mile-square grid over the Appalachian wilderness, across the Ohio Valley, and into the Great Plains. Seventy-five years later, the Homestead Act further divided each square mile into "quarter sections," still plainly visible as one flies across the country. As a result, the quarter section is by far the most common size for housing subdivisions. Conveniently, it corresponds to the ideal neighborhood size, which is a five-minute walk from edge to center.

land gives few hints as to where to begin, a complex site tells the designer pretty clearly what it wants to be. A good example of this phenomenon is the quirky plan of Middleton Hills, in which every major decision arose directly out of the site's topography and watersheds.

Entering from the south, one passes through a sequence of two forks. At the first fork, which frames the corner store, veering right allows the visitor to bypass the neighborhood and continue north on a country highway. The left fork leads to the base of a hill, like the hull of an overturned ship, that splits the road again. This prominent site has been reserved for a civic building. Here, a left turn leads along the "low road" to the west—the retail main street— while a right turn ascends the "high road," along the crest of the eastern hills, which provide views of the state capitol across Lake Mendota.

The low road ends at the wetlands preserve, a swamp that has been expanded into a fifty-acre natural park. As in most historic neighborhoods, this park is not privatized behind the backyards of houses but surrounded by a public parkway so that it belongs to all residents equally. The wetland is fed by a watershed that sits a saddle to the northeast. The saddle's shape has determined the diagonal orientation of this part of the plan, which recalls the same condition in the nearby Madison grid. Running down the middle of this saddle is the swale-centered avenue, which terminates on a second civic site at the peak of the hill. At the top center of the plan, at the very highest point, a third prominent site has been reserved for an elementary school, surrounded by a hillside prairie. The rest of the plan is an attempt to connect these unique features efficiently without damaging the natural slopes of the hillside.

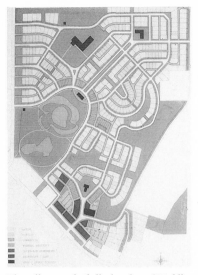

The village on the hill: the plan of Middleton Hills was largely determined by sloping site conditions

Middleton Hills: the southern entry and downtown

Middleton Hills: the wetland park and "saddle"

The Middleton Hills plan demonstrates the approach demanded by distinctive sites. Wetlands, lakes, ponds, streams, hills, tree stands, hedgerows, and other significant features are not only retained but celebrated. Fronted by public roads rather than by private yards, they are formalized into greens, squares, and parks, the kinds of traditional public spaces that add value to the surrounding blocks. In larger developments, green areas between neighborhoods are carefully connected into continuous corridors, in the manner of Olmsted's Emerald Necklace in Boston. These greenways can serve as natural drainage ways and areas for habitat continuity, and often provide recreational opportunities and pedestrian paths.[•]

THE DISCIPLINE OF THE NEIGHBORHOOD

Middleton Hills is a good example of a single neighborhood, sized around the measure of a five-minute walk from its edge to its center. The five-minute walk—or *pedestrian shed*—is roughly one-quarter mile in distance. It was conceptualized as a determinant of neighborhood size in the classic 1929 New York City Regional Plan, but it has existed as an informal standard since the earliest cities, from Pompeii to Greenwich Village. If one were to map the neighborhoods of most prewar cities, they would average about one-quarter mile from edge to center. While some flexibility is advisable—the

[•] Developing new neighborhoods with this approach to the natural environment is logical enough. Restoring environmental integrity in already urbanized areas is a more complex undertaking. The work of Bill Morrish and Catherine Brown has begun to show the way for a long-term approach to reconceiving the built environment. For continued reading, we recommend their book *Planning to Stay: Learning to See the Physical Features of Your Neighborhood.*

West Coast designer Peter Calthorpe recommends a ten-minute walk in order to engage a larger number of households to a transit stop, and college students seem to put up with twenty minutes, even in icy Wisconsin—most new traditional town plans are designed around the five-minute measure. One-quarter mile is usually the distance from which you can actually spot your destination. More important, experience suggests that it is a distance short enough that most Americans simply feel dumb driving, making it a perfect rule of thumb for our auto-dependent times.

The first step in designing an open site is to use its natural features to locate the centers and edges of five-minute-walk neighborhoods. Neighborhood centers are typically located at the geographic center of the available land, but can be shifted in response to site conditions, such as a view or a major road at one edge. At Seaside, where Highway 30-A passes to the southern edge of the property, the center sits on the highway, which is also the gateway to the beach. For sites large enough to hold multiple neighborhoods, two organizational options are available: the neighborhoods can be distinct, separated by a greenbelt, in which case each remains a village, or the neighborhoods can be directly adjacent, sharing a boulevard at their seam, in which case they can coalesce into a town or even a city. In both cases, the overall structure links neighborhood centers with avenues in a fairly direct transit loop. This approach can be clearly seen in the design for Cornell, a new town in Markham, Ontario. Cornell is a fairly pure application of the neighborhood concept, the only modification being that a high density allows several of the neighborhood centers to stretch out into longer main streets. The result is two pedestrian sheds that are ovals rather than circles.

Cornell is an interesting story. We designed its 2,400 acres over

The plan of Cornell, Ontario: a new town divided into distinct neighborhoods

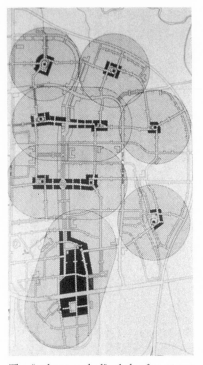

The "pedestrian shed" of the five-minute walk applied to the plan of Cornell: almost every residence is within five minutes of shopping and a bus stop

The radical innovation: a street of single-family houses in Cornell

two years for the Province of Ontario. When we had almost finished it, a newly elected government decided to sell it for revenue. The unbuilt project was purchased by a powerful conventional developer. It is as yet unclear how faithfully he will implement the original plan; so far, construction has largely followed the original urban design, but the architecture is much busier than what is advocated here. Using an anti-sprawl sales pitch—"Cornell will be a complete community"—the developer sold over three hundred houses in the first five months of operations.

Cornell is located at what may be the international epicenter of anti-sprawl activity. Led by a strong planning commissioner named Lorne McCool and several visionary councilors, the Town of Markham decided eight years ago to take a proactive role in fighting sprawl, a remarkable stance given that Markham mostly *was* sprawl. The town retained our firm to design two large sectors, and established a neighborhoods-only approach for new development at the periphery. The resulting land plan reads like an uncanny inversion of the typical North American city: classic sprawl at the center, surrounded on all sides by a consistent gridded urbanity. Ideally, these new neighborhoods will follow the rules laid out in this chapter, but we must remain skeptical, as some of the town's best efforts are being contested by a clever and recalcitrant homebuilding cartel.

Once the center and the edge of a neighborhood have been located, the distribution of uses follows naturally. The areas of highest density and urbanity surround the center, which is the location of a major public space such as a plaza, square, or green, depending on the local tradition.• The center is also the location for shops and

---

• Plazas are primarily paved, and tend to occur in places with a Mediterranean tradition, such as New Mexico. Squares are mostly green, but are formally arranged, and are com-a transit stop. From the center outward, housing densities fall, such that, in villages, the conditions at the edge can be downright rural. Different building types are "zoned," not by use, but by size, and changes in zoning occur at mid-block rather than mid-street, so that each street tends to have the same building types on both of its sides. This is quite different from the asymmetrical experience typically encountered in suburbia.

The standard practice: a street of single-family houses in a nearby subdivision

As one leaves the center and approaches the neighborhood edge, building densities decrease and there occurs a corresponding shift in the design of the street. Every single aspect of the public realm transforms from urban to rural. Closed curbs and gutters become open swales; trees stop lining up and become more varied in species; sidewalks narrow and eventually disappear; and front yards become gradually deeper. In this way, there is an authentic and gentle transition from culture to nature. This sort of detailing, which is essential to giving a neighborhood a unique sense of place, requires designers and developers to exercise a degree of care that is now rare. One can only hope that the financial success of the new places designed in this manner will eventually encourage more developers to invest in such precise design.

An inverted city: the plan of Markham, Ontario, with a central core of sprawl surrounded by subsequent layers of traditional street network (Cornell is at the extreme right)

The gradual transition from center to edge occurs most clearly in villages, which by definition are single neighborhoods sitting free in the landscape. In towns or cities, where multiple neighborhoods meet across shared main streets, the neighborhood edges may instead be designed as areas of increased density and activity. In this case, the

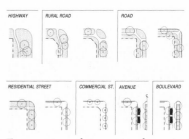

From most rural to most urban: street frontages vary in response to their location within the neighborhood

---

mon throughout the United States, particularly in the old South and the Midwest. Greens, a New England specialty, are grassy and informal, as if a piece of pasture has been captured by the city. The dominance of different urban spaces in different locations reminds us that planning has certain cultural determinants that often overrule the social, economic, and environmental determinants.

A typical Cornell neighborhood: a main street at one edge, a school at another, a commercial central square, and a playground in each quarter

urban/rural transition is reserved for the outer edge of the entire collection of neighborhoods.

In addition to this radial organization, the neighborhood also possesses a Cartesian substructure, as shown at left. The larger streets that lead to the center divide the neighborhood into quadrants, each of which is sized to be the independent realm of the small child. As such, each is equipped with nothing but the slowest roads, and contains a local "pocket park"—often no bigger than a single house lot—located within a three-minute walk of every dwelling. The neighborhood thus grants freedom of motion and a certain degree of autonomy even to its youngest citizens.

MAKING TRANSIT WORK

The neighborhood structure is naturally suited for public transit, be it light rail, trolleys, buses, or jitneys. But there are also three rules that transit must follow in order to appeal to users, regardless of the urban framework:

1. Transit must be frequent and predictable. The challenge is not to prove this obvious principle but to create a transit system in which frequency is economically viable. This objective can be achieved only at certain densities; studies suggest that a minimum of seven units per acre is necessary if transit is to be self-supporting.[*] For lower densities, the careful organization of neighborhood centers, to be served by smaller vehicles, can result in a successful net-

---

[*] The conventional wisdom among transit analysts is that a minimum of seven dwellings per acre is needed to support bus service every thirty minutes, and fifteen units per acre can support bus service every ten minutes (Joint Center for Environmental and Urban Problems, *Florida's Mobility Primer,* 38).

work. This network, however, would likely require financial support.

2. *Transit must follow a route that is direct and logical.* Riders shy away from transit systems in which the path is not efficient and easy to understand conceptually. Anyone who has ever taken a shared hotel bus to the airport knows how intolerable an uncertain, zigzagging route can be. Yet bus routes often dogleg interminably. The desire for a trustworthy, unchanging route is one factor that helps explain riders' preference for light rail over buses.

3. *The transit stop must be safe, dry, and dignified.* In most suburban communities, transit passengers are made to feel like impoverished transients, waiting by the side of the road on a graffiti-covered bench or inside an ungainly plastic bubble. No wonder, then, that the only people who take the bus are those who have no choice, creating a self-perpetuating underclass ridership. In contrast, the structure of the traditional neighborhood offers the possibility of a transit experience that is both comfortable and civilized. When the transit stop is located at the neighborhood center, next to the corner store or the café, the commuter has the opportunity to wait for the bus or trolley indoors with a cup of coffee and a newspaper, with some measure of comfort and dignity. For this condition to occur with regularity, transit routes and urban plans must be developed in concert. Ideally, transit authorities should also work directly with shop owners, who typically welcome the extra business that a transit stop can generate.

THE STREETS

We have already discussed pavement width, but we must be more specific. On well-traveled streets within a neighborhood, there is no

A yield street: a single travel lane handles traffic in both directions

justification for travel lanes wider than ten feet and parking lanes wider than seven feet. If either are any wider, the cars speed. However, on less-traveled residential streets, another logic should prevail, that of the "yield street." Common in almost every prewar American neighborhood—but now summarily rejected by public works departments—the yield street uses a single travel lane to handle traffic *in both directions*. When two cars approach each other, they both slow down, and one eases slightly into a parking lane while the other passes. Because traffic is necessarily slow, accidents are virtually unheard of on such streets. While inappropriate for heavy volume, yield streets cause few delays when used for minor residential streets in low-density neighborhoods.

Although this type of street is endorsed in the engineers' official manual,[*] it is virtually impossible to get one approved. Almost everywhere we've worked, our demand for yield streets has threatened to delay our projects. It seems irrelevant that these streets exist in every older city, and that we have all driven on them regularly without incident.

A decisive battle in the *Traffic Engineering versus Reality* war was fought recently in Kentlands. One of the key compromises demanded by the local public works department pertained to Tschiffely Square Road, the town's main drive. It is a divided avenue, with twenty-four feet of pavement in each direction, owing unsurprisingly to the requirements of the fire chief. In addition to

[*] The famous "Green Book," the manual of the American Association of State Highway Transportation Officials, recommends yield streets as follows: "The level of inconvenience occasioned by the lack of two moving lanes is remarkably low in areas where single-family units prevail . . . In many residential areas, a 26-ft-wide roadway is typical. This curb-face-to-curb-face width provides for a 12-ft center travel lane and two 7-ft parking lanes. Opposing conflicting traffic will yield and pause on the parking lane until there is sufficient width to pass" (AASHTO, 436).

this generous width, the public works department forced the developer to add left-hand turning lanes at every intersection, based upon their calculation of expected traffic loads; we were told that traffic jams were imminent. Seven years later, it was no surprise to hear that traffic congestion was not the problem; speeding was. In response to an outcry from the citizens, the city of Gaithersburg agreed to return the avenue to its original design at considerable expense. In subsequent projects, the city has been much more receptive to the use of traditional street widths.

THE BUILDINGS

A good town plan is not enough to generate a desirable public realm; individual private buildings must also behave in a manner that contributes to pedestrian life. Once again, a study of how the most valued historic neighborhoods differ from conventional sprawl uncovers the rules for a pedestrian-friendly architecture.

While conditions should vary throughout the neighborhood, houses should generally be placed close to the street in order to define its space, with fronts that are relatively simple and flat. Setbacks should range from about ten feet near the neighborhood center to about thirty feet near the neighborhood edge. To encourage sociability, the front yard should include porches, balconies, stoops, bay windows, or other semi-private attachments. These attachments should be allowed to encroach *within* the setback area, so that they represent a gain in space rather than a loss for those who build them. With the proper incentives, front porches need not be mandated, although the town planner who wishes to create streets and squares of dependable character may do so in specific areas.

Attached row houses, a common urban type, should generally be placed closer to the sidewalk than freestanding houses—right up against it, with room only for the stoop. In this case, the first floor must be raised at least two feet off the ground for privacy. People don't seem to mind sipping tea directly adjacent to passing pedestrians if those pedestrians can't easily see over the windowsill. Residential spaces within five feet of a sidewalk must never be located at ground level, period. If one must place a ground-level room within ten feet of a sidewalk, it must be protected by a porch or a dense garden.

For retail buildings, the setback rule is straightforward: don't have one. Traditional retail, to be successful, must pull directly up to the sidewalk, so that people can see the merchandise in the window. Parking lots in front are of course forbidden: there is little that is more destructive to pedestrian life. All parking that cannot be handled on the street can be provided by mid-block lots that are hidden behind buildings. The connection from mid-block parking to street-shop entrances is a tricky one, and must be handled with extreme care. The most effective technique is the traditional *pedestrian passage,* illustrated here in Winter Park, in which a carefully detailed walkway—often articulated with trellises, fountains, stairways to second-floor apartments, and landscaping—connects the rear parking lot to the street. Experienced retailers recognize this passage as a merchandizing opportunity, and flank it with windows and indoor/outdoor displays. In Palm Beach, a series of charming "paseos" helps to make Worth Avenue one of America's most successful shopping destinations.

Whether commercial or residential, taller buildings are to be encouraged because they use land more efficiently while doing a better job defining the public space. Most houses should be a mini-

The pedestrian passage: handling the transition from Main Street to hidden parking

mum of two stories tall. One-story shops and offices, the suburban standard, fail to provide for mixed use and are a waste of valuable land. They should be combined with each other or with housing whenever possible. Where no other mechanism exists to make this happen, municipalities should direct their housing subsidies to the construction of apartments above shops.

There is one last rule that much of suburbia needs to follow: traditional architectural detailing, if used at all, should be used accurately, or it results in parody. There is no specific argument or justification for this rule, except for the horrible feeling that one gets when it is broken. Unfortunately, many modern architects put so much effort into fighting all traditional architecture—a losing battle—that they fail to distinguish between good historicism and tack-on kitsch, which is where they could exert a more positive influence.

PARKING

When building new places, one quickly finds that the amount of dwellings, shops, and offices that one can provide depends primarily on the amount of parking that can be accommodated. As one of our clients puts it, "parking is destiny." Unfortunately, parking is often a very anti-urban destiny, as most municipalities' parking requirements make higher densities impossible without multilevel parking garages, something that most developers can't afford to build. The high cost of structured parking—$12,000 per place, versus $1,500 in a surface lot—is the reason why almost every new suburban building is either less than three stories tall or more than ten stories tall; only a tower can pay for a parking garage.

When new towns are being built in the suburbs, parking requirements cannot be dismissed, as they can be in an older city. Most developers and their lenders insist on ample parking, anyway. The key to sizing parking lots properly in the suburbs is to recognize that the existing requirements are written for the purest sprawl, in which no alternatives to driving exist, and on-street parking is rarely allowed. Each of the factors that distinguishes traditional towns from sprawl—on-street parking, mixed use, transit (when present), pedestrian viability, etc.—also reduces the number of parking spaces that are needed. For example, mixed use means that a school and a cinema can share a parking lot, since they have complementary schedules; the same is true of an office building and an apartment house. Therefore, it is improper to apply the standard suburban parking requirements—often as high as five off-street parking spaces for every thousand square feet of construction—to a mixed-use neighborhood. A more appropriate requirement is three per thousand, *including on-street spaces*. This is the number that acknowledges the opportunity for shared parking.

That's still a lot of parking, enough to undermine most attempts at urbanity. But it is important to remember that *where* is more significant than *how much,* and that the quality of the street space comes first. An essential rule of thumb is to provide no more off-street parking than can be concealed behind buildings, and no more buildings than that amount of parking can support.

THE INEVITABLE QUESTION OF STYLE

Traditional neighborhood design has little or nothing to do with the issue of architectural style. This point may seem obvious to lay readers, but the question of style must be addressed for one reason: it is the architectural style of most Traditional Neighborhood Developments that causes them to be dismissed as "nostalgic" by much of the design profession. While the word *style* is hardly used in architectural circles—"What style is your architecture?" is a question that makes most designers cringe*—the fact is that the current architectural establishment could be accurately described as violently allergic to traditional-style architecture. For many architects, it is impossible to see past the pitched roofs and wooden shutters of Seaside and Kentlands to the progressive town-planning concepts underneath.

Why the negative reaction? Because modernist architects associate it with ideology, style takes on moral overtones. In an age of technology and diversity, they believe that it is morally unacceptable to build with techniques of an earlier era or in styles used by repressive societies.■ Now, there is no denying that the avant-garde has contributed tremendously to the vitality of our culture, from urban skyscrapers to war memorials. It has fared less well, however, in the common vernacular—the suburban building for everyday uses—where, at odds with the human need for communication and

---

* *Style* seems superficial in an age of ideas. To a modern sensibility, the role of classification historically played by *style* is instead played by *ideology*. *Style* is about a building's looks; *ideology* is about the ideas that cause it to look that way. *Ideology* implies valuation, since some ideas are more significant, more appropriate, or simply better than others. Because certain ideas lead to certain looks, style and ideology are inevitably associated. For this reason, traditional architecture may no longer be considered simply in its own terms but instead as representative of a traditional outlook and all that implies.

■ By this logic, Classicism is *verboten* because of its attractiveness to the Third Reich, British imperialists, and Southern slave owners, among others—including, paradoxically, democratic Greeks, Jeffersonian Republicans, and the Works Progress Administration under Roosevelt. Unfortunately, this sort of guilt-by-association quickly turns into a no-win game. For example, modernism was appropriated by some of the worst totalitarian regimes, so by the same logic, it should no longer be an acceptable style. One can imagine a future in which, as every new style eventually becomes associated with some villain government or evil corporation, the only acceptable style remaining is the one that hasn't been invented yet.

personalization, it has been thoroughly debased. Renamed "contemporary," it is a weak and confused style that even most modernists are unable to stomach. Meanwhile, the haphazard introduction of modernist impulses to traditional building has made a mess of it as well, so that most "traditional" housing looks nothing like its supposed inspiration.

As a result, there now exist essentially three different types of architecture: cutting-edge modernist, authentic traditional, and a gigantic middle ground of compromise that includes lazy historicism, half-hearted modernism, and everything in between, most of which could be called kitsch. While cutting-edge modernism has proved popular for monuments, commercial structures, some apartment buildings, and the spectacular houses of well-to-do patrons, it has not penetrated the middle-class housing market. The vast majority of home buyers are only interested in traditional architecture or, sadly, the middle ground of compromise.

It is on this ravaged battlefield that the campaign for traditional town planning is being waged. Most of our audience—the citizens and public servants who must approve our projects if they are to be built—do not appreciate or trust modernist architecture. To present the ideas of neighborhood design in an underappreciated modernist vocabulary would bring them up against insuperable skepticism, even more than they already face for being different. It is hard enough convincing suburbanites to accept mixed uses, varied-income housing, and public transit without throwing flat roofs and corrugated metal siding into the equation.

Some critics think of this as pandering, and suggest that we are playing to the lowest common denominator. For them, we are absolutely forthright in affirming that, when necessary, we are prepared to sacrifice architecture on the altar of urbanism, because all architecture is meaningless in the absence of good urban design. Behind six acres of parking, a true cantilever is no more ethical than a fake arch.

Other critics condemn the use of style codes, which they consider to be autocratic restrictions on the creativity of the individual architect.[*] These critics make two false assumptions. The first is that every individual building should have the opportunity to be—and indeed, bears the responsibility of being—a work of art, a singular, dramatic manifestation of the spirit of the age and the skill of the artist. Most great cities do indeed contain such unique, expressive public buildings, but they are inevitably surrounded by repetitive and undistinguished private buildings. If every building were to croon at once, nothing could be discerned from the cacophony. The second false assumption is that, in the absence of architectural restrictions, what would emerge would be a harmonious landscape of structures that looked as if they had been designed by Richard Meier or Frank Gehry. Somehow, from the perspective of the schools and the magazines, the default setting for unrestricted architecture appears to be modernism. If only this were the case! The default setting for architecture in America is not modernism but vulgarity. To confirm this assertion, the architecture magazines need only look at the advertisements that fill the pages between the masterpieces they display.

That 'said, there is absolutely no incompatibility between

---

[*] Colleagues who complain to us about Seaside usually have two criticisms. The first is the restrictiveness of the architectural code, and the second is the significant number of overdecorated "gingerbread" cottages there. They are usually surprised to learn that the gingerbread houses at Seaside demonstrate not the requirements of the (largely style-neutral) code but the code's inability to overcome the traditional tastes of the American housing consumer. The only way to wipe out the hated traditional architecture would have been to tighten the hated code.

South Beach: modern architecture flourishing in a traditional urban framework

traditional urbanism and modernist architecture—far from it: modernist architecture looks and works its best when lining the sidewalks of traditional cities. Some truly great places—Miami's South Beach, Rome's EUR District, Tel Aviv—consist largely of modernist architecture laid out in a traditional street network. These places do not suffer in any way from their modernist vocabulary, and neither do neighborhoods that combine many different eras of architecture in a true urban fabric. Such is the power of the traditional street.

We look forward to the time when American designers can address the problems associated with sprawl as effectively in a modernist building vocabulary as in a traditional one—something that is already happening in Europe. Until then, we hope that those architects who would rather fight the style wars than take on larger social issues will eventually recognize that our current urban crisis makes their concerns irrelevant.

A NOTE FOR ARCHITECTS

If an obsession over style were the only problem troubling the architectural profession, we could all rest easier. Unfortunately, many of the smartest architects suffer from an additional malaise that is no less threatening to the quality of the built environment. It could perhaps be called Intentional Alienation Syndrome.

The last fifty years have witnessed a decline in the relevance and influence of the architectural profession in America. While architects used to lead the design team on most large projects, they are now more likely to be one of many subconsultants to a general contractor, often providing no more than the decoration for someone else's concept. More and more projects are being completed with hardly any architects involved at all, especially in the suburbs.

In response to their growing sense of insignificance, some architects have tried to regain a sense of power through what can best be described as mysticism. By importing arcane ideas from unrelated disciplines—such as contemporary French literary theory (now outdated)—by developing illegible techniques of representation, and by shrouding their work in inscrutable jargon, designers are creating increasingly smaller realms of communication, in order that they might inhabit a domain in which they possess some degree of control. Nowhere is this crisis more evident than in the most prestigious architecture schools.

To understand the problem, one need only review the studio publication of any leading school. A reader can easily flip through a dozen projects before discovering one that is even vaguely recognizable as a building. For the incredulous, here is a typical passage from an Ivy League design publication, describing the plan for a single-family house:

A typical drawing from the architectural schools: somehow, vaguely related to the act of building (we presume)

> These distortions elicit decipherment in terms of several virtual constructs that allow the house to analogize discourse and call for further elucidation. These constructs are continually motivated and frustrated by conflicts in their underlying schemata and the concrete form in which they are inscribed. They refer to the ideal or real objects, organizations, processes and histories which the house approximately analogizes or opposes.•

• (*Harvard Graduate School of Design News,* Winter/Spring 1993, 13.) In all fairness, it must be acknowledged that the academy is aware of its own neuroses. Jorge Silvetti, the chairman of Harvard's architecture program, has written, ". . . we are becoming more

This text was written by a well-respected professor of first- and second-year graduate students. No illustration of the accompanying design is needed to demonstrate how the withdrawal into mysticism only contributes to the irrelevance of the profession.

Further, the entrenched academic embrace of deconstruction—not the style but the philosophy—has proved, with its distrust of objectivity, to be a short cut to nihilism and impotence among students, since there is no clear right or wrong and thus no trustworthy principles of design. In the studio, a deconstructive approach is often an excuse for sloppy reasoning, since carefully constructed arguments are regarded with suspicion.• Still, deconstruction remains much in vogue as a way to feel superior to a society that is apparently not smart enough to value architects more highly.

Although engagement with society at large sometimes has the unpleasant effect of reminding architects of their limited power, it is the only way to begin to increase that power. Trained to be among the most wide-ranging problem-solvers in the world, architects need to rededicate themselves to their communities, whether those communities seem to want them or not. Those few architects who have made consistent efforts to engage the public will insist that it is indeed a rewarding endeavor.

---

and more like alchemists or magicians—every project becoming a private and arcane search for a secret formula for bliss, or a 'voodoo' act of magic empowerment" (Jorge Silvetti, "The Symptoms of Malaise," 108).

• Needless to say, in such an intellectually limiting environment, the concepts of traditional neighborhood design are dismissed immediately as too black-and-white, too pro-business, and much too . . . traditional. Students in these schools who advocate traditional neighborhood design are generally regarded, by their own account, as campus nerds par excellence.

11

WHAT IS TO BE DONE

THE VICTORY MYTH; THE ROLE OF POLICY; WHAT PUBLIC SERVANTS

CAN DO AT THE MUNICIPAL, COUNTY, REGIONAL, STATE,

AND FEDERAL LEVELS; WHAT ARCHITECTS CAN DO;

WHAT CITIZENS CAN DO; THE ARMCHAIR URBANIST

———

Civil courage in an ecological age means not only demanding social
justice, but also aesthetic justice and the will to make judgements of
taste, to stand for beauty in the public arena and speak out about it.
—JAMES HILLMAN AND MICHAEL VENTURA,
*WE'VE HAD A HUNDRED YEARS OF PSYCHO-
THERAPY, AND THE WORLD'S GETTING WORSE*
(1993)

———

THE VICTORY MYTH

While it has been an uphill struggle, there are many successes
worth celebrating in the fight against sprawl. Federal agencies and
local civic groups are promoting smart growth. Architects are creating pedestrian-friendly, transit-oriented neighborhood plans. Traffic
engineers are rewriting their once-destructive standards. Planners are
throwing out their sprawl-generating land-use codes. Economists
are identifying the real costs of suburban growth and recording the

financial success of new traditionally designed neighborhoods. A new breed of developer is emerging, committed to building community, not just product. Environmentalists are promoting urban infill as a nature-conservation strategy. Mayors and other elected officials are spearheading community revitalization efforts. For the first time, American presidential candidates and governors are including anti-sprawl language prominently in their campaign platforms, with strong grass-roots support. An international organization called the Congress for the New Urbanism, now with over one thousand members, has dedicated itself to the eradication of sprawl. (Its charter is provided in Appendix B.)

But this is not enough. People regularly tell us that "we've won"; the problem is that no one seems to have told the developers. While there is a broadening consensus that neighborhoods are preferable to sprawl, dozens of new housing subdivisions, shopping centers, and office parks break ground daily. Clearly, something else is needed if we are to stop sprawl any time soon.

Toward that end, we offer this final chapter as a call to arms and a brief primer on stopping sprawl. But first, it is important to point out that there are essentially only three tools for manipulating the physical environment: design, policy, and management. It is important to recognize which tool can effect which results. Crime, for example, is an urban problem that responds to all three tools. Design: public spaces can be organized to be easily monitored by people in the surrounding buildings, to eliminate hiding places for would-be attackers, and to exhibit a high standard of civic care through the use of beautiful and durable materials. Policy: zoning regulations can require buildings to have entries and windows facing public spaces, to populate those spaces and make them easy to supervise. Management: the neighborhood cop, on foot or on bicycle, can get to know neighborhood residents and visitors and develop a personal relationship with the adolescents of the neighborhood.

In this book we have explained a variety of design techniques that can either create or destroy community. Our town planning practice is based on the understanding of these techniques, but we have also come to understand that, alone, they are insufficient. Policy and management can work hand-in-hand with design to ensure results or, likewise, can conspire to make such results impossible.

For example: if trash is strewn about your street, the problem is not one of design but one of management. It is the responsibility of local government. If people are speeding down your street, however, that is more complicated. Most likely, people speed because the street is too wide. Street widths may be determined through local municipal standards, which may have been predetermined by a county or state standard, which in turn may have been pre-predetermined by a national labor union standard. In our attempts to reduce speeding in Dade County, we were repeatedly frustrated by a huge street-width standard based upon the maneuverability of fire trucks much larger than the county's low-rise neighborhoods required. When we asked the county why it didn't buy smaller fire engines for such neighborhoods, we were told that the firefighters' union requires a minimum number of firefighters per truck, regardless of truck size. Given this requirement, the fire chief had long ago determined that efficiency was best served by purchasing only the largest trucks. Through a circuitous chain of events, the desire of firefighters for job security resulted in speeding on neighborhood streets.

Very often, unsatisfying physical environments are the unintended result of such complex interactions, whose unraveling may be long and costly.* In such cases, we must remember that all three tools of design, policy, and management are at our disposal. As designers, we sometimes forget that the best way to make lasting change is often to identify and act upon the policies that make good design impossible to implement.

THE ROLE OF POLICY

From local zoning codes to federal automobile subsidies, there is a long list of regulatory forces that have proved destructive to communities in unexpected ways. Because government policy has played a major role in getting us where we are today, it can also help us to recover.

The following policy proposals demand a commitment to community at every level of government. The promotion of community may seem to be an obvious role for the public sector, especially at the local level; some would suggest that it is the public sector's primary responsibility. Yet it can become a sticky constitutional issue

---

* In our "highly evolved" regulatory system, this process is most often accomplished through expensive lawsuits, as documented in *The Death of Common Sense.* In light of this situation, a number of not-for-profit organizations have arisen over the years—the *National Resources Defense Council,* the *Environmental Defense Fund,* Ralph Nader's *Public Citizen*—capable of throwing legal firepower at otherwise unresolvable problems. As of yet, there is no such advocate for the built environment. But the sophisticated legal strategies that have succeeded in attacking air pollution and corporate negligence are also available to activists concerned similarly about their cities. Tough times call for tough measures, and activists should not shy away from using every means at their disposal in defense of their urban environment.

when brought face-to-face with the American ideology of rugged individualism. This is particularly true when it comes to property rights, people's ability to do whatever they want with their land.

In this regard, we must turn to the first question of political philosophy: Is it the role of government to promote individual rights while defending the common good, or to promote the common good while defending individual rights? To those of us who are concerned with creating and maintaining community, it seems obvious that our government has too long favored the former objective, and that it is time for a correction. Real estate developers, whom Americans entrust to build their communities, adhere to regulations set by government policy. If the public sector does not actively involve itself, with vision and power, private action cannot be anything but self-interested and chaotic.

This state of affairs may seem inevitable, but the first quarter of the twentieth century provides evidence of an alternative. The City Beautiful movement was a period of urban rebuilding and new-town construction in which civic pride, beauty, and community were a consensus agenda, promoted to an optimistic populace by wise leaders at both the local and federal levels. Of course, some things have changed since the enlightened building of that progressive era—the development of new transportation and communication technologies, enormous social flux, and the globalization of markets—but our governments would do well to acknowledge that these changes have only intensified the need for properly designed communities.

This is not merely an issue of aesthetics. Building strong neighborhoods and cities is a matter of social, economic, and environmental health that determines our quality of life and thereby

America's ability to compete in the global marketplace. When we visit countries that—in marked contrast to the United States—actually develop and maintain their cities with an eye to past successes and failures, we can't help but conclude that the United States will soon find itself at a competitive disadvantage to Europe. We watch in frustration as our governments refuse to play an active role in the construction of community, typically leaving that task to the ad hoc creators of tangible failures.*

For the growing number of public servants who share our frustration and hope to make a difference, we offer the following policy proposals. As should become clear, these proposals are not about increasing the size of government but about reforming its influence on the built environment. They are structured from the bottom up, from the local to federal level.

MUNICIPAL AND COUNTY GOVERNMENT

Put community design back on the agenda. Elected leaders who want to leave behind a place worth caring about must make design a part of their public agenda. People have trouble recognizing the pro-

---

* Only a brief explanation is necessary to demonstrate why the private sector alone cannot be trusted to make places of lasting value. Anyone with a fair amount of business training knows that corporations make investment decisions based upon their "cost of capital." Cost of capital, narrowly defined, is the interest rate at which money is borrowed, but it could be more accurately described as *the income that could be earned on a given amount of money were it invested elsewhere.* For most successful companies, this cost of capital is well over 10 percent, and in the high-risk field of real estate, it is often well over 20 percent. When contemplating an investment, businesses create cost-and-income spreadsheets in which all future earnings are discounted at this rate. A dollar earned next year is worth about ninety cents this year, since it could have been invested

found effect that our physical surroundings have on daily life. When the topic of physical planning does surface, it is usually in the form of bitter citizen outcry over something gone wrong or about to go wrong, almost always perceived to be perpetrated from above. Sprawl is a disease so chronic that people have grown accustomed to living with it, and they attack only the symptoms rather than the underlying condition.

That condition can be traced back to rules and regulations that are instituted with little understanding of their likely physical outcome. Words and numbers are printed on paper and enforced without any guidance from drawings or other visual models. No wonder the result is so often an unpleasant surprise. Drawings, unlike words and numbers, are something that people can relate to and judge. As quality of life becomes a national concern, design becomes increasingly useful as both a decision-making tool and a generator of value. In order to be effective—and discussed effectively—policy that impacts the physical environment must be preceded and justified by a specific physical vision.

Rewrite the regulations. If our communities are to recover from sprawl, they need both new regulations and a new regulatory environment. Existing zoning ordinances—typically outdated, over-

---

elsewhere at 10 percent. The effect that this technique has on long-term value is straightforward: at a 10 percent discount rate, a dollar earned ten years from now is worth only thirty-five cents today. A dollar earned twenty years from now is worth only twelve cents. When investing in a new building or public space, a wise developer knows that any income earned from that building after thirty years is essentially worthless. Therefore, a developer who invests extra money to create a long-lasting building is making a poor business decision, and, quite literally, hurting his colleagues and shareholders. Given these circumstances, it is utter nonsense to believe that we can entrust the making of community to forces that are, by definition, primarily interested in making money.

complicated, and vulnerable to influence peddling—are often discredited but rarely discarded. The flaws of these ordinances are too many to mention here, but can be gleaned through even cursory reading. Most need radical restructuring just to open the door for traditional development. New regulations, in addition to making traditional neighborhoods possible, must support the character of older places through the compatible filling in of existing neighborhoods. This is the opposite of what happens in most historic communities today, where modern building codes force new construction to take a form drastically distinct from that of its neighbors.[*]

These problems led us to write the *Traditional Neighborhood Development Ordinance,* an alternative zoning code based on the evident advantages of America's older cities, towns, and villages.[■] The TND Ordinance can replace existing land-use codes, or be instituted as an optional alternative. Obviously, the first path is the preferable one, but the second is more politically viable. The TND deals succinctly with the criteria essential to making authentic neighborhoods. The code is broken down into two sections: *Urban Infill,* which addresses existing neighborhoods, and *Greenfield*

---

[*] This situation typically brings down property values, for one of two reasons. Either the new construction sticks out like a sore thumb, creating an incoherent streetscape, or the construction creates a newness standard against which its older neighbors are judged inferior. Modern building codes are also destructive in that they often make renovating historic buildings prohibitively expensive, evidenced by the dozen still-vacant office towers above the Art Deco theaters of Los Angeles' Broadway. It is simply not affordable to reoccupy these buildings under existing ordinances. If they truly wish to encourage historic preservation, municipalities (and states) must enforce a less strenuous coding standard for older structures.

[■] The TND Ordinance was first developed in 1988 with the engineer Rick Chellman, of White Mountain Survey, Inc., for a project in Bedford, New Hampshire. Mr. Chellman has gone on to become the Institute of Traffic Engineers' leading authority on traditional neighborhood street design.

Development, which deals with the creation of new neighborhoods from scratch. In both cases, new growth is modeled on the old patterns that people cherish.

The TND is not the only instrument of its kind. Other groundbreaking zoning ordinances include Sacramento County's *Transit Oriented Development Ordinance,* Pasadena's *City of Gardens Code,* and Loudon County, Virginia's *Rural Village Ordinance.* Municipalities that are currently making use of customized TND-style ordinances include Miami–Dade County, Orlando, Columbus, Santa Fe, and Austin. These ordinances demonstrate the TND's adaptability to a wide range of local conditions.

With any luck, the TND Ordinance and others like it will exert a powerful influence over the shape of America's towns and cities in the near future. Much of the disappointing form of our communities can be attributed to the widespread dissemination of the pro-sprawl zoning codes of the 1960s. If the new ordinances are circulated in an equally effective fashion, there may yet be a day when sprawl is suppressed by traditional urbanism.

One warning: Experience suggests that it is a mistake to try to fix old zoning codes. Attempting to change a typical words-and-numbers ordinance into a physical-form-based ordinance through deletions and additions, chewing gum and baling wire, will result in a new ordinance that is even more confusing and difficult to implement than the old one.

In most municipalities, the best way to thoroughly upgrade a development code is to start from scratch, which is not in itself a difficult task. The problem lies not in creating a new ordinance but in throwing out the old one. Since zoning plays such a large role in determining the value of private property, any modification of the status quo may have profound economic consequences. Even a slight change in terminology can generate or obliterate millions of dollars in earnings for large-scale landowners, who typically have strong political connections and can stop change in its tracks. Worse yet, they'll sue, and win. Recent court judgments have decided in favor of developers demanding compensation for losses caused by changes in land-use regulations. For that reason, it is wisest to keep the old code intact, while offering the new code as a parallel alternative. It would be optional, but made attractive by an accelerated permitting process. The result, as discussed in Chapter 9, would be a regulatory environment in which projects based on neighborhood design principles are much easier, faster, and therefore cheaper to build than the conventional alternative. In the time-sensitive game of real estate, in which the interest clock is always ticking, such an approach could be extremely effective.

Make government proactive. The local planning department must be empowered and encouraged to propose development patterns *ahead* of the private sector. "You call this planning?" is a common cry of outrage as a new, seemingly random building project takes shape. This should come as no surprise. Most municipal planners are entirely *reactive* in their approach to development; often, their only role is to interpret the codes. Some will even argue that it's entirely up to the market to decide what gets built where. So much for planning! And even when the municipal staff exhibit an enthusiasm and aptitude for design, they rarely have the mandate to produce plans for urban change. Given these limitations, how can government encourage the development and improvement of cohesive neighborhoods? Probably the best solution is to commission a professional public plan and then provide incentives for its private implementation. This approach works well with the fast-track permitting technique described earlier.

The public sector should also take the lead in the planning and development of public-benefit facilities such as convention centers, sport stadiums, and arenas. When initiated by the private sector, these projects rarely benefit anyone but their big-business sponsors. One ideal model for such development is downtown Baltimore's Camden Yards baseball park, which was developed with government guidance, is accessible to all, and remains a source of civic pride. By way of contrast, Miami's suburban Pro Player Stadium was developed privately on a cheap site far from transit, intruding on an existing residential community. Although highway improvements were provided to help counter its remote location—funded, of course, by the taxpayers—Pro Player Stadium remains inaccessible to many sports fans and contributes nothing to the city's vitality.

Think globally, act locally, but plan regionally. Local municipalities must act with the understanding that the most meaningful planning occurs at the regional scale. This broad perspective stems less from a desire to help one's neighbors than from simple self-preservation—more than one community has seen its own planning efforts sabotaged by the actions of another town nearby. Circling the wagons by, say, closing streets may be a temporary solution, but if the problem is a regional traffic crisis, traffic will be relieved only until surrounding communities do the same. When making local planning decisions, a municipality must consider the impact of its initiatives on the entire region. And the community that wishes to truly determine its future will take the additional step of advocating for the creation of a regional planning authority.

True citizen participation: a public design workshop brings planning out into the open

Plan with public participation. Citizen participation in the planning process—a horrifying prospect to some administrators—has proved to be the most effective way to avoid mistakes. In San Francisco, Indianapolis, and many other cities, we have seen a participatory process revive civic responsibility and action. Residents of West Palm Beach are now actively involved, from volunteering in the workshops that created the city's new Master Plan, to monitoring the projects that must follow its guidelines. True participatory planning should not be confused with occasional orchestrated set pieces or legally mandated public hearings; rather, it should include community design workshops, citizen's advisory committees, constant media coverage, and an ongoing feedback process.

That said, it is painful but necessary to acknowledge that the public process does not guarantee the best results. In fact, on certain issues, such as transit, population density, affordable housing, and facilities for special-needs populations, the public process seems to produce the *wrong* results. Acting selfishly, neighbors will typically reject a Lulu (locally undesirable land use) even if its proposed location has been determined based on regional, social, or even ethical considerations. One might posit that it is precisely because there is no process for public participation at the regional scale that such projects are often successfully opposed by local residents.

In the absence of a truly representative public process, decision-makers must rely on something above and beyond process, something that may be called *principles*. Affordable housing must be fairly distributed. Homeless shelters must be provided in accessible locations. Transit must be allowed through. The environment must be protected. Many of these principles have been outlined in this book, and we hope that they will provide a foundation upon which to make difficult decisions on behalf of the public good.[*]

Practice what you preach. At every level of government, public servants can begin their battle against sprawl by reconsidering the location and design of their own office buildings. To set a good example, but also to avoid harming existing communities, governments must eschew the practices of past decades. Don't leave the city center for a workplace at the perimeter. Don't locate offices away from easy transit access. Don't abandon historic structures. Don't consolidate services in a single location when they could enliven a dozen main streets. Don't pull the building back behind a parking lot, or face blank walls to the sidewalk. From the post office to the Pentagon, every government building has the opportunity and the responsibility to make its neighborhood better.

REGIONAL GOVERNMENT

The greatest challenge to regional planning is the scarcity of regional government; few of our cities have governing authorities of a scope appropriate to the metropolis. To create such an agency can be difficult, as it should be built with resources distributed from

[*] Unfortunately, principles are often forgotten in the name of a democratic process. At a 1996 conference on the celebrated town planner John Nolan in Madison, we were handed a flyer describing that city's ongoing regional planning effort. Rather than explaining the proper solution to Madison's incipient sprawl, the flyer listed ten distinct approaches for addressing the crisis; all were presented as equally desirable, even though three of them were nothing but more sprawl. Unsurprisingly, the citizens who had initiated the planning process were furious, and the plan was failing, because it dodged the difficult decisions. Thanks to its public nature, planning is perhaps the only profession whose practitioners feel compelled to please everyone at once, no matter the cost.

existing governments to avoid increased taxation. Once a regional-scale agency is established, however, its mandate is clear. Those issues which can be handled effectively only at a regional level—transportation, environmental quality, water and waste management, social services, affordable housing, economic development, higher education, etc.—must be addressed comprehensively, so that individual cities and towns no longer have to struggle with them alone or, worse yet, in competition. Individual issues must be addressed in the context of a comprehensive Regional Plan, a plan based upon a clearly stated and well-publicized set of goals.

Regional planning efforts should not stop short of creating detailed physical plans for the development and redevelopment of neighborhoods, especially for areas near transit stations. Merely zoning for higher density in these locations is not enough to give confidence to early investors and cannot ensure the sort of pedestrian-friendly environment that supports transit. The most effective plans are drawn with such precision that only the architectural detail is left to future designers. These plans must be created through a public process in the presence of the residents and leaders of the surrounding communities.[*]

Contrary to current opinion, it is not un-American to engage in regional planning. American history is replete with examples of such work, the fruits of which we still enjoy today, such as the Appalachian Trail. Even the L'Enfant plan for Washington, D.C.—

---

[*] This is already beginning to happen. After a first generation of zoning increases intended to support transit station densification, which did little more than encourage real-estate speculation, a new cycle of transit-oriented redevelopment designs for these still-empty parcels—often initiated by local shareholders—appears to be heading toward success.

spanning fifty square miles and encompassing several existing towns and a good portion of the Potomac ecosystem—must be considered, by the scale of its time, a regional plan. Today, Portland, Seattle, San Diego, and other cities are engaged in regional planning efforts that enjoy public support and contribute to their growing popularity.

Those concerned about the future of their urban region will work to establish metropolitan planning agencies, even if only for economic reasons. As work—especially well-paid work—becomes increasingly independent of place, those cities which lack a healthy regional organization will gradually lose their most productive residents to places that offer shorter commutes, cleaner air, and easier access to both nature and culture.

STATE GOVERNMENT

Owing to the scarcity of regional governments, cities typically rely upon state governments for leadership on regional issues. Therefore, state lawmakers must attempt to enact legislation that effectively accomplishes regional planning. This may be done in two ways: either through new growth management laws, or through the modification of existing laws and funding vehicles.* Maryland recently committed itself to a smart-growth agenda, to be accomplished through the careful allocation of infrastructure financing.

---

* Indeed, new laws that are apparently unrelated to sprawl can also be used to encourage healthy growth. For example, any program that offers state (or federal) funding to local municipalities can tie that funding to smart-growth criteria. This would mirror President Johnson's use of Medicare as a tool to desegregate Southern hospitals, by denying Medicare dollars to whites-only facilities.

Florida and New Jersey, in turn, have enacted top-down growth management legislation. Georgia, Vermont, Maine, Oregon, and Washington are also fighting sprawl, through a variety of less direct measures.

New Jersey's visionary law establishes a clear ideal for the full range of models, from rural conservation to urban redevelopment. If there is a flaw, it is the absence of a strong compliance review process. Such a process is the strength of Florida's growth management laws, which, conversely, lack the clear vision of New Jersey's. Over time, the success or failure of these pioneer states in fighting sprawl will show other states which model is worth emulating. The most promising solution may be New Jersey's recently initiated "tough love" incentive program, in which cities and towns must practice smart growth in order to receive state funding for infrastructure and education. The success of such a program depends on sustained leadership from a strong governor, as every state agency must participate in a coordinated way.

States that truly hope to control sprawl must also combine regional planning and transportation planning into a single activity. Most existing Metropolitan Planning Organizations are misnamed, as they deal only with transportation plans. State departments of transportation (D.O.T.s) are more often than not a part of the problem, as they largely ignore the interrelationship between transportation systems and land-use patterns. State transportation planners, intending to reduce traffic congestion, routinely commission the new roadways that further disperse the population and only make traffic worse. By mistaking *mobility* for *accessibility,* they undermine the viability of both new and old places by focusing entirely on moving cars through them. The result—already well documented—is a landscape lacking in destinations worth getting to. Florida has begun to address this phenomenon by refusing to fund the construction of new highways containing more than three non-car-pool lanes in either direction. As a result, in congested cities such as Miami, some transportation funds are now flowing to public transit.

If they wish to play a role in the creation of healthy communities, state D.O.T.s must come to view transportation policy as an integral component of a regional land use plan, not just as an autonomous problem with a financial solution. They might learn to assess their effectiveness by how little money they need to spend, rather than by how many federal highway dollars they can grab. Unlike education and policing, fields in which more funding may produce better results, increased highway funding consistently makes traffic worse. Additional funds for public transit, however, not only alleviate the traffic problem but also create jobs at an astounding rate, as shown in Chapter 5. But even embracing transit—as more states are beginning to do—is insufficient without a comprehensive plan for high-density pedestrian-oriented development at rail stations. In this regard, Portland and San Diego are implementing state-assisted programs that deserve to become models for the nation.

Of course, if state transportation departments cannot be reformed, they can be overruled. This is the proposal of Georgia's Governor Roy Barnes, whose Regional Transportation Authority would have power over the Georgia D.O.T. Apparently, he gave up on G.D.O.T. after it failed to bring Atlanta into compliance with the Federal Clean Air Act, a failure that may have lost the state millions in federal funding. The most significant undertaking of the new authority is expected to be the planning of a new light rail line for Atlanta's northern suburbs.[1]

State governments are also active in the funding of affordable housing, which is most often provided with little concern for the greater goal of creating viable communities. Tax credit programs, in their well-intentioned effort to protect public moneys, enforce criteria that are antithetical to the creation of neighborhoods. Following the old highway engineering adage of "fast, safe, and cheap"—which betrays a preference for efficient production over the needs of the user—the resulting housing is isolated on large tracts far from shopping, schools, and transit, and bunched together by the hundreds according to generic plans. This formula contradicts all that is known about creating successful communities, and further burdens poor families with multiple car ownership.

Correcting troubled "projects" must take precedence over the creation of new ones, with investment directed to infill housing in existing neighborhoods. Affordable housing must be provided in a form and a place that allow for affordable living, even if it comes at greater cost. Although land may be cheaper on the urban fringe, that location fails to provide residents with easy access to jobs and services. Similarly, the cheaper cookie-cutter housing designs often make infill development impossible, because they don't fit in with their neighbors. And the financial mandate to provide cheap housing in gigantic increments creates ghettoes of concentrated poverty.

State law also establishes rules for local property taxes, which often determine what the private sector does with its real estate. The higher tax assessments that follow rezoning and precede rebuilding often displace long-time residents, encourage speculation by absentee landlords, and lead to the destruction of historic buildings. Recognizing this problem, some states have passed laws allowing cities and towns to allocate tax credits or abatements for historic properties. Other states are permitting municipalities to tax land at a higher rate than buildings—"site-value taxation"—to discourage demolitions and land speculation, and to encourage construction where it might ordinarily occur last.

Finally, states set school policy and therefore must acknowledge that educational goals, busing costs, and community design principles all support the same conclusion: smaller schools are better. Recommendations for larger facilities almost always result from a shortsighted focus on administrative efficiency. Moreover, many states require unjustifiably oversized building sites, and as a result schools become neighborhood separators rather than community centers.[•] At their worst, these requirements even impose dispersed suburban layouts in dense urban areas, effectively preventing new city school construction. These rules must be changed. In addition, new real estate developments should be required to include neighborhood-based schools that children can walk to. Similarly, any new citywide magnet schools should be located at public transit hubs to be accessible to all.

In sum: the federal government is distant, local government is myopic, and regional government is lacking. In this context, state government is best able to promote regional planning. Whether it is purchasing land for conservation, mandating urban boundaries, or restricting low-density development, state leadership is needed to foster awareness and to sponsor smart growth.

[•] The overly large school sites often result from requirements for one-story buildings, voluminous parking, future portable-classroom additions, and redundant playing fields. As schools follow this pattern they become Lulus (locally undesirable land uses), requiring distant siting and generating heavy traffic.

What has been most needed at the federal level is the admission that we have a problem. Happily, after ten years of media coverage of the ills of sprawl—*Newsweek* covers, *Nightline* episodes, well-publicized local stories—the topic is finally of national political interest. In 1999, for the first time in history, an American president and vice president took a swing at sprawl. One hopes that this does not turn it into a partisan issue, since advocates for smart growth have thus far spanned the political spectrum.

There is an urgent need for national policy on community design. It must be on the public agenda, alongside crime reduction, health care, and family preservation. It is in the nation's interest to grow healthily, if for no other reason than to maintain its competitive advantage in the global marketplace. Just as it regulates aviation and broadcasting on behalf of its citizens, the federal government should advocate smart growth.

The necessary initiatives are now obvious. The best strategy, in the simplest terms, would be the systematic reversal of those policies which decanted America's cities into their suburbs after World War II. To begin with, our government's dedication to subsidizing automotive transportation should be balanced by increased support for public transit. The gasoline tax, whatever its size, should aim to benefit transit as much as highways. After all, if we tax cigarettes to pay for anti-smoking ads, we can certainly tax gasoline to pay for trolleys.* Then, to create transit systems that actually work, federal

---

* Of the current gasoline tax, 15 percent does go to transit, but 85 percent still goes to highways (*Tea-21 User's Guide,* 7). The comparison to smoking is not as farfetched as it seems, since the number of "excess deaths" from breathing air pollution in the United

funding criteria should regulate the urban design within a half-mile radius of all new stations.

Tax and mortgage policies must be revamped to encourage renovation as much as new construction. Federal incentives to convince developers to do business downtown are necessary but not sufficient. They must be supplemented by programs that remove the disincentives embedded in current industry regulations, such as redlining nonconforming uses and structures built according to earlier codes. Such disincentives often prevent smaller businesses from investing in existing communities, and they require specific attention, as they have become institutionalized into lending and insurance underwriting practices. The Community Reinvestment Act, which requires banks to invest in neighborhood renovation, is working and must be renewed and strengthened. Those federal programs that target neighborhoods, such as *Enterprise Zones* and *Empowerment Zones,* must be assessed and improved. Rather than perpetually introducing new (i.e., untested) ideas for dramatic political impact, successive administrations should simply extend effective programs and improve partially successful efforts.

Congress must also establish a mandate for balanced resources among school systems, similar to the federal mandate for transregional air quality. In the final analysis, this is perhaps the critical component of any plan for making urban areas attractive to families of all incomes. For young parents, the single most important factor in choosing a new home is usually its school district, and the inner city can never truly compete without competitive schools.

States is between 50,000 and 125,000 annually, and each gallon of gas pumps 5.5 pounds of carbon into the atmosphere (Andrew Kimbrell, "Steering Toward Ecological Disaster," 35; and Bill McKibben, *The End of Nature,* 6).

For the federal Department of Transportation, the mandate is clear. If we truly want to curtail sprawl, we must acknowledge that automotive mobility is a no-win game, and that the only long-term solutions to traffic are public transit and coordinated land use. Given the well-documented case of Atlanta, where road construction did nothing but lengthen commuting times, every inch of proposed pavement must be scrutinized to determine its likely contribution to sprawl.[*]

Finally, a federal initiative is needed to better coordinate those policies which now govern the apparently distinct objectives of affordable housing provision, business assistance, job creation, and social services. To be effective, these policies must be focused together at *specific places,* initiated nationally but customized locally. Each of these programs addresses only one aspect of community life, so they must be approached and applied as a group. HUD's new initiatives emphasizing community design, not just housing construction, are a step in the right direction.

These policy recommendations, at every level, are focused upon generating public-sector support for private-sector initiatives in the building and rebuilding of communities. After decades of govern-

---

[*] The D.O.T. must also reconsider its current approach to funding transit, in which it contributes little to the operation of the new systems it helps to build. Trains and trolleys are quite distinct from highways, in that they require drivers, administrators, and constant tuning and replacement. For many cities, receiving a new transit system without an operating budget is like receiving a Christmas toy without its batteries. This situation can be especially problematic, as local citizens will often vote down funding for the only form of transportation that serves the non-voting poor. Since shortsighted decisions are easy to make at the local level, it is in the federal government's best interest to provide dedicated funding sources for the operation of transit, much as it does for the FAA.

ment policies that seem to have been dedicated to the building business rather than to building communities, we have much to change. While there are encouraging trends in the real estate industry, government policy must be overhauled if we are to see lasting results. This is not about more government, but about smarter government: to the degree that government policies influence the market, this influence must consciously support community, not inadvertently destroy it.

ARCHITECTS

Many different professions contribute to the making of sprawl, and they all need to change. We have not shied away from criticizing the planners, traffic engineers, and land-use attorneys, and greater scrutiny needs to be applied by those practitioners to their own work. As architects, we are best qualified to discuss the negative contributions of our own profession. This may come as a surprise, since it has not been the habit of architects to air their dirty laundry.

The previous chapters have already laid out in detail the specific techniques that architects may use to counter sprawl. But there is a larger lesson to impart, which is that architects can truly make a difference. In this case, making a difference requires architects to accept a proposal that may run counter to their schooling: *design affects behavior.*

Disputing this truism may seem silly, yet for some reason it is still a topic of heated debate at architecture schools. The persistence of this non-issue is probably due to the way it gets confused with another, more esoteric inquiry, which is whether the design of the environment exerts any influence on human nature itself. While it is easy to have strong feelings about that question as well, there is no need to answer it; human nature is not at issue here, but simply whether people behave differently in different physical surroundings. For us, that question is as obvious as asking whether locking a door keeps someone out of a room, or whether creating an environment in which nothing is nearby causes people to drive. One does not have to believe that front porches encourage sociability to accept that unwalkable streets discourage it.*

This state of affairs has a complex and lamentable history. It developed in response to the arrogance of modernism, an ethos that believed unquestioningly in the beneficial power of design. Inspired by the unrealized utopias of the Enlightenment, early-modern architects were convinced that they possessed the means for solving society's problems. By applying theories from the incipient quasi-sciences of psychology and sociology, architects invented new forms of buildings and cities that they believed would transform their inhabitants into the most benevolent of creatures. These forms were actually built in places such as Pruitt Igoe and Cabrini Green,

---

* The nonsensical argument that "design can't affect behavior" is so persistent that one must always be armed with evidence to the contrary. A recent article in *The Wall Street Journal* was particularly compelling. It described the old town of Rhineland, Missouri, which was relocated to a bluff one mile away to escape the flooding Missouri River. All but one of 160 residents moved their houses up the hill, but they were rearranged into a suburban configuration of six curving roads without sidewalks. More significantly, the town's post office, daycare center, and tavern stayed in the valley. Now "the residents of Rhineland seem to have lost their sense of community. In the six years since the floods, the town hasn't had another August block party. Few residents stroll the streets; most prefer now to drive around town. And neighbors who used to while away the afternoons at the local tavern don't speak quite as often anymore." As one resident reported, "We used to go over and talk to our neighbors. You don't see that now . . . We were just closer down there" (Jeanne Cummings, "Swept Away: How Rhineland, Mo., Saved Itself But Lost a Sense of Community," A1, A8).

with disastrous results: entire projects were subsequently abandoned and demolished, as they continue to be. The antisocial behavior that immediately developed in these places was far from what had been predicted.

These failures were fresh in the minds of our professors when we arrived at architecture school. The lesson was clearly stated by the sociologist Nathan Glazer: "We must root out of thinking the assumption that the physical form of our communities has social consequence."[2] With that single statement, architects were absolved of all responsibility to society. The profession retreated into itself, and we were encouraged to avoid social issues and address only topics that were strictly architectural and largely self-referential. Thus began the pursuit of *form for its own sake* that continues today.

What is now clear is that our generation learned the wrong lesson from the failure of modernism. The abysmal performance of the social housing projects of the fifties and sixties, rather than confirming the independence of design and behavior, proved just the opposite: if one builds cities based upon the untested theories of flawed science, they are likely to fail. Good design may not generate good behavior, but bad design can generate bad behavior.•

The real lesson is that the design of new places should be modeled on old places that work. Invention is welcome, but must be laid

The wrong lesson learned: failed modernist housing schemes taught architects to stop trying to solve society's problems

---

• Viable albeit poor neighborhoods were demolished and their inhabitants conscripted into these experiments, which went bad almost immediately. Any number of additional factors can also be held responsible for the crime and violence of these projects—including concentrated poverty, poor administration, and inadequate policing—and it is not clear that these places, if traditionally designed, would have been successful. But few people now doubt that design played a significant role in their demise. Similarly, few people are surprised that Ray Gindroz's traditionally organized low-income projects dramatically reduce crime.

upon the solid foundation of precedent, as it is in medicine and jurisprudence.[*] While this approach may be less entertaining than inventing a new building style every Monday morning—and thus far less popular in the architecture schools—it affords the designer a degree of expertise and authority that is lacking in the profession today.

Architects who accept the challenge of being not just inventors but experts will find ample opportunity to confront suburban sprawl. It is common knowledge which types of buildings constitute sprawl, just as it is understood which buildings create a pleasant, pedestrian-scale environment. How to turn the former into the latter, in a way that developers can live with, is also becoming better known. For architects who wish to become a part of the solution, the task is clear.

CITIZENS

Citizens can begin by understanding how much their environment affects—or, in fact, generates—their quality of life. Once this relationship is recognized, it becomes obvious how we can best serve our own needs by improving our physical surroundings. In an

---

[*] The intentional ignorance and dismissal of precedent that dominates many architecture schools is an inevitable outgrowth of the modern image of the architect as heroic genius. First codified in Ayn Rand's *The Fountainhead,* this image encourages young architects to think of each new commission as an opportunity to stand out rather than to fit in, and thus works strongly against the creation of physically coherent communities. This frenzy of self-glorification is further encouraged by an architectural fashion press that promotes novelty at the expense of urban performance, such that architects design their buildings less for their surrounding neighborhoods than for the cover of *Architecture* magazine.

increasingly diverse nation, in which our social, intellectual, and spiritual realities can be as varied as our genealogy, the physical world is the one thing that we truly share. All the more important, then, that we work on it together.

Indeed, concern over one's surroundings has the potential to create community among the most diverse populations. An urban or suburban neighborhood may be home to people of many backgrounds, but all share the same concern for the health and safety of their families and for their quality of life. Even if a neighborhood improvement effort fails at first, that effort can create the relationships that make future success more likely.

Among other things, this book is an appeal to the "armchair architect" to become an armchair urbanist. Armchair architects rarely have the opportunity to put their knowledge and energy to work. Since most buildings are designed without public participation, the mere citizen—unless wealthy enough to initiate private projects—is confined to the role of critic. The most influence an armchair architect can exert on a building is to block it.

In contrast, the armchair urbanist has a new opportunity every day to make a constructive contribution to the creation and improvement of the public realm. Thanks to several decades of activism, more and more urban-scale projects are being developed with the active participation of citizens in the design process. Their common sense is a necessary foil against the technical expertise of the specialists.

Furthermore, every citizen can initiate the improvement of the physical environment. Whether it be raising awareness of design issues at the grass-roots level, convincing local government of the need for a master plan or TND Ordinance to stop sprawl, or promoting a main street revitalization effort, private individuals have abundant opportunity to positively influence their surroundings. Many successful neighborhood improvement efforts can trace their origins back to the kitchen table of a concerned citizen.

Finally, armchair urbanists can begin to undermine the hegemony of sprawl simply by spreading the word. As this book should make clear, there are too many misconceptions about the American suburb. Most of us are not in the habit of thinking critically about our environment, or about how its form can dramatically affect the quality of our lives. Just raising the topic is a valuable start. Indeed, it is the only start. None of the government reforms discussed above will even be initiated without voters clamoring for change.

With empowerment comes responsibility. Now that citizens have earned a position in the planning process, it is their duty to become experts in good design, and to demand the same from those in charge. In this regard, it is worth repeating the five truths most often misconstrued by citizens and government alike:

- Growth cannot be stopped; it never has been. The only hope is to shape it into a more benevolent form, the neighborhood.
- The profit motive is not the problem with development. The best neighborhoods in America were built for profit.
- Most issues are interrelated. Traffic, housing, schools, crime, and the environment can be successfully addressed only if taken together, within the context of the neighborhood.
- Planners and other professionals are specialists who, when left to themselves, distort the issues. Only generalists can be trusted to offer reasonable advice.

- The role of the generalist must be played by citizens, but citizens can forfeit that role by becoming the specialists of their own backyard. A Nimby is nothing but a specialist who lacks formal training.

This book attempts to create expert generalists, and we hope that it will help its readers participate in a positive way. However, we admit that the issues at stake are quite complex, and that the path of reason may not always be clear. In such situations, it may be best to simply remember this refrain:

> No more housing subdivisions!
> No more shopping centers!
> No more office parks!
> No more highways!
> Neighborhoods or nothing!

Of course, the ultimate goal must not be limited to the cessation of sprawl. For our country to prosper, Americans must also concern themselves with the building of community. The immediate challenge, however, is not to convince people to support community but to confirm what they already know in their hearts: community flourishes best in traditional neighborhoods. When this fact is widely acknowledged, government officials, designers, and citizens will begin to act with the confidence that what is good for neighborhoods is good for America. Then, the work of rebuilding can begin.

APPENDIX A
THE TRADITIONAL NEIGHBORHOOD
DEVELOPMENT CHECKLIST

———

This book describes the qualities that distinguish Traditional Neighborhood Development from suburban sprawl. While some of these distinctions are either too subtle or too complicated to be easily summarized, the following checklist represents an attempt to distill the book's arguments into a brief, easy-to-use document.

This list was compiled with a particular type of project in mind: the development of a new town, neighborhood, or village of twenty-five acres or more. Many of its criteria apply both to smaller projects and to inner-city rehabilitation, but not all. For example, the mixture of housing types—from apartments to mansions—is appropriate for a new suburban development, but perhaps not for a downtown site surrounded by high-rises. The list would need to be significantly modified for inner-city use.

This checklist can serve different groups in different ways. It allows developers to review their current plans to determine whether they can expect to realize the market premium that has been demonstrated to accrue to TNDs. It enables planning officials to determine whether submitted plans are likely to provide the social benefits associated with TNDs, in order that they may qualify for incentives such as automatic permitting or increased density allocation. Of course, municipalities that truly wish to implement the policies represented by this list should take the additional step of legislating a Traditional Neighborhood Development Ordinance, as described in Chapter 11.

There are always exceptions, but the majority of Traditional Neighborhood Developments correspond to the majority of the rules that follow. All these principles have a significant impact on the quality of a development, but those marked with an asterisk (*) are essential and nonnegotiable.

THE REGIONAL CONTEXT

__ Is the TND location consistent with a comprehensive regional plan that preserves open space and encourages public transit?*

__ Is the TND connected in as many locations as possible to adjacent developments and thoroughfares?*

__ Do highways approaching the TND either pass to its side or take on low-speed (25 mph maximum) geometries when entering the neighborhood proper?*

__ Does the TND provide a relatively balanced mix of housing, workplace, shopping, recreational, and institutional uses?*

THE SITE CONTEXT

__ Are lakes, ponds, wetlands, and other natural resources retained and celebrated?*

__ Are significant natural amenities at least partially fronted by thoroughfares or public tracts rather than privatized behind backyards?*

__ Is the site developed in such a way as to maximize the preservation of high-quality trees and significant groups of trees?*

___ Does the plan locate neighborhood centers and sub-centers such as squares, greens, and parks at significant tree-save areas and other natural amenities?*

___ Does the plan accommodate itself to the site topography to minimize the amount of grading necessary to achieve a viable street network?*

___ Are significant hilltops celebrated with public tracts and/or civic buildings, and are mountaintops and major ridges kept clear of private development?

THE PLAN STRUCTURE

Is the plan divided into neighborhoods, where each neighborhood has the following characteristics:

___ Is it roughly a five-minute walk—a quarter mile—from edge to center? (Centers can be peripherally located in response to a site condition, such as a beach, major thoroughfare, or railroad station.)*

___ Does housing density increase from the edge to the center?*

___ Is the neighborhood center the location of retail space—a corner store is required (subsidized if necessary)—and office space, ideally located in mixed-use buildings?*

___ Is there a dry, dignified place to wait for transit at the neighborhood center?*

___ Is there a civic space such as a plaza or green at the neighborhood center?*

___ Does the neighborhood reserve at least one prominent, honorific site for a civic building?*

— Are there small parks distributed evenly through the neighborhood, roughly within one-eighth mile of every dwelling?*

— Are elementary schools and recreational facilities located within one mile of most dwellings, sized accordingly, and easily accessible on foot?*

— Are lots zoned not by use but by compatibility of building type?*

— Do most zoning changes in allowable building type occur at mid-block rather than mid-street?

— Is the neighborhood edge bordered by either a natural corridor or the edge of an adjacent neighborhood across a pedestrian-friendly boulevard?

— Are any large areas of open space between neighborhoods connected into continuous natural corridors?

— Do all public tracts within the neighborhood correspond to well-understood open-space types, such as park, green, square, or plaza?

THE THOROUGHFARE NETWORK

— Are streets organized in a comprehensible hierarchical network that manifests the structure of the neighborhood?*

— Do blocks average less than 600 feet in length and less than 1,800 feet in perimeter?*

— Are all streets fronted by public or private property, rather than serving as collector roads with no purpose other than handling traffic?*

— Are cul-de-sacs avoided when natural conditions do not demand them?*

___ Are unconventional roadway geometries provided to calm traffic, such as forks, triangles, and staggered intersections?

___ Are most street vistas terminated by a carefully sited building, a public tract, a view of a natural feature, or a curve in the street?

___ Do most streets that curve maintain roughly the same cardinal orientation (except where steep grades dictate otherwise)?

THE STREETSCAPE

___ Is there a hierarchy of streets,* including:

   ___ Main street, approximately 34 feet wide, with marked parking on both sides;

   ___ Through streets, approximately 27 feet wide, with marked parking on one side;

   ___ Standard streets, approximately 24 feet wide, with unmarked parking allowed to stagger from side to side;

   ___ Local streets, medium density, approximately 26 feet wide, with unmarked parking on both sides;

   ___ Local streets, low density, approximately 20 feet wide, with unmarked parking on one side;

   ___ Commercial rear alleys, approximately 24 feet wide within a 24-foot right-of-way;

   ___ Rear lanes, approximately 12 feet wide within a 24-foot right-of-way?

___ Do all streets other than alleys and lanes have a sidewalk on at least one side, 4 to 5 feet in width?* (Exceptions are granted in extremely rural or low-traffic conditions.)

___ Does every street include, between the roadbed and the sidewalk, a tree strip 4 to 10 feet in width, of indigenous shade trees planted approximately 30 feet apart, 10-foot minimum height at planting (located in grated sidewalk planters on commercial streets)?*

___ Are curb radiuses at intersections a maximum of 15 feet, with a typical measurement of 10 feet at local intersections?*

___ Are all parking lots located at the center of enlarged blocks, such that only their access is visible from adjacent streets?*

___ Are all parking lot aisles separated by a tree strip approximately 5 feet in width, planted with indigenous shade trees approximately 30 feet apart, 10-foot minimum height at planting?

___ Are all unsightly transformers, lift stations, utility meters, HVAC equipment, and other machinery located not in the front streetscape but at the rear lane or alley?

___ For neighborhoods that are located adjacent to nature, does the streetscape become more rural as it approaches the edge of the neighborhood, with curbs becoming open swales and trees becoming more informal in their placement?

THE BUILDINGS

___ Is there a diversity of housing types located within close proximity to each other?* Ideally, there should be a 5 percent minimum representation of at least five of the following eight categories:

   ___ Apartments above commercial space;

   ___ Multifamily apartment buildings;

- __ Two- and three-family houses;
- __ Row houses;
- __ Live/work row houses;
- __ Bungalows and patio houses on small lots (30–40 feet wide);
- __ Houses on standard lots (40–70 feet wide);
- __ Houses on large lots (over 70 feet wide).

__ Is each house lot permitted to contain a small ancillary dwelling unit in the rear yard, such as an apartment over the garage?*

__ Is subsidized housing provided in an increment of approximately one subsidized unit per ten market-rate units?

__ Is subsidized housing architecturally indistinguishable from market-rate housing?*

__ Are residential buildings placed relatively close to the street, such that they are generally set back the equivalent of one-quarter the width of the lot?

__ Do the front setbacks permit the encroachment of semipublic attachments, such as stoops, porches, bay windows, and balconies?*

__ Do most lots smaller than 50 feet wide (and apartment house lots) access their parking via a rear lane (or alley), with front driveways prohibited?*

__ Are all garages that are served from the street front set back a minimum of 20 feet from the front of the house, or rotated so that the garage doors do not face adjacent streets?*

__ Do all houses served by alleys have a 3-to-6-foot-tall privacy fence, wall, or shrubs on their rear property line?*

__ Do all row houses have 5-to-7-foot-tall privacy walls or fences on shared side property lines?*

___ Do all commercial buildings directly front the sidewalk, with all parking lots located behind the buildings?*

___ Are buildings permitted to satisfy their parking requirements with spaces located both off-street and on-street within one eighth of a mile of the building itself?

___ Do all commercial buildings with parking at the rear have shopping entrances only at the front?

___ Does the transition from mid-block parking to main-street shopping take place in a pleasant pedestrian passage lined with shop windows?

___ Do all commercial buildings have a second story (or more) for other uses?

___ Are all residential buildings other than bungalows and patio homes at least two stories tall?*

___ Does each house on a corner lot have its front door facing the larger street, the exceptions being end-unit row houses, which must always turn the corner, and houses against high-speed roadways?

___ Do buildings have relatively flat fronts and simple roofs, with most wings and plan articulations set at the rear?

APPENDIX B
THE CONGRESS FOR
THE NEW URBANISM

—

Advocates for a return to traditional urbanism seem to defy political classification. While academics call the neighborhood model reactionary and homebuilders call it radical, the new neighborhoods movement has been profiled enthusiastically in publications ranging from *The American Enterprise* to *The Utne Reader*. Of course, making news and causing change are two entirely different things, especially in today's media-saturated culture.

One encouraging development in the attempt to effect change has been the founding of the Congress for the New Urbanism, an international organization dedicated to the replacement of sprawl with a neighborhood-based alternative. First organized in 1994, the CNU was modeled on CIAM (*Congrès Internationaux d'Architecture Moderne*), the celebrated series of conferences first convened in 1928 which, for better or worse, had a profound effect on the shape of the world's cities.* The CNU was founded by a coalition of architects, urban designers, planners, engineers, journalists, attorneys, public servants, and concerned citizens who have all been

---

* It is fair to say that CIAM, more than any other single organization, can be credited or blamed for the shape of the modern city. While CIAM writings loosely promoted the concept of the neighborhood, it was the drawings and early buildings produced by its members that had the greatest long-term influence. As one regards the cruciform towers of New York's Co-op City or the automotive urbanism of Tyson's Corner, Virginia, one cannot help but think of Le Corbusier's landscape of freestanding buildings isolated in open space and connected by high-speed motorways.

working independently toward the same goals for many years. Like CIAM, the CNU was first intended to be dissolved at the completion of its Charter—signed in 1996 at the Fourth Congress by 300 attendees, including HUD Secretary Henry Cisneros. But conferences have continued on an annual basis owing to both an ongoing interest in the material and a shared sense that much work remains to be done. Congress VII, in Milwaukee, was attended by over one thousand members.

The stated principles of the Congress for the New Urbanism are straightforward: In order to promote community, the built environment must be diverse in use and population, scaled for the pedestrian, and capable of supporting mass transit as well as the automobile. It must have a well-defined public realm supported by buildings reflecting the architecture and ecology of the region. These principles are further described in the CNU Charter, included below.

The New Urbanism goes by many names, but the Congress chose this one for its political neutrality, and for the accuracy with which it conveys an enthusiasm for urban form. It is also favored among architects and academics, who tend to love the city, warts and all. However, this name is a bit of a hurdle for many others, from developers and homebuilders to journalists and citizens, for whom the word *urban* carries a stigma of poverty and crime. This is a pity and an embarrassment, but in order to make the concept palatable to home buyers, some planners have also come to identify it as Neotraditionalism. This term leaves much to be desired when it comes to progressiveness and political correctness—and it in turn has alienated a number of architects and academics—but in some ways it is even more accurate in communicating the nature of the work.

The term *neotraditional* was coined by the Stanford Research Institute to describe the ethos of the baby-boom generation, the generation that is expected to be culturally dominant until the year 2030. Its foremost characteristic is that it is nonideological to its core, which sets it apart from both traditionalism and modernism. Ideologies are easy to spot, as the behaviors that they spawn defy common sense. Traditionalists like to live in old-fashioned houses, but they don't stop there. The front porch light is fed by gas, and the bathroom contains a claw-footed tub encircled by a flimsy curtain that sticks to your body when you take a shower. Modernists—our parents' generation—live in houses without attics or basements, and own silverware which is so beautifully streamlined that it hardly picks up food. These are people who are prepared to suffer for their beliefs.

Neotraditionalists, in contrast, happily pick and choose whatever works and looks best. The image that Stanford Research provided as epitomizing neotraditionalism was a black Braun alarm clock sitting on a white Victorian mantelpiece. One obvious neotraditional product is the Mazda Miata, a car that looks, sounds, and handles like a British roadster but maintains the rate-of-repair record of a Honda Civic. The typical neotraditional house, which populates many New Urban neighborhoods, has an airy, free-flowing interior enclosed within a colonial shell.

Neotraditionalism is an apt term to describe the New Urbanism, because the New Urbanism's intention is to advocate what works best: what pattern of development is the most environmentally sensitive, socially responsible, and economically sustainable. As is often the case, what seems to work best is a historic model—the traditional neighborhood—adapted as necessary to serve the needs of modern man.

The commonsense nature of the New Urbanism bodes well for its future. The fact that it was not invented, but selected and adapted from existing models, dramatically distinguishes it from the concepts of total replacement that preceded it. It took many years and many failures for planners and architects to reach this point, but so many new inventions have fared so badly that designers have been forced to put some faith in human experience. Further experience will no doubt modify the precepts and techniques of the New Urbanism, but that is as it should be.

THE CHARTER OF THE NEW URBANISM

INTRODUCTION

The Congress for the New Urbanism views divestment in central cities, the spread of placeless sprawl, increasing separation by race and income, environmental deterioration, loss of agricultural lands and wilderness, and the erosion of society's built heritage as one interrelated community-building challenge.

We stand for the restoration of existing urban centers and towns within coherent metropolitan regions, the reconfiguration of sprawling suburbs into communities of real neighborhoods and diverse districts, the conservation of natural environments, and the preservation of our built legacy. We recognize that physical solutions by themselves will not solve social and economic problems, but neither can economic vitality, community stability, and environmental health be sustained without a coherent and supportive physical framework.

We advocate the restructuring of public policy and development practice to support the following principles: neighborhoods should be diverse in use and population; communities should be designed for the pedestrian and transit as well as the car; cities and towns should be shaped by physically defined and universally accessible public spaces and community institutions; urban places should be framed by architecture and landscape design that celebrate local history, climate, ecology, and building practice.

We represent a broad-based citizenry, composed of public and private sector leaders, community activists, and multidisciplinary professionals. We are committed to reestablishing the relationship between the art of building and the making of community, through citizen-based participatory planning and design.

We dedicate ourselves to reclaiming our homes, blocks, streets, parks, neighborhoods, districts, towns, cities, region and environment.

We assert the following principles to guide public policy, development, practice, urban planning, and design:

The Region: The Metropolis, the City, and the Town

1. Metropolitan regions are finite places with geographic boundaries derived from topography, watersheds, coastlines, farmlands, regional parks, and river basins. The metropolis is made of multiple centers that are cities, towns, and villages, each with its own identifiable center and edges.

2. The metropolitan region is a fundamental economic unit of the contemporary world. Governmental cooperation, public policy, physical planning, and economic strategies must reflect this new reality.

3. The metropolis has a necessary and fragile relationship to its agrarian hinterland and natural landscapes. The relationship is environmental, economic, and cultural. Farmland and nature are as important to the metropolis as the garden is to the house.

4. Development patterns should nor blur or eradicate the edges of the metropolis. Infill development within existing urban areas conserves environmental resources, economic investment, and social fabric, while reclaiming marginal and abandoned areas. Metropolitan regions should develop strategies to encourage such infill development over peripheral expansion.

5. Where appropriate, new development contiguous to urban boundaries should be organized as neighborhoods and districts, and be integrated with the existing urban pattern. Noncontiguous development should be organized as towns and villages with their own urban edges, and planned for a jobs/housing balance, not as bedroom suburbs.

6. The development and redevelopment of towns and cities should respect historical patterns, precedents, and boundaries.

7. Cities and towns should bring into proximity a broad spectrum of public and private uses to support a regional economy that benefits people of all incomes. Affordable housing should be distributed throughout the region to match job opportunities and to avoid concentrations of poverty.

8. The physical organization of the region should be supported by a framework of transportation alternatives. Transit, pedestrian, and bicycle systems should maximize access and mobility throughout the region while reducing dependence upon the automobile.

9. Revenues and resources can be shared more cooperatively among the municipalities and centers within regions to avoid destructive competition for tax base and to promote rational coordination of transportation, recreation, public services, housing, and community institutions.

The Neighborhood, the District, and the Corridor

1. The Neighborhood, the District, and the Corridor are the essential elements of development and redevelopment in the metropolis. They form identifiable areas that encourage citizens to take responsibility for their maintenance and evolution.

2. Neighborhoods should be compact, pedestrian-friendly, and mixed use. Districts generally emphasize a special single use, and should follow the principles of neighborhood design when possible. Corridors are regional connectors of neighborhoods and districts; they range from boulevards and rail lines to rivers and parkways.

3. Many activities of daily living should occur within walking distance, allowing independence to those who do not drive, especially the elderly and the young. Interconnected networks of streets should be designed to encourage walking, reduce the number and length of automobile trips, and conserve energy.

4. Within neighborhoods, a broad range of housing types and price levels can bring people of diverse ages, races, and incomes into daily interaction, strengthening the personal and civic bonds essential to an authentic community.

5. Transit corridors, when properly planned and coordinated, can help organize metropolitan structure and revitalize urban centers. In contrast, highway corridors should not displace investment from existing centers.

6. Appropriate building densities and land uses should be within walking distance of transit stops, permitting public transit to become a viable alternative to the automobile.

7. Concentrations of civic, institutional, and commercial activity should be embedded in neighborhoods and districts, not isolated in remote, single-use complexes. Schools should be sized and located to enable children to walk or bicycle to them.

8. The economic health and harmonious evolution of neighborhoods, districts, and corridors can be improved through graphic urban design codes that serve as predictable guides for change.

9. A range of parks, from tot-lots and village greens to ballfields and community gardens, should be distributed within neighborhoods. Conservation areas and open lands should be used to define and connect different neighborhoods and districts.

The Block, the Street, and the Building

1. A primary task of all urban architecture and landscape design is the physical definition of streets and public spaces as places of shared use.

2. Individual architectural projects should be seamlessly linked to their surroundings. This issue transcends style.

3. The revitalization of urban places depends on safety and security. The design of streets and buildings should reinforce safe environments, but not at the expense of accessibility and openness.

4. In the contemporary metropolis, development must adequately accommodate automobiles. It should do so in ways that respect the pedestrian and the form of public space.

5. Streets and squares should be safe, comfortable, and interesting to the pedestrian. Properly configured, they encourage walking and enable neighbors to know each other and protect their communities.

6. Architecture and landscape design should grow from local climate, topography, history, and building practice.

7. Civic buildings and public gathering places require important sites to reinforce community identity and the culture of democracy. They deserve distinctive form, because their role is different from that of other buildings and places that constitute the fabric of the city.

8. All buildings should provide their inhabitants with a clear sense of location, weather, and time. Natural methods of heating and cooling can be more resource-efficient than mechanical systems.

9. Preservation and renewal of historic buildings, districts, and landscapes affirm the continuity and evolution of urban society.

For CNU membership information, please contact:
The Congress for the New Urbanism
The Hearst Building
5 Third Street, Suite 725
San Francisco, CA 94103
415-495-2255
www.cnu.org

For more information about the Traditional Neighborhood Development Ordinance (TND), please contact:
Duany Plater-Zyberk & Co.
1023 SW 25th Avenue
Miami, FL 33135
305-644-1023
www.dpz.com

ACKNOWLEDGMENTS

Many people contributed to the creation of this book, offering both inspiration and assistance. Its intellectual underpinnings can be found in the turn-of-the-(twentieth-)century writings of Ebenezer Howard, Raymond Unwin, Camillo Sitte, Hermann Josef Stübben, and the other wonderfully unspecialized planners and designers of the progressive era. They understood that the physical creation of community was the work of generalists, to be undertaken by artists and scholars rather than by single-minded engineers and technocrats. Their legacy, the sparkling downtowns of the City Beautiful movement and the elegant suburbs of the teens and twenties, appropriately redefined town planning as *Civic Art*.[*]

Indeed, we are equally indebted to the places that these planners created, many of which were brought to our attention by Robert A. M. Stern and John Massengale's early 1980s book and exhibition, *The Anglo-American Suburb*. Our excitement upon first discovering these neglected masterpieces is difficult to imagine now, but at the time it was quite palpable, as many of them had been discredited or simply ignored by the dominant modernist ethos. During our education, Ken Frampton, Robert Venturi, and Allan Greenberg also bucked convention by including in their lectures the historic models that continue to inspire our work. We are also deeply indebted to our professor Vincent Scully, who, more

[*] Images of this period's achievement were concisely presented in 1922 by Werner Hegemann and Elbert Peets in *The American Vitruvius: An Architect's Handbook of Civic Art*. Recently reprinted, this continues to be a valuable design manual.

than anyone, encouraged us to look admiringly at history during the apex of modernist architectural production.

We have been inspired in both our writing and our practice by our friend and colleague Leon Krier. His words and sketches, which we at first found shocking and scandalous, ultimately formed the foundation for our work. His brilliant cartoon synopsis of sprawl remains, even after two decades, the most elegant and convincing document on the subject.

A number of writers on cities have influenced our work, most notably William Whyte, Christopher Alexander, Kevin Lynch, Herbert Gans, and, of course, Jane Jacobs, whose *Death and Life of Great American Cities,* published almost forty years ago, is required reading for all who care about the built environment. We still refer to our dog-eared copy whenever we feel the need for some sage advice.

In the recent intensification of the war against sprawl, a number of journalists and authors have worked continually to keep the subject prominent in the public discourse. These include Peter Katz, Philip Langdon, and James Kunstler, who have been our partners in arms for many years. Mr. Kunstler's dyspeptic rants never fail to rally his friends in their efforts.* We must also acknowledge the many idealistic professionals who have joined us in battle, most notably our colleagues in the Congress for the New Urbanism. Our co-founders of the Congress—Peter Calthorpe, Liz Moule, Stef Poly-

---

* Indeed, some of what has been written here can also be found in James Howard Kunstler's two books, *The Geography of Nowhere* and *Home from Nowhere.* Those ideas that appear here without credit are printed with his permission; Mr. Kunstler acknowledges that their original source was our own lectures and writings. We are grateful to Jim for his success in bringing these ideas into the open well before we had the opportunity to complete this book.

zoides, and Daniel Solomon—have played no small part in the development of the ideas advanced here.

Before there was a Congress for the New Urbanism, this book's principles were nurtured over many years in two extremely supportive environments. One is the University of Miami, where a true *school* of historically informed architectural practice has developed around the shared objective of building community. The other is the office of Duany Plater-Zyberk & Co., where a talented group of young designers constantly challenges and reinvigorates the principles and techniques behind our work. The projects and drawings of DPZ neighborhoods pictured in this book are of course the product of many hands, and we are more than grateful for their efforts.

We thank the architect and urbanist Peter Brown for his great enthusiasm and intelligence in reviewing our original manuscript. We are also obliged to the author, educator, and critic Witold Rybczynski for his appropriately critical reaction to an early text. Vital data and fact-checking were generously provided by many members of the anti-sprawl community, including Rick Chellman, Robert Gibbs, Ruben Greenberg, Roy Keinitz, Christopher Kent, Walter Kulash, Christopher Leinberger, David Petersen, Patrick Pinnell, Randall Robinson, Peter Swift, and Mike Watkins. Finally, for their tremendous assistance in the completion of this book, we thank Corey Drobnie at Duany Plater-Zyberk & Co., Neeti Madan at Charlotte Sheedy Literary Agency, and our skillful and patient editor, Ethan Nosowsky, at North Point Press/Farrar, Straus and Giroux.

NOTES

———

3. The House That Sprawl Built

1. From the U.S. Census Bureau's 1997 report on Geographical Mobility.
2. Edward Blakely and Mary Gail Snyder, *Fortress America,* 24.
3. Ibid., 7.
4. Peter Calthorpe, *The Next American Metropolis,* 19.

4. The Physical Creation of Society

1. "Parking Lot Pique," A26.
2. Jonathan Franzen, "First City," 91.
3. Jonathan Rose, "Violence, Materialism, and Ritual," 145.
4. Le Corbusier, *The City of Tomorrow and Its Planning,* 129.
5. Jane Jacobs, *The Death and Life of Great American Cities,* 129.

5. The American Transportation Mess

1. Jane Jacobs, *The Death and Life of Great American Cities,* 183.
2. Donald D.T. Chen, "If You Build It, They Will Come," 4.
3. Ibid., 6.
4. Stanley Hart and Alvin Spivak, *The Elephant in the Bedroom,* 122.
5. Jane Holtz Kay, *Asphalt Nation,* 129.
6. Hart and Spivak, *The Elephant in the Bedroom,* 111; James Howard Kunstler, *Home from Nowhere,* 67, 99.
7. Hart and Spivak, *The Elephant in the Bedroom,* 166.

6. Sprawl and the Developer

1. Data from the *Survey of Surveys,* a comprehensive study compiled by Brooke Warrick's *American Lives.*
2. Christopher Kent, *Market Performance,* 3.
3. Charles Tu and Mark Eppli, *Valuing the New Urbanism,* 8.

7. The Victims of Sprawl

1. Julie V. Iovine, "From Mall Rat to Suburbia's Scourge," 62–63.
2. Stephanie Faul, "How to Crash-Proof Your Teenager," 8.
3. Ibid.
4. Donna Gaines, *Teenage Wasteland*, 85–86.
5. William Hamilton, "How Suburban Design Is Failing American Teen-Agers," B1.
6. Jane Holtz Kay, "Stuck in Gear," D1.
7. Philip Langdon, *A Better Place to Live*, 11.
8. Brett Hulsey, *Sprawl Costs Us All*, 8.

8. The City and the Region

1. Jane Holtz Kay, *Asphalt Nation*, 64.
2. Benton MacKaye, *The New Exploration*, 179.
3. Todd S. Purdum, "Suburban Sprawl Takes Its Place on the Political Landscape," A1.

9. The Inner City

1. "For Pedestrians, NYC Is Now Even More Forbidding," A11.

10. How to Make a Town

1. Keat Foong, "Williams Goes Urban to Differentiate Post," 42.
2. Data from Christopher A. Kent, P.A., C.R.E., Real Estate Broker and Counselor.

11. What Is to Be Done

1. Kevin Sack, "Governor Proposes Remedy for Atlanta Sprawl," A14.
2. Edmund P. Fowler, *Building Cities That Work*, 72.

BIBLIOGRAPHY

———

American Association of State Highway and Transportation Officials. *A Policy on Geometric Design of Highways and Streets (the "Green Book")*. Washington, D.C.: AASHTO, 1990.

Aschauer, David. "Transportation, Spending, and Economic Growth." Report by the American Public Transit Association, September 1991.

Benefield, F. Kaid; Matthew D. Raimi; and Donald D.T. Chen. *Once There Were Greenfields: How Urban Sprawl Is Undermining America's Environment, Economy, and Social Fabric*. New York: National Resources Defense Council, 1999.

Beyond Sprawl: New Patterns of Growth to Fit the New California. Report by the Bank of America, the Resources Agency of California, the Greenbelt Alliance, and the Low Income Housing Fund, 1995.

Blakely, Edward, and Mary Gail Snyder. *Fortress America: Gated Communities in the United States*. Washington, D.C.: Brookings Institute Press, 1997.

Boddy, Trevor. "Underground and Overhead: Building the Analogous City." *Variations on a Theme Park*. Michael Sorkin, ed. New York: Noonday Press, 1992: 123–53.

Byrne, John A. *The Whiz Kids: Ten Founding Fathers of American Business and the Legacy They Left Us*. New York: Doubleday, [n.d.]

Calthorpe, Peter. *The Next American Metropolis: Ecology, Community, and the American Dream*. New York: Princeton Architectural Press, 1993.

Carroll, James. "All the Rage in Massachusetts." *The Boston Globe*, July 22, 1997: A14–A15.

Chellman, Chester E. (Rick). *City of Portsmouth, New Hampshire: Traffic/Trip Generation Study*. Report by White Mountain Survey Company, December 1991.

———. *Traditional Neighborhood Development Street Design Guidelines: A Recommended Practice of the Institute of Transportation Engineers*. Washington, D.C.: Institute of Transportation Engineers, 1999.

Chen, Donald D.T. "If You Build It, They Will Come . . . Why We Can't Build Ourselves Out of Congestion." *Surface Transportation Policy Project Progress* VII.2 (March 1998): 1, 4.

269

Chira, Susan. "Is Smaller Better? Educators Now Say Yes for High School." *The New York Times,* July 14, 1993: A1, B8.

Collins, George, and Christiane Crasemann Collins. *Camillo Sitte: The Birth of Modern City Planning.* New York: Rizzoli, 1986.

Crawford, Margaret. "The World in a Shopping Mall." *Variations on a Theme Park.* Michael Sorkin, ed. New York: Noonday Press, 1992: 3–30.

Cummings, Jeanne. "Swept Away: How Rhineland, Mo., Saved Itself But Lost a Sense of Community." *The Wall Street Journal,* July 15, 1999: A1, A8.

Davis, Mike. *City of Quartz: Excavating the Future in Los Angeles.* New York: Vintage, 1990.

Dean, Andrea Oppenheimer. "At AIA, Gore Pledges Support for More 'Livable' Communities." *Architectural Record,* February 19, 1999: 49.

Dillon, David. "Big Mess on the Prairie." *Dallas Morning News,* October 2, 1994: 1c–2c.

Dittmar, Hank. "Congressional Findings in Tea-21." *Surface Transportation Policy Project Progress* VIII:4 (June 1998): 10.

————. "Tea-21: More than a Free Refill." *Surface Transportation Policy Project Progress* VIII:4 (June 1998): 1, 3.

Downs, Anthony. *New Visions for Metropolitan America.* Washington, D.C.: The Brookings Institute, 1995.

Duany, Andres, and Elizabeth Plater-Zyberk. "The Second Coming of the American Small Town." *The Wilson Quarterly* XVI:1 (Winter 1992): 19–50.

Easterling, Keller. *American Town Plans: A Comparative Time Line.* New York: Princeton Architectural Press, 1993.

Faul, Stephanie. "How to Crash-Proof Your Teenager." *Car and Travel* (American Automobile Association) (February 1996): 8–9.

Fishman, Robert. *Bourgeois Utopias: The Rise and Fall of Suburbia.* New York: Basic Books, 1987.

Foong, Keat. "Williams Goes Urban to Differentiate Post." *Multi-Housing News* (November 1998): 1, 42–43.

"For Pedestrians, NYC Is Now Even More Forbidding." *The Boston Globe,* December 30, 1997: A11.

Fowler, Edmund P. *Building Cities That Work.* Montreal: McGill-Queens University Press, 1992.

Franzen, Jonathan. "First City." *The New Yorker,* February 19, 1996: 85–92.

Gaines, Donna. *Teenage Wasteland: Suburbia's Dead-End Kids.* Chicago: University of Chicago Press, 1998.

Garland, Michelle, and Christopher Bender. "How Bad Transportation Decisions Affect the Quality of People's Lives." *Surface Transportation Policy Project Progress* IX:2 (May 1999): 4–7.

Garreau, Joel. *Edge City: Life on the New Frontier.* New York: Anchor, 1991.

Gerstenzang, James. "Cars Make Suburbs Riskier than Cities, Study Says." *Los Angeles Times,* April 15, 1996: A1, A20.

Gladwell, Malcolm. "Blowup." *The New Yorker,* January 22, 1996: 32–36.

Goodman, Percival, and Paul Goodman. *Communitas: Ways of Livelihood and Means of Life.* New York: Columbia University Press, 1960.

Graz, Roberta Brandes, with Norman Mintz. *Cities Back from the Edge: New Life for Downtown.* New York: John Wiley and Sons, 1998.

Hall, Peter. *Cities of Tomorrow.* London: Basil Blackwell, 1988.

Hamilton, William. "How Suburban Design Is Failing American Teen-Agers." *The New York Times,* May 6, 1999: B1, B11.

Hart, Stanley, and Alvin Spivak. *The Elephant in the Bedroom: Automobile Dependence and Denial; Impacts on the Economy and Environment.* Pasadena, Calif.: New Paradigm Books, 1993.

Harvard Graduate School of Design News (Winter/Spring, 1993).

Harvard University Graduate School of Design. *Studio Works 3.* Cambridge, Mass.: Harvard University, 1995.

Hegemann, Werner, and Elbert Peets. *The American Vitruvius: An Architect's Handbook of Civic Art.* New York: Princeton Architectural Press, 1990.

Howard, Ebenezer. *To-morrow: A Peaceful Path to Real Reform.* London: Swan Sonnenschein, 1898.

Howard, Philip K. *The Death of Common Sense: How Law Is Suffocating America.* New York: Random House, 1994.

Hulsey, Brett. *Sprawl Costs Us All: How Uncontrolled Sprawl Increases Your Property Taxes and Threatens Your Quality of Life.* Report by the Sierra Club Midwest Office, 1996.

Institute of Transportation Engineers, Transportation Planning Council Committee 5P-8. *Traditional Neighborhood Development Street Design Guidelines.* Washington, D.C.: Institute of Transportation Engineers, 1997.

Iovine, Julie V. "From Mall Rat to Suburbia's Scourge." *The New York Times Magazine,* October 2, 1994: 19, 62–63.

Jackson, Kenneth. *Crabgrass Frontier: The Suburbanization of the United States.* New York: Oxford University Press, 1985.

Jacobs, Allan B. *Great Streets.* Cambridge, Mass.: MIT Press, 1993.

Jacobs, Jane. *The Death and Life of Great American Cities.* New York: Random House, 1961.

Johnson, Dirk. "Population Decline in Rural America." *The New York Times,* September 11, 1990: A20.

Joint Center for Environmental and Urban Problems—Florida Atlantic/Florida International Universities. *Florida's Mobility Primer.* Draft report, November 1992.

Jouzatis, Carol. "39 Million People Work, Live Outside City Centers." *USA Today,* November 4, 1997: 1A–2A.

———. "You Can't Get There from Here." *USA Today,* November 4, 1997: 2A.

Katz, Peter. *The New Urbanism.* New York: McGraw Hill, 1993.

Kay, Jane Holtz. *Asphalt Nation: How the Automobile Took Over America, and How We Can Take It Back.* New York: Crown, 1997.

———. "Stuck in Gear." *The Boston Globe,* October 6, 1996: D1.

Kent, Christopher. *Market Performance: The Town of Seaside.* Report written 1991, updated 1999.

Kilborn, Peter T. "No Work for a Bicycle Thief: Children Pedal Around Less." *The New York Times,* June 7, 1999: A1, A21.

Kimbrell, Andrew. "Steering Toward Ecological Disaster." *The Green Lifestyle Handbook.* Jeremy Rifkin, ed. New York: Owl/Henry Holt, 1990.

Krieger, Alexander, ed. *Andres Duany and Elizabeth Plater Zyberk: Towns and Town Making Principles.* New York: Rizzoli, 1991.

Krier, Leon: *Choice or Fate.* Windsor: Papadakis, 1998.

———. *Houses, Palaces, Cities.* London: AD Editions, 1984.

Kruse, Jill. "Remove It and They Will Disappear: Why Building New Roads Isn't Always the Answer." *Surface Transportation Policy Project Progress* VII:2 (March 1998): 5, 7.

Kulash, Walter. "The Third Motor Age." *Places* (Winter, 1996): 42–49.

Kunstler, James Howard. *The Geography of Nowhere: The Rise and Decline of America's Manmade Landscape.* New York: Simon and Schuster, 1993.

————. *Home from Nowhere: Remaking Our Everyday World for the Twenty-first Century.* New York: Simon and Schuster, 1996.

Lancaster, Osbert. *Here, of All Places: The Pocket Lamp of Architecture.* London: John Murray, 1959.

Langdon, Philip. *A Better Place to Live.* Amherst: University of Massachusetts Press, 1994.

Lasch, Christopher. *The Revolt of the Elites and the Betrayal of Democracy.* New York: W. W. Norton, 1995.

Le Corbusier. *The City of Tomorrow and Its Planning.* London: John Rodher, 1929.

————. *The Radiant City.* London: Faber and Faber, 1967.

"Living with the Car," *The Economist,* June 22, 1966: 4–18.

Lynch, Kevin. *The Image of the City.* Cambridge, Mass.: MIT Press, 1960.

MacKaye, Benton. *The New Exploration: A Philosophy of Regional Planning.* New York: Harcourt, Brace, 1928.

MacKenzie, James; Roger Dower; and Donald Chen. *The Going Rate: What It Really Costs to Drive.* Report by the World Resources Institute, 1992.

McKibben, Bill. *The End of Nature.* New York: Doubleday, 1989.

Mohney, David, and Keller Easterling. *Seaside: Making a Town in America.* New York: Princeton Architectural Press, 1992.

Morrish, William R., and Catherine R. Brown. *Planning to Stay: Learning to See the Physical Features of Your Neighborhood.* Minneapolis: Milkweed Editions, 1994.

"Most Americans Are Overweight." *The New York Times,* October 16, 1996: C9.

Mumford, Lewis. *The City in History.* New York: Harcourt, Brace, Jovanovich, 1961.

————. "Regions—to Live In." *Survey* 54 (1925): 152–53.

Newman, Oscar. *Defensible Space: Crime Prevention Through Urban Design.* New York: Collier Books, 1972.

Newman, Peter, and Jeff Kenworthy. *Winning Back the Cities.* Sydney: Photo Press, 1996.

Norquist, John. *The Wealth of Cities: Revitalizing the Centers of American Life.* New York: Perseus Books, 1999.

Nyhan, David. "For the Planet's Sake, Hike the Gas Tax." *The Boston Globe,* November 28, 1997: A27.

Orfield, Myron. *Metropolitics: A Regional Agenda for Community and Stability.* Washington, D.C.: The Brookings Institute, 1997.

Palmer, Thomas. "Pacifying Road Warriors." *The Boston Globe,* July 25, 1997: A1, B5.

"Parking Lot Pique." *The Boston Globe,* May 16, 1997: A26.

Petersen, David. "Smart Growth for Center Cities." *ULI on the Future: Smart Growth—Economy, Community, Environment.* Washington, D.C.: Urban Land Institute, 1998: 46–56.

Phillips, Michael. "Welfare's Urban Poor Need a Lift—to Suburban Jobs." *The Wall Street Journal,* June 12, 1997: B1.

Pierce, Neal. "The Undefinable Mega-Issue." *The Washington Post Writers Group* (Web broadcast), September 13, 1998.

Popper, F. J. *The Politics of Land Use Reform.* Madison: University of Wisconsin Press, 1981.

Purdum, Todd S. "Suburban Sprawl Takes Its Place on the Political Landscape." *The New York Times,* February 6, 1999: A1, A7.

Regional Growth Management Plan. Report by the Southern California Association of Governments, 1989.

Replogle, Michael. *Transportation Conformity and Demand Management: Vital Strategies for Clean Air Attainment.* Report by the Environmental Defense Fund, April 30, 1993.

Rising, Nelson. Speech at the second Congress for the New Urbanism, Los Angeles, May 21, 1994.

Road Kill: How Driving Solo Runs Down the Economy. Report by the Conservation Law Foundation, 1994.

Rogers, Will. The Trust for Public Land membership letter. San Francisco (unpublished), May 1999.

Rose, Jonathan. "Violence, Materialism, and Ritual: Shopping for a Center." *Modulus 23: Towards a Civil Architecture in America* (August 1994): 137–51.

Rusk, David. *Cities Without Suburbs.* Washington, D.C.: Woodrow Wilson Press, 1993.

Rybczynski, Witold. *City Life: Urban Expectations in a New World.* New York: Scribner, 1995.

Sack, Kevin. "Governor Proposes Remedy for Atlanta Sprawl." *The New York Times,* January 26, 1999: A14.

Schumacher, E. F. *Small Is Beautiful: Economics As If People Mattered.* New York: Harper Collins, 1973.

Scully, Vincent. *Between Two Towers: The Drawings of the School of Miami.* New York: Monacelli Press, 1996.

———. *The Natural and the Man-Made.* New York: St. Martin's Press, 1994.

Sennett, Richard. *The Fall of Public Man.* New York: Norton, 1974.

Sert, Jose Luis. *Can Our Cities Survive? An ABC of Urban Problems, Their Analysis, Their Solutions, Based Upon the Proposals Formulated by the International Congress for Modern Architecture.* Cambridge, Mass.: Harvard University Press, 1947.

Sewell, John. *The Shape of the City: Toronto Struggles with Modern Planning.* Toronto: University of Toronto Press, 1993.

Sharp, T. *Town and Countryside: Some Aspects of Urban and Rural Development.* London: Oxford University Press, 1932.

Sierra Club. *The Dark Side of the American Dream.* Report, 1998.

Silvetti, Jorge. "The Symptoms of Malaise." *Progressive Architecture* (March 1992): 108.

Solomon, Daniel. *ReBuilding.* New York: Princeton Architectural Press, 1992.

Staats, Eric. "The Renewal of Stuart." *Naples Daily News,* April 25, 1994: 1a, 10a.

Stern, Robert A.M., and John Massengale. "The Anglo-American Suburb." *Architectural Design* (October–November 1981) (full double issue).

Stilgoe, John R. *Borderland: Origins of the American Suburb, 1820–1939.* New Haven: Yale University Press, 1988.

Surface Transportation Policy Project. "Campaign Connection." *Surface Transportation Policy Project Progress* IX.2 (May 1999): 8.

———. *Tea-21 User's Guide: Making the Most of the New Transportation Bill.* Report, 1998.

Swift, Peter. "Residential Street Typology and Injury Accident Frequency." Report by Swift Associates, 1997.

Tu, Charles, and Mark Eppli. *Valuing the New Urbanism: The Case of Kentlands.* Report by the George Washington University Department of Finance, 1997.

Unwin, Raymond. *Town Planning in Practice.* New York: Princeton Architectural Press, 1994.

U.S. Department of the Interior. *The Secretary of the Interior's Standards for Rehabilitation and Guidelines for Rehabilitating Historic Buildings.* Washington, D.C.: U.S. Government Printing Office, 1990.

Vest, Jason; Warren Cohen; and Mike Tharp. "Road Rage." *U.S. News & World Report,* June 2, 1997: 24–30.

Warrick, Brooke. *Survey of Surveys.* Report by *American Lives,* 1995.

White, Morton and Lucia. *The Intellectual vs. the City: From Thomas Jefferson to Frank Lloyd Wright.* New York: Mentor, 1962.

Whyte, William. *City: Rediscovering the Center.* New York: Doubleday, 1988.

Winner, Langdon. "Silicon Valley Mystery House." *Variations on a Theme Park.* Michael Sorkin, ed. New York: Noonday Press, 1992: 31–60.

Zuckerman, Wolfgang. *The End of the Road: From World Car Crisis to Sustainable Transportation.* Vermont: Chelsea Green, 1993.

SOURCES OF ILLUSTRATIONS

———

The images in this book have been collected from a wide range of sources, some of which have, unfortunately, been forgotten. Those images of uncertain provenance are marked "unknown," and we welcome correct attributions so that we may change future printings. All images not listed below are believed to be the property of Duany Plater-Zyberk & Co. We are grateful to the many people who generously contributed these photographs and illustrations.

Page	*Source*
4 (top)	© Landslides: Alex S. MacLean
6 (top)	© Landslides: Alex S. MacLean
7 (bottom)	© Robert Cameron
12	City of Virginia Beach, Va.
15	© Robert Cameron
18 (top)	City of Coral Gables, Fla.
18 (bottom)	Unknown
25 (bottom)	Rick Chellman
29 (top)	© Craig Studio
29 (bottom)	© Steve Dunwell
30 (bottom)	Unknown
33	© David King Gleason Collection
34	Unknown
36 (top)	Raymond Unwin, *Town Planning in Practice*, 249.
36 (bottom)	© *The Miami Herald*
41 (top)	Unknown
46	© Robert Cameron
48 (top)	© Harry Connolly
52	City of Charleston, S.C.
55 (both)	Urban Design Associates, Inc.
61	© *The Miami Herald*
68	City of Portland, Oreg.

Page	Source
72 (top)	Virginia Department of Transportation
77	Unknown
81 (bottom)	Richard McLaughlin
91	© Tom Toles, Universal Press Syndicate
100 (bottom)	Unknown
103	Felix Pereira
106 (bottom)	© Landslides: Alex S. MacLean
112	© Jacuzzi, Inc.
119	© *The New York Times*
120	© *AAA Car and Travel*, Jan.–Feb., 1996, 9.
121 (bottom)	© Landslides: Alex S. MacLean
136 (top)	© Landslides: Alex S. MacLean
150 (bottom)	Unknown
159 (top)	William Whyte, *City*, 204.
159 (bottom)	Unknown
188 (top)	Marshall Erdman and Associates, Inc.
188 (bottom)	© Rob Steuteville, New Urban News
189	© Steve Hinds Photography
192	© Steven Brooke Studios
193	© Landslides: Alex S. MacLean
200 (bottom)	Law Development Group
201 (middle)	Town of Markham, Ontario
212	Unknown
213	Harvard University Graduate School of Design, *Studio Works 3*, 13.
239	Unknown

INDEX

———

developers, 99–113; changes in land-use regulations opposed by, 224; conventional wisdom of, 105–9; decline of, 99–101; inner city, 170–71, 174, 177*n*, 178; market experts and, 101–5; of new towns and villages, 187–88; permitting process for, 178–80; regional planning and, 141, 145–47; and rising expectations of consumers, 154–55

Diggstown (Norfolk, Virginia), 55

dingbats, 175–76

disinvestment, 130

Disney World, 63

downtown business districts: decline of, 9; revitalization of, 136, 186*n*; *see also* inner cities

Durning, Alan Thein, 120*n*

Eastward Ho! civic initiative, 141

economic factors: discrimination based on, *see* income, segregation by; greenfield development and, 185; regional planning and, 141–42

education, *see* schools

Eisner, Michael, 113

elderly, suburban, 122–24

emergency-vehicle response time, 66, 67

Emery, Mary, 100

Empowerment Zones, 235

enclosure, sense of, 74–79

Enterprise Zones, 235

environment: greenfield development and, 184, 185; protection of, 226; regional planning and, 140, 141, 144; site planning and, 196–98

Environmental Defense Fund, 218*n*

environmental movement, 149–51

Environmental Protection Agency, 150

Everglades, 140, 141

extended family, housing for, 52

"eyes on the street," 73

façade design, 76–77, 109–10

face-block, 75*n*

Fannie Mae, 56*n*, 112

farmers' markets, 169

farmland, preservation of, 144

Federal-Aid Highway Act (1956), 87*n*

Federal Housing Administration (FHA), 7–8

federal policies, 234–36

Federal Realty, 29

Ferrara, Rick, 54

festival-oriented marketing, 166

financing of developments, 105

fire departments, 66–69, 82, 217

Fishman, Robert, 11*n*

five-minute walk neighborhoods, 15, 198–202

Floor Area Ratio (F.A.R.), 176–77*n*

Florida, 44, 150, 230; Department of Transportation, 36, 231; *Eastward Ho!* civic initiative, 141; *see also specific municipalities*

Ford, Henry, 135

Fort Lauderdale (Florida), 62*n*

Franklin (Wisconsin), 127–28

Franzen, Jonathan, 61

gable orientation, 17

Gaithersburg (Maryland), 185–86*n*; *see also* Kentlands

gangs, teenage, 119–20

garage apartments, 51, 73

Garland, Michelle, 62

gasoline, cost of, 95

gated communities, 44–46

Gehry, Frank, 211

General Motors, 8*n*

gentrification, 172–73

Georgia, 230; Regional Transportation Authority, 231; *see also specific municipalities*

Germany, urban development in, 186*n*

Gibbs, Robert, 165

Gindroz, Ray, 55, 239*n*

Glazer, Nathan, 239

global marketplace, 219, 220, 234

global warming, 95*n*, 96

"tough love" incentive program, 230
tourism: historic preservation–induced, 174–75*n*; Main Street as destination for, 28, 169; street width and, 78; traffic generated by, 24
towers-in-the-park approach, 65, 66*n*
towns, new, *see* new towns and villages
Traditional Neighborhood Development Checklist, 146, 186, 245–52
Traditional Neighborhood Development Ordinance, 146, 177, 222–23
traditional neighborhoods, 3–4; affordable housing in, 55; alleys in, 81–82; construction costs for, 107–9; environmental concern for, 151; fundamental rules of, 15–17; homebuilders and, 109–10, 113; income variance in, 44, 46–47; market experts and, 102–4; mass transit and, 138; new, development of, *see* new towns and villages; plans for, 18–20; profitability of, 113–14; property values in, 106–7; in regional planning, 145, 148; sense of enclosure in, 75–76; size of, 198–99; street design for, 72; traffic flow in, 23–24; urban, 136, 156, 181; width of streets in, 78
traffic, 7; congested, reasons for, 22–24; induced, 88–94; regional planning and, 225; unimpeded flow of, 65; *see also* roadways
traffic calming, 37, 69*n*
traffic lights, 160
trains, commuter, *see* rail transport
transit, *see* public transit
Transportation, U.S. Department of, 236
transportation planning, 85–97; automobile subsidies and, 94–97; induced traffic and, 88–94; regional, 140, 230–31; relationship of highways to towns in, 86–88
trees: in parking lots, 13, 31; along streets, 16, 79, 158
Trenton (New Jersey), 167*n*
trucking, 95–96
Turley, Henry, 113, 173
"twenty-minute house," 76

Unwin, Raymond, 36
urban codes, 176–78; master plans and, 181
urban entertainment centers, 156*n*
Urban Growth Boundary, 143, 144
urban infill, 93, 141, 145, 185, 222, 232
Urban Land Institute (ULI), 104*n*
urban poor, 129–33
urban/rural transition, 201–2
USA Today, 89
U.S. News & World Report, 62*n*
U.S. Postal Service, 128
Utah, 193–94
utilities, underground, 82

Ventura, Michael, 215
Vermont, 126*n*, 230
Vero Beach (Florida), 107
Veterans Administration (VA), 7–8
villages, new, *see* new towns and villages
Virginia Beach (Virginia), 12–16
Virginia Department of Transportation, 16
Visual Preference Survey, 103–4

walkable neighborhoods, *see* pedestrian-friendly design
Wall Street Journal, The, 238*n*
Warwick (New York), 193
Washington, George, 15
Washington, D.C., 7, 92*n*, 131, 137; Georgetown, 46–47, 49, 75–76, 106, 156*n*, 184; L'Enfant plan for, 228–29; Rock Creek Park, 144
Washington State, 230; *see also* Seattle
welfare reform, 131
West Hollywood (California), 169
West Palm Beach (Florida), 136, 172*n*, 179, 226
wetlands, 197
white flight, 130
White Mountain Survey, Inc., 222*n*
Whiz Kids, 11
Who Framed Roger Rabbit (film), 8*n*
Whyte, William, 9
Williamsburg (Virginia), 17*n*